The Psychology of
Women at Work

The Psychology of Women at Work

Challenges and Solutions for Our Female Workforce

Volume 3
Self, Family, and Social Affects

Edited by
MICHELE A. PALUDI

Praeger Perspectives

Women's Psychology

**Westport, Connecticut
London**

Library of Congress Cataloging-in-Publication Data

The psychology of women at work : challenges and solutions for our female workforce / edited by Michele A. Paludi
    p. cm. — (Women's psychology, ISSN 1931-0021)
    Includes bibliographical references and index.
    ISBN 978-0-275-99677-2 ((set) : alk. paper) — ISBN 978-0-275-99679-6 ((vol. 1) : alk. paper) — ISBN 978-0-275-99681-9 ((vol. 2) : alk. paper) — ISBN 978-0-275-99683-3 ((vol. 3) : alk. paper)
    1. Women—Employment—Psychological aspects. 2. Work and family. 3. Women—Job stress. 4. Women—Psychology. I. Paludi, Michele Antoinette.
    HD6053.P75 2008
    158.7082—dc22   2008004119

British Library Cataloguing in Publication Data is available.

Library of Congress Catalog Card Number: 2008004119
ISBN: 978-0-275-99677-2 (set)
       978-0-275-99679-6 (vol. 1)
       978-0-275-99681-9 (vol. 2)
       978-0-275-99683-3 (vol. 3)
ISSN: 1931-0021

First published in 2008

Praeger Publishers, 88 Post Road West, Westport, CT 06881
An imprint of Greenwood Publishing Group, Inc.
www.praeger.com

Printed in the United States of America

The paper used in this book complies with the Permanent Paper Standard issued by the National Information Standards Organization (Z39.48–1984).

10 9 8 7 6 5 4 3 2 1

For Antoinette and Michael Paludi, who encouraged me
to define what women's work is for myself

Contents

Acknowledgments

I thank Debbie Carvalko at Praeger for her encouragement and support throughout the writing of these three volumes. It is an honor to work with her. I also thank the graduate students in my human resources classes for their comments about the changing nature of work for women. I am confident that they will make a difference in the lives of the next generation of women employees and their families. I am grateful to Carrie Turco and Sharon Butler for their comments on earlier versions of the introduction.

The following family, friends, and colleagues have been invaluable during the preparation of these three volumes. Thank you to Rosalie Paludi, Lucille Paludi, Presha Neidermeyer, and Paula Lundberg Love. I especially acknowledge Carmen Paludi, Jr., for his friendship and sage advice. Together we continue to make the dreams of our grandparents on Weaver Street into realities.

Finally, I wish to thank William Norton Dember, my advisor and mentor in graduate school, who, like my parents, told me to seek my own career path and be tough-minded and kindhearted at the same time. I started drafting these books after I last saw Bill in May 2006, when we discussed my career since graduate school (it had been 26 years since I received my PhD). He reminded me that I came to work with him as a graduate student at the University of Cincinnati because I was interested in the psychology of women's work and achievement motivation. Moreover, he inquired why I hadn't written or edited a book in that field during the course of my career. These three volumes are in response to Bill's question. Bill died in September 2006. These books are in tribute to him as a psychologist, mentor, professor, colleague, and friend.

Introduction

Because I am a woman, I must make unusual efforts to succeed.
If I fail, no one will say, "She doesn't have what it takes."
They will say, "Women don't have what it takes."

—Clare Boothe Luce

Clare Boothe Luce's sentiment was once again highlighted during the preparation of these three volumes of *The Psychology of Women at Work: Challenges and Solutions for Our Female Workforce,* when Senator Hillary Rodham Clinton announced her candidacy for the presidency of the United States. Throughout the initial part of Senator Clinton's candidacy, comments about a woman president received media attention. Polls from CNN.com (July 24, 2007) and YouTube (January 21, 2007; March 5, 2007) reported the following quotations:

"Hillary Clinton needs to wear a dress or skirt now and then. Her always making public appearances in pants gives a sense she is trying to 'fit in' with the boys, which is never going to be the case."

"Hillary is cute. Those are her qualifications for prez."

"It'll be nice to have a woman president but you know white America won't let her."

"Women, above all, should reject hillary. Missus clinton is the biggest misogynist of all."

"hillary clinton running must be a joke! A woman for president! Ha! Now that['])s a joke."

Elizabeth Edwards, whose husband, John Edwards, also declared his candidacy for president, joined the chorus in criticizing Hillary Clinton. Elizabeth Edwards stated the following:

She [Hillary Clinton] and I are from the same generation. We both went to law school and married other lawyers, but after that we made other choices. I think my choices have made me happier. I think I'm more joyful than she is.

Elizabeth Edwards also stated, "Sometimes you feel you have to behave as a man and not talk about women's issues."

Mrs. Edwards's comments prompted a comparison of the two women—one perceived as "feminine" and the other "masculine." Responses from a CNN.com poll (July 24, 2007) included the following: "It would be awesome if Hillary was more like Elizabeth. But Hillary lacks the compassion and realness Elizabeth possesses."

Tucker Carlson, host of MSNBC's *Tucker,* asked a guest, "I mean, let's take this critique [by Elizabeth Edwards] seriously—is Hillary Clinton too manly to be president?"

This is in direct contrast to the view that many people had of Congresswoman Patricia Schroeder, who, when she dropped out of running for U.S. president in 1984, cried. This raised the question of whether a woman was too "emotional" to be president. Schroeder (1998) wrote, "Crying is almost a ritual that male politicians must do to prove they are compassionate, but women are supposed to wear iron britches."

In 1870, when Victoria Woodhull, the first woman to run for president, declared her candidacy, the *New York Herald* commented: "She is rather in advance of her time. The public mind is not yet educated to the pitch of universal woman's [sic] rights" ("Woman's Idea of Government," 1870, p. 6). In 2008 we are still hearing arguments that the United States is not ready for a woman president—a view expressed not only to Victoria Woodhull but also to other women candidates for president before Hillary Clinton: Margaret Chase Smith (in 1964), Shirley Chisolm (in 1972), Patricia Schroeder (in 1984), Elizabeth Dole (in 2000), and Carolyn Moseley Braun (in 2004). Similar comments were directed toward Geraldine Ferraro, the first woman to be placed on a national presidential ticket (as Walter Mondale's vice president in 1984). Ferraro was criticized for wearing short-sleeved dresses while campaigning because her arms wobbled when she waved (considered not "feminine").

"The emotional, sexual, and psychological stereotyping of females begins when the doctor says, 'It's a girl,'" Shirley Chisholm once noted. Gender-role stereotypes about "appropriate" and "inappropriate" occupations for women still abound. Gender stereotyping is a psychological process that illustrates a structured set of beliefs about the personal attributes of females and males (Ashmore & DelBoca, 1981; Doyle & Paludi, 1997; Fiske & Stevens, 1993). When asked to describe a woman, for example, individuals commonly cite "caring," "nurturing," "sensitive," and "passive." When asked to name a woman's occupation, individuals cite "nurse," "elementary school teacher," or "social worker," but not "president of the United States."

I have frequently used the following riddle when students and train-ees indicate that they believe that they themselves do not hold gender-role stereotypes about occupations:

One afternoon, a man and his son go for a drive through the countryside. After an hour or so they get into a terrible car crash. The father dies instantly. The son is taken by a helicopter to the nearest hospital, where a prominent surgeon is called to help save the boy's life. Immediately on entering the operating room and looking at the boy, the surgeon exclaims, "I can't possibly operate on this boy ... he's my son." How can this be?

The responses I have received to this question have ranged from "The father didn't really die—he sustained only minor injuries and could perform the surgery" to "It was the boy's stepfather who died, and his biological father was the surgeon" to "The boy's adoptive fa-ther is the surgeon, and his biological father was with him in the car." Individuals rarely solve this riddle: The surgeon is the boy's mother. When the answer is revealed, these individuals are angry with them-selves that they initially stated that they hold no occupational stereo-types for women and men. Individuals also usually "mark" an occupation if they believe that the gender of the person performing the job is atypical. Thus, they say "male nurse," "female physician," "female professor," and "male model" (Paludi, Paludi, & DeFour, 2004). Markings alert listeners or readers to something atypical for the occupation—that it is held by an individual of the sex other than the one with which it is traditionally associated.

An awareness of the contents of occupational stereotypes related to gender begins in the preschool years and is well developed by first grade (Betz, in press; Gottfredson, 1981; Heyman & Legare, 2004; Hughes & Seta, 2003; Sczesny, 2003). Among 6-year-olds, there is research evidence of gender stereotypes in the kinds of occupations that children consider for future employment. Girls commonly choose the occupations of nurse, teacher, or flight attendant. Boys, on the other hand, select police officer, truck driver, architect, or pilot. Children's ranges of occupations are difficult to change once they are set (Betz, in press; Eccles, Wigfield, & Schiefele, 1999).

Levy, Sadovsky, and Troseth (2000) reported that a stereotypic view of the world reinforces many of the common gender-role stereotypes and is a factor in prompting young boys' interest in more than twice as many occupations as that of young girls. Girls thus restrict their occupational aspirations. In addition, girls have a more limited concept than boys do of the career possibilities available to them in math- and computer-related occupations (Burger et al., 2007; Creamer & Laughlin, 2005; Naua, Epperson, & Kahn, 1998; White & White, 2006). Girls focus on occupations that are associated with less status, less satisfaction, and less pay than the occupations considered by boys (Heyman, 2000; Richardson & Sandoval (2007).

Siegel and Reis (1998) reported that although teachers perceived gifted girls as working harder and doing better work than gifted boys, these teachers gave higher grades to the boys. Similarly, Fennema and colleagues (1996) found that teachers perceived that boys are better than gifted girls at math and science. Kerr, Colangelo, and Gaeth (1988) reported that gifted girls are concerned about the negative effects of being gifted on their peers' attitudes toward them. The researchers found that, by the sophomore year of college, most gifted women changed their majors to less intellectually challenging ones. Furthermore, Kerr, Colangelo, and Gaeth found that, by their senior year, these gifted women reduced the level of their career goals.

Brody (1977) reported a decline in self-esteem among girls but not boys in elementary, middle, and high school. For example, 55% of elementary school girls agreed with the following statement: "I am good at a lot of things." This percentage declined to 29% in middle school and 23% in high school. The American Association of University Women (AAUW) (1992) reported that girls who pursued math and science courses and participated in sports maintained their self-esteem from elementary school through high school.

Hall and Sandler (1982) and Allan and Madden (2006) argued that, for girls and women, the educational system is a "chilly climate." Girls and women are discouraged from classroom participation, are sexually harassed by teachers as well as peers, receive a lack of mentoring, and are advised by guidance counselors to lower their expectations for a career (AAUW, 2001; Paludi, Martin, & Paludi, 2007; Richardson & Sandoval, 2007).

As can be seen from this brief review, an important manifestation of gender-role stereotyping is a progressive decrease in girls' and women's career aspirations (Betz, 2007; Farmer, 1997). "The test for whether or not you can hold a job should not be the arrangement of your chromosomes," Bella Abzug once protested.

Lacampagne, Campbell, Herzig, Damarin, and Vogt (2007) reported that gender differences are significant in math-related careers and in career aspirations. For example, of students who took the SAT in 2005, 5% of boys and 1% of girls reported planning to major in computer science. In addition, 10% of boys and 2% of girls were planning to major in engineering (College Board, 2005).

Career education programs continue to be gender-segregated; 90% of women in training programs are in traditionally female fields—for example, office technology and health care (AAUW, 2002). More than 90% of teachers (preschool, elementary, and special education), secretaries, child-care workers, waitresses, hairdressers, speech therapists, occupational therapists, dental hygienists, and teacher's aides are women (U.S. Department of Labor, 2003). Betz (in press) reported that women remain underrepresented in technical and scientific fields as well as in managerial positions in education, government, business, and the military.

In a recent study conducted by Catalyst (2007), gender-role stereotyping was linked to women's participation as leaders in business. According to this report, "Gender stereotyping, one of the key barriers to women's advancement in corporate leadership, leaves women with limited, conflicting and often unfavorable options no matter how they choose to lead."

Catalyst found that women constitute more than 50% of management and professional occupations but are only 15.6% of Fortune 500 corporate officers and 14.6% of Fortune 500 board directors. Ilene Lang, president of Catalyst, comments on this as follows:

> When companies fail to acknowledge and address the impact of gender stereotypic bias, they lose out on top female talent.... Ultimately, it's not women's leadership styles that need to change. Only when organizations take action to address the impact of gender stereotyping will they be able to capitalize on the "full deck" of talent.

Women earn less than 20% of the bachelor's degrees in fields such as engineering and physics and less than 10% of the graduate degrees in engineering (Betz, 2007). Women represent only about 14% of engineers, 30% of computer systems analysts, and 25% of computer programmers (U.S. Department of Labor, 2003, 2005). Women account for 8% of physicists and astronomers, 7% of air traffic controllers, 5% of truck drivers, 4% of pilots, 5% of firefighters, and 2% of carpenters and electricians (Betz, 2007).

Equally important, women are paid less for full-time employment than men are; women make only 77% as much as men do when both are employed full-time (U.S. Department of Labor, 2005). This income disparity is greater for Black, Asian, Native American, and Hispanic women than for White women, and for middle-age and older women than for younger women.

"We haven't come a long way," noted Elizabeth Janeway, "we've come a short way. If we hadn't come a short way, no one would be calling us baby."

These realities of the psychology of women at work require an in-depth look at not only the barriers to women's success but also the strategies for empowering women at the individual, organizational, legal, and societal levels. These three volumes provide an overview of the scholarly research on the issues related to women and work.

Volume 1, "Career Liberation, History, and the New Millennium," provides an overview of research on comparisons of men and women in gender-relative (i.e., stereotypical masculine and feminine) communication styles, women as bosses, women as entrepreneurs, personality factors that impact women in the workplace, feminist competing values leadership, career preparation programs in high school, and sexual harassment.

Volume 2, "Obstacles and the Identity Juggle," offers reviews on the double standard for women in the workplace; sexual harassment; women and leadership; the glass ceiling; pay inequalities; incivility toward women in the workplace; women in the sciences, technology, engineering, and math; and the economics of women in the workplace.

Volume 3, "Self, Family, and Social Affects," discusses women and self-esteem, the impact of work on women's physical health, mental health issues for women in the workforce (especially women who have experienced discrimination), women's relationships with male co-workers, and religion and women at work.

In addition to the scholarly reviews of research on the psychology of women at work, I have included women's personal accounts of their career development, especially their experiences in the labor force. A variety of careers is represented in these personal accounts—attorney, human resource manager, college president, chiropractor, and psychologist—as well as students who are pursuing careers. For many years researchers have defined for women what success is, what work is, and what achievement striving should be. These definitions have typically contained masculine biases (Paludi & Fankell-Hauser, 1986). Thus, these personal accounts of women's experiences recognize that women differ in the strength of their striving for achievement and in the roles that elicit their striving, taking into account the effects of family, friends, role models, and partners. It is the goal of these volumes that these personal accounts stimulate additional research, legislation, and advocacy on behalf of female students and employees so that a woman running for the United States presidency will be accepted and encouraged.

REFERENCES

Allan, E., & Madden, M. (2006). Chilly classrooms for female undergraduate students: A question of method? *Journal of Higher Education, 77,* 684–711.

American Association of University Women (AAUW). (1992). *The AAUW report: How schools shortchange girls.* Washington, DC: Author.

American Association of University Women (AAUW). (2001). *Hostile hallways: Bullying, teasing, and sexual harassment in school.* Washington, DC: AAUW Educational Foundation.

American Association of University Women (AAUW). (2002). *Title IX at 30: Report card on gender equity.* Washington, DC: Author.

Ashmore, R., & DelBoca, F. (1981). Conceptual approaches to stereotypes and stereotyping. In D. Hamilton (Ed.), *Cognitive processes in stereotyping and intergroup behavior*. Hillsdale, NJ: Erlbaum.

Betz, N. (2007). Women's career development. In F. L. Denmark & M. Paludi (Eds.), *Psychology of women: A handbook of issues and theories* (2nd ed.). Westport, CT: Greenwood Press, pp. 717–752.

Brody, J. E. (1997, November 4). Girls and puberty: The crisis years. *The New York Times*, p. B8.

Burger, C., Abbott, G., Tobias, S., Koch, J., Vogt, C., & Sosa, T. (2007). Gender equity in science, engineering and technology. In S. Klein (Ed.), *Handbook for achieving gender equity through education* (pp. 255–279). Mahwah, NJ: Erlbaum.

Catalyst. (2007). *The double-bind dilemma for women in leadership: Damned if you do, doomed if you don't*. New York: Author.

College Board. (2005). *2005 College-bound seniors: Total group profile report*. Available online at www.college-board.com

Creamer, E., & Laughlin, A. (2005). Self-authorship and women's career decision making. *Journal of College Student Development, 46*, 13–27.

Doyle, J., & Paludi, M. (1997). *Sex and gender: The human experience*. New York: McGraw-Hill.

Eccles, J., Wigfield, A., & Schiefele, U. (1999). Motivation to succeed. In N. Eisenberg (Ed.), *Handbook of child psychology: Vol. 3. Social, emotional and personality development* (pp. 1017–1095). New York: Wiley.

Farmer, H. S. (1976). What inhibits achievement and career motivation in women? *Counseling Psychologist, 6*, 12–14.

Farmer, H. S. (1997). *Diversity and women's career development*. Thousand Oaks, CA: Sage.

Fennema, E., Carpenter, T. P., Franke, M. L., Levi, L., Jacobs, V., & Empson, S. (1996). A longitudinal study of learning to use children's thinking in mathematics education. *Journal for Research in Mathematics Education, 27*, 403–434.

Fiske, S., & Stevens, L. (1993). What's so special about sex? Gender stereotyping and discrimination. In S. Oskamp & M. Costanzo (Eds.), *Gender issues in contemporary society*. Newbury Park, CA: Sage.

Gottfredson, L. S. (1981). Circumscription and compromise: A development theory of occupational aspirations. *Journal of Counseling Psychology, 28*, 545–579.

Hall, R., & Sandler, B. (1982). *The classroom climate: A chilly one for women*. Washington, DC: Project on the Status and Education of Women.

Heyman, J. (2000). *The widening gap*. New York: Basic Books.

Heyman, G., & Legare, C. (2004). Children's beliefs about gender differences in academic social domains. *Sex Roles, 50*, 227–239.

Hughes, F., & Seta, C. (2003). Gender stereotypes: Children's perceptions of future compensatory behavior following violations of gender roles. *Sex Roles, 49*, 685–691.

Kerr, B., Colangelo, N., & Gaeth, J. (1988). Gifted adolescents' attitudes toward their giftedness. *Gifted Child Quarterly, 32*, 245–247.

Lacampagne, C., Campbell, P., Herzig, A., Damarin, S., & Vogt, C. (2007). Gender equity in mathematics. In S. Klein (Ed.), *Handbook for achieving gender equity through education* (pp. 235–253). Mahwah, NJ: Erlbaum.

Levy, G., Sadovsky, A., & Troseth, G. (2000). Aspects of young children's perceptions of gender-typed occupations. *Sex Roles, 42,* 993–1006.

Naua, M., Epperson, D., & Kahn, J. (1998). A multiple-groups analysis of predictors of higher level career aspirations among women in mathematics, science and engineering majors. *Journal of Counseling Psychology, 45,* 483–496.

Paludi, M., & Fankell-Hauser, J. (1986). An idiographic approach to the study of women's achievement strivings. *Psychology of Women Quarterly, 10,* 89–100.

Paludi, M., Martin, J., & Paludi, C. (2007). Sexual harassment: The hidden gender equity problem. In S. Klein (Ed.), *Handbook for achieving gender equity through education* (pp. 215–229). Mahwah, NJ: Erlbaum.

Paludi, M., Paludi, C., & DeFour, D. (2004). Introduction: *Plus ca change, plus c'est la meme chose* (The more things change, the more they stay the same). In M. Paludi (Ed.), *Praeger guide to the psychology of gender* (pp. xi–xxxi). Westport, CT: Praeger.

Richardson, B., & Sandoval, P. (2007). Impact of education on gender equity in employment and its outcomes. In S. Klein (Ed.), *Handbook for achieving gender equity through education* (pp. 43–58). Mahwah, NJ: Erlbaum.

Schroeder, P. (1998). *24 Years of housework ... and the place is still a mess: My life in politics.* Kansas City, MO: Andrews McMeel.

Sczesny, S. (2003). A closer look beneath the surface: Various facets of the think-manager-think-male stereotype. *Sex Roles, 49,* 353–363.

Siegel, D., & Reis, S. M., (1998). Gender differences in teacher and student perceptions of gifted students' ability and effort. *Gifted Children Quarterly, 42,* 39–47.

U.S. Department of Labor, Bureau of Labor Statistics. (2003). *Facts on women workers.* Washington, DC: U.S. Government Printing Office.

U.S. Department of Labor, Bureau of Labor Statistics. (2005). *Women in the labor force: A data book.* Washington, DC: U.S. Government Printing Office.

White, M., & White, G. (2006). Implicit and explicit occupational gender stereotypes. *Sex Roles, 55,* 259–266.

Woman's idea of government. (1870). *New York Herald,* p. 6.

Chapter 1

Aggressive Men and Witchy Women: The Double Standard

Susan Strauss

Labeling a man *aggressive* is stereotypically associated with strength, decisiveness, and power (Harris, 1994; Johnson, 1997), but when a woman behaves in the same or in a similar manner, she might be labeled as a *witch*, a word commonly used to insult and demean women (Johnson). This discrepancy of labels implies hostility toward women and establishes a double standard, which is reinforced by both women and men (Conway & Vartanian, 2000; Heim, 1995; Johnson; Ledet & Henley, 2000; Wood & Karten, 1986). Turkel (2004) asserted that when a man is direct he is considered strong, but when a woman is direct she is considered overbearing. When women are assertive, they are often labeled aggressive and are then hesitant to express their ideas or to disagree with others (Turkel).

Several theories have been examined in the scholarly literature to explain the phenomenon of judging women more harshly than men: sexism (Glick & Fiske, 1996; Masser & Abrams, 2004), sex role stereotyping (Deaux, 1995; Devine, 1989; Fiske & Stevens, 1993), patriarchy (Johnson, 1997), oppression (Johnson, 1997; Stout & McPhail, 1998), and competition (Loya, Cowan, & Walters, 2006), to name a few. Most of the literature measured the perceptions of gender behavior within the workplace milieu; however, a few researchers associated women's hostility toward women as a reflection of jealousy caused by current beauty and body image standards (Forbes, Collinsworth, Jobe, Braum, & Wise, 2007; Loya et al., 2006). This chapter will explore these theories that provide a rationale for both women and men viewing women as *witchy*.

STEREOTYPES AND GENDER ROLE THEORY

Research has demonstrated that stereotypes often operate unconsciously (Devine, 1989), are used to evaluate situations and people (Deaux, 1995), and have not changed much over time (Eagly, 1987). Fiske (1993) asserted that stereotyping is more prevalent with those individuals who hold power, and Eagly, Makhijani, & Klonsky (1992) found that women in leadership roles tend to be devalued compared to men in leadership roles. Both women and men cultivate expectations about their own and the opposite gender's behavior based on their beliefs about what is appropriate for both genders, which Eagly (1987) labeled gender-role theory. A stereotype is a complex construct in which researchers have hypothesized female gender subtypes. Fiske and Glick (1995) categorized three subtypes for women: sex object (sexually desirable and potentially sexually available), traditional woman (weak, vulnerable, and powerless), and the nontraditional woman (strong, competitive, and difficult). Kanter's (1977) four female subtypes are similar: mother (sympathetic), seductress (sex object), pet (girlish, cute, admires male antics), and iron maiden (strong, competitive, tough, threatening, unfeminine). Iron maidens face hostility from their coworkers and are often viewed as less agreeable and cooperative (Fiske & Glick).

According to Fiske and Stevens (1993), all stereotypes are comprised of both *descriptive* and *prescriptive* elements. The prescriptive element of the stereotype identifies how an individual ought to behave on the basis of membership within the particular group. The researchers found that gender stereotypes are more likely to be prescriptive and therefore more rigid about what constitutes acceptable behavior. Several scholars (Burgess & Borgida, 1999; Franke, 1997; Schultz, 1998) asserted that prescriptive stereotypes may result in discrimination against women who violate these stereotypes and defy behavioral expectations; these women may be subjected to sexual harassment or receive a poor performance evaluation. Franke's legal perspective suggested that when sexual harassment, a form of gender discrimination, punishes individuals who do not conform to prescriptive stereotypes, it reinforces the prescriptive gender stereotypes of both genders. The descriptive element of the stereotype reflects what others believe about members of the specific group. For example, the male stereotype is that men are aggressive, daring, rational, strong, and self-confident (Johnson, 1997). In contrast, the female stereotype describes a woman who is nurturing, soft-spoken, compliant (Eagly, 1987), illogical, emotional, passive (Burgess & Borgida), weak, and lacking in self-control (Johnson). Therefore, if a woman is generally believed to be less competent than a man, then she will be evaluated less positively and perceived as having less ability than her male counterpart (Deaux, 1995). Both women and men share the descriptive element of gender stereotypes but differ in their prescriptive gender stereotypes, resulting in both genders being likely to discriminate (Burgess & Borgida).

Both prescriptive and descriptive female gender stereotypes were critical in not granting a partnership to Ann Hopkins when she was employed at Price Waterhouse, a prominent accounting firm, because she was seen to lack femininity (*Price Waterhouse v. Hopkins*, 1989). She was a strong and ambitious woman, competent and well thought of by her clients. She was also perceived as lacking skills in coworker relationships and engaging in more typically male behavior. For example, she was told to "walk more femininely, talk more femininely, dress more femininely, wear makeup, have her hair styled, and wear jewelry" (Fiske, Bersoff, Borgida, Deaux, & Heilman, 1991, p. 1050). Fiske and Stevens (1993), in referring to the Price Waterhouse case, captured the dilemma many women experience:

> The issue no longer is acknowledgment of competence. Rather this aspect of the stereotyping process explains the penalties that result from perceived violation of acceptable sex-role appropriate behaviors. Because many behaviors considered inappropriate for women are the very ones deemed necessary to be competent in a traditionally male job, sex stereotypes create a double bind for women. Their competence is undervalued if they behave in traditionally feminine ways, while their interpersonal skills are derogated and their mental health is questioned if they behave in traditionally masculine ways. (p. 218)

Women who work in male-dominated jobs, who therefore do not fit their gender stereotype, are more likely to be viewed negatively (Eagly & Mladinic, 1994), be victims of male backlash (Faludi, 1992), and experience discrimination and harassment (Fiske & Glick, 1995). According to Glick (1991), male-dominated jobs are seen as requiring specific knowledge and skills that set men up as superior to women, so when women are able to do the jobs, men's self-esteem and gender identity are threatened. This nontraditional woman is likely to experience hostility from some of the men with whom she works. A hostile work environment results in an attempt to alienate and denigrate the women who have moved into male-dominated roles and have entered male turf (Fitzgerald, 1993; Gutek, 1985).

Expectancy-value theory (Troyer & Younts, 1997) is similar to Fiske and Stevens' (1993) model of descriptive and prescriptive stereotypes. Expectancy-value theory is a model of social order of interacting with others and supports a status hierarchy based on a number of variables including gender, seniority, race, and so on. The theory consists of first-order and second-order expectations for social interactions. The researchers found that first-order expectations, similar to descriptive stereotypes, is what an individual expects of her or his own behavior, and second-order expectations, similar to prescriptive stereotypes, include the expectations that are held for others. If first-order and second-order expectations are in conflict with one another, second-order expectations carry more weight in influencing the social action of the individual. In other words, the greatest influence on an individual's social interaction is what the other person's expectations are of her or him. When men and women are interacting while involved in a specific task, the gender beliefs of both individuals will shape what each expects from the other gender, resulting in a double standard for evaluating performance with women seen as less competent (Biernat & Kobrynowicz, 1997).

In a study of college students' expectations about female and male candidates for professorships, sex-role stereotypes emerged in the students' evaluations of the candidates based on altered application materials (Wall & Barry, 1985). If a woman's name was used in the materials, the students indicated that she seemed to be too focused on the business side of her career and didn't seem to exhibit much personality. Conversely, if a man's name was used on the materials, no reference was made regarding his career emphasis or personality. The researchers also discovered that students judged women professors more severely than men, expecting the women to be more devoted to students by spending more time with them than the male professors were expected to spend. The authors suggested that female professors may be unfairly evaluated when students praise male professors even when it was the females that were more attentive to students. The reasoning was that women, in acting more nurturing and providing more time with students, are merely doing what is expected of them as women, whereas a male professor, when providing time and attention to students, is exceeding students' expectations.

Women leaders whose style tends to fit the male stereotype of leadership (i.e., autocratic and direct) received more negative evaluations than their male peers who used the same style, and the women were viewed as less effective leaders as well (Eagly, Karau, & Makhijani, 1995). Men are more harsh when evaluating female leaders than are women (Eagly et al., 1992). Eagly and Johnson's (1990) meta-analysis of women's natural leadership styles demonstrated that women generally act in ways that are consistent with prescriptive stereotypes—participatory and democratic—and will purposely use those skills in their management role. Kanter (1977) presented a sociological study of an actual corporation she labeled Indsco. Her study contrasted roles of women and men at work with both genders incorporating the stereotypical behavior of their gender within the organization's climate. As a result, Kanter postulated that stereotypical behavior is not based solely on individuals but rather is imbedded within the organizational system, as for example, sex-segregated jobs. Sex-role spillover, a theory suggested by Gutek and Morasch (1982), states that women and men carry over their gender-based roles into the workplace even when those roles are inappropriate. This phenomenon is most likely to occur when the gender ratio is skewed toward either women or men and is most obvious when women work in male-dominated jobs. When a woman works in a male-dominated job, her sex is salient in her position, leading to both her female and male coworkers questioning whether she is as capable as a man, which reflects the coworkers' gender bias.

As these researchers have demonstrated, stereotypes appear to play an essential role in how women and men are perceived and expected to behave. A deviation from their prescribed role may be viewed as a violation of the social order and may lead to the double standard of women being devalued and viewed as witchy and less competent. As a result women are caught in a double bind of balancing strength and autonomy with warmth and wanting to be liked; they can be discriminated against for their membership in any of the female stereotype subtypes, and the female stereotype works against them in a male-dominated environment. The stereotypes reflect sexist beliefs that require examination.

SEXISM

Sexism is defined by Forbes, Collinsworth, Jobe, Braum, and Wise (2007) as "the assignment of roles and privileges as a function of gender (p. 266) ... [and] plays a central role in implementing and justifying the oppression of women" (p. 267). Glick and Fiske (1996, 1997, 2001) have further divided sexism into two interrelated components, hostile and benevolent sexism. The researchers defined benevolent sexism as "attitudes toward women that are sexist in terms of viewing women stereotypically and in restricted roles but that are subjectively positive in feeling or tone (for the perceiver) and also tend to elicit behaviors typically categorized as prosocial (e.g., helping) or intimacy seeking (e.g., self-disclosure)" (1996, p. 491). Benevolent sexism, however, stems from the belief that women are inferior to men and that they require special attention or privileges because they are not men's equals (Forbes et al.). Glick and Fiske (2001) define hostile sexism as "an adversarial view of gender relations in which women are perceived as seeking to control men whether through sexuality or feminist ideology" (p. 109). According to Glick and Fiske (1996, 1997, 2001, 2002), hostile and benevolent sexism are complementary to each other, with both demonstrating the inequality between women and men. For example, men who hold benevolent sexist beliefs about women (perceived by some as positive characteristics) likewise believe in hostile sexism (negative stereotypes) (Glick & Fiske, 1996).

Sibley and Wilson (2004) found that the complementary effect between hostile and benevolent sexism by men is evident in men's belief of the various female stereotype subtypes. These results mirror the findings of Glick, Diebold, Balley-Werner, and Zhu (1997). This means that women who display attributes of the traditional subtype of women may be more likely to experience a more positive experience with men, whereas nontraditional women may bear the brunt of men's negative actions. Hostile sexism is associated with negative evaluations of women, especially those who are perceived as threatening male hegemony within the workplace (Masser & Abrams, 2004). Masser and Abrams' findings were in contrast to other researchers who found that benevolent sexism was the best predictor of negative evaluations of women candidates for positions within a male-dominated organization (Abrams, Viki, Masser, & Boehner, 2003; Glick et al.). Glick et al. asserted that when women's behavior is in violation of the traditional gender role, they receive negative evaluations from those with benevolent sexism beliefs. Glick et al. and Masser and Abrams noted that men who display hostile sexism may also judge nontraditional women negatively; however, their judgments appear to be in response to feeling intimidated or threatened by these women.

Lee's (2002) qualitative research suggested that failure to conform to gender stereotypes was the basis for gendered bullying. She provided examples of women who were bullied because they didn't adhere to *appropriate* female workplace conduct. In some cases, the bullying resulted in low performance-related pay and promotions, which is discrimination. Other examples suggested that women who were assertive were bullies, but women who were perceived as compliant and quiet, characteristics associated with femininity, were treated more favorably.

In the communication study conducted by Conway and Vartanian (2000), women tended to demonstrate verbal passive-aggressive behavior. Terms defining verbal passive-aggressive communication in their study were nagging, complaining, fussy, and whiny. The researchers raised the question as to whether the behavior of complaining is labeled as nagging because it is coming from a woman, and wondered if the same term would be applied if a man were complaining. Passive-aggressive communication may be considered more acceptable for women than aggressive behavior.

Women are not supposed to be aggressive so that men *can* be aggressive and demonstrate their manhood (Johnson, 1997). When women don't abide by this unspoken rule, it interferes with men's ability to separate themselves from women, if women can be like men. This in turn interferes with male privilege. Women who fail to follow the stereotype of their gender by acting assertively are viewed negatively and become the all-encompassing *witch*.

Not all women who violate female stereotypes are judged negatively. According to Glick et al. (1997), hostile sexists do not routinely evaluate career women negatively and may view them quite positively when evaluating their work prowess. Women's interpersonal skills, however, were viewed negatively by evaluators using words such as "aggressive, selfish, greedy and cold" (p. 1330). Women managers, then, are more likely to be disliked because they violate the prescriptive gender stereotype; they may be seen as unable to relate well to coworkers, yet may be respected from a competency perspective.

Sexism and sex-role stereotypes are closely aligned in the double standard of aggressive men and witchy women. They both can be observed in action in the communication styles that both genders use.

COMMUNICATION

Women and men communicate differently (Arliss, 1991; Stout & McPhail, 1998; Tannen, 1990, 1994). This gendered communication demonstrates a subtle and sometimes invisible sexism that is effective in diminishing a woman's status, demeaning her humanity, and minimizing her power (Stout & McPhail, 1998). Tannen (1990) stated that "language keeps women in their place" (p. 241). She indicated that women have a choice to make in their communication style—that of being perceived as a "strong leader or a good woman" (p. 241). Women who are assertive are labeled *domineering, aggressive, witchy,* or *worse.* Words such as *bitch, nag, whore,* and *cunt* are on the severe end of hostile and demeaning labels for women (Arliss), particularly when women step out of their social stereotype and are verbally aggressive and/or argumentative. Tannen contrasted a male speaker's and female speaker's style and how others perceive them in the following quote:

> [A man may] find himself commanding more attention in public if that is what he wants. And in the process, he would better fit the model of masculinity in our culture. But women who attempt to adjust their styles of speaking louder, longer, and with more self-assertion will also better fit the model of masculinity. They may command more attention and be more respected, but they may also be disliked and disparaged as aggressive and unfeminine. (p. 239)

Nicotera and Rancer (1994) found that men are significantly more likely to be argumentative and to express verbal aggression. Men who are not aggressive are often labeled *wimps* (Tannen, 1994). According to Infante (1981, 1985), those who are highly argumentative are viewed more positively than those who are not likely to argue. Men are expected to be more aggressive and forceful on the basis of their perceived higher status (Conway & Vartanian, 2000). Infante (1985) stated that an individual's credibility is enhanced if he is argumentative. Women, then, may be perceived as less credible than men on the basis of lower argumentative behavior. Tannen (1994) asserted that women who do not display "angry outbursts" (p. 182) may set themselves up for exploitation because their behavior may be perceived as avoidance of conflict. Smith et al. (1990) found, however, that when women are angry, they violate gender stereotypes, risk rejection, and will be viewed more negatively than angry men.

Women are concerned with being liked and getting along so they have learned conflict-avoidant behavior and are more likely to seek consensus (Smith et al., 1990). Women typically enjoy using consensus as the preferred style rather than a style of ruling with an iron fist (Tannen, 1994). Infante (1987) stated that "according to the cultural sex-role expectations model, arguing ... is compatible with expectations for male behavior but incompatible with expectations for female behavior" (p. 175). Women perceive argumentativeness more negatively than men regardless of which gender is displaying the behavior (Nicotera & Rancer, 1994). Perceptions and evaluation of aggressive behavior varies on the basis of the gender of the individual (Harris & Knight-Bohnhoff, 1996). Argumentativeness and aggression are not the only forms of communication in which women and men are judged differently. The ways in which both genders are addressed differs on the basis of gender, with women more likely to be called by their first names.

Using a woman's first name in addressing her, rather than addressing her with her title, such as Dr. or Ms., is common, whereas men are more likely to be addressed with their titles (Stout & Kelly, 1990). Stout and Kelly found in their study that 72% of the time women managers were called by their first names yet only 28% of the time were men referred to by their first names. Titles are indicators of one's status and demonstrate respect and equality when used by all individuals in communication. When titles are not equally used, for example when male physicians call female nurses by their first names yet nurses are expected to use the title of *Doctor* when addressing a physician, it is a subtle demeaning of women and demonstrates male hegemony.

According to Stout and McPhail (1998), "language has been used to exclude women from participation as equals and thus keeps women as invisible outsiders" (p. 81). One of the most common yet insidious examples of excluding women is the use of the default gender pronoun *he* or use of the word *man*, such as in mailman, policeman, mankind, etc. Though progress has been made in correcting the error, it is still a common communication trait. Wood's (1994) study concluded that people do not think of women but automatically think of men when hearing or seeing in print the generic word *man*.

Communication, both overt and covert, expresses the stereotypes and sexism that demean women at work and in society. It is the tool used by both genders to enact the double standard that portrays women negatively. But these three constructs—gender stereotypes, sexism, and communication—are cogs in a wheel of a patriarchal system.

PATRIARCHY AND OPPRESSION

Johnson (1997) asserted that "a society is patriarchal to the degree that it is male-dominated, male-identified, and male-centered ... and involves as one of its key aspects the oppression of women" (p. 5). The world is viewed through a gendered lens using the male standard as the norm, yet the lens isn't merely about women and men—it is a systemic framework of power, control, and competition. The framework is about leadership traits that are masculine, and according to Johnson, recognize that "power looks sexy on men but not on women" (p. 7). Patriarchy is "a culture embodied by everything from the content of everyday conversation to literature and film ... ideas about the nature of things ... about social life and how it is supposed to be ... what's expected of people and about how they feel ... standards about feminine beauty and masculine toughness ... valuing of masculinity and maleness and the devaluing of femininity and femaleness" (Johnson, pp. 84–85).

Both sexism and sex-role stereotypes are part of the patriarchal system that serves to negate women and maintain the framework of male hegemony, cultural misogyny, and the oppression of women (Johnson, 1997). According to Johnson, sexism is prejudice against women because it supports a culture of male privilege by supporting patriarchy and oppression. In contrast, anti-male stereotypes are not anchored in a culture that espouses maleness as disgusting and inferior as with femaleness. Femaleness is devalued in cultures throughout the world, supporting the oppression of women similar to the way racial minorities, the disabled, and gays and lesbians are devalued and oppressed in a patriarchal system. According to Friere (1968) and Johnson, oppression is a system of inequality where one group dominates another group and benefits from the subordination. The oppressed internalize the thoughts and behavior of the oppressor and follow the oppressor's prescribed behavior. Members of oppressed groups believe that the actions of the oppressor toward them are undertaken for their sake when instead it is for the oppressor's best interests. Gradually members begin to internalize their oppression and their marginalization and believe that it is their own deficiencies, described by the oppressor, that are responsible for their low self-esteem, powerlessness, and hopelessness, and eventually they learn to hate themselves and the group to which they belong.

The misuse of power lays the framework to oppressed group behavior (Friere, 1968; Johnson, 1997). The oppressor uses his power to cause the oppressed to submit and be compliant. Lee and Saeed (2001) posited that members of oppressed groups are reactive rather than rational and intentional. This reactive behavior continues to support the oppression. According to Freire (1968), members of oppressed groups are often silent when there is cause to express their concerns. Their silence reflects feelings of shame and embarrassment about their oppression. There is a resistance in acknowledging that as humans we are part of the patriarchal and oppressive system, and therefore we often fail to acknowledge its dynamic. Friere declared that oppression is successful because it is not recognized and can therefore become internalized. Internalized oppression occurs when women have learned to internalize the negative beliefs about women touted by their oppressor, often feeling inferior to men (Stout & McPhail, 1998). Women will often take on the voice of men, their oppressor, by stating, for example, that they would rather work with men than women, or would rather work for a male boss than a female boss. In essence, then, women become judgmental and critical of their own gender—they internalize the misogyny of the patriarchal system. It's misogyny that changed the concept of the word *witch* from being that of a wise woman healer or midwife to that of an evil-doer, resulting in burning "witches" at the stake during the Middle Ages because of their healing abilities (Ashley, 1976; Ehrenreich & English, 1973; Johnson).

Not all women necessarily experience oppression the same just because they are women, however. Race, sexual orientation, religious beliefs, and other aspects of womanhood influence the degree of oppression one may both experience and internalize (Johnson, 1997). Pheterson (1986) provided a more detailed definition of the construct of internalized oppression:

> Internalized oppression is the incorporation and acceptance by individuals within an oppressed group of the prejudices against them within the dominant society. Internalized oppression is likely to consist of self-hatred, self-concealment, fear of violence, and feelings of inferiority, resignation, isolation, powerlessness, and gratefulness for being allowed to survive. Internalized oppression is the mechanism within an oppressive system for perpetuating domination not only by external controls but also by building subservience into the minds of the oppressed groups. (p. 148)

When women and men label women who are assertive, or who display what are typically labeled male characteristics, or who work in male-dominated occupations, as *witchy*, it serves to maintain the patriarchal system by keeping women "in their place" and promoting male privilege (Johnson, 1997).

One aspect of oppression is horizontal hostility (HH) (Stone, 2007), also called horizontal violence (Friere, 1968; Lee & Saeed, 2001). HV occurs when the oppressed direct their anger and sense of helplessness and hopelessness about their oppression to members of their own group. This is a result of often being unable to exhibit feelings of aggression against the dominant group for fear of reprisal. They also tend to lack pride with their own group and are hesitant to align themselves with those members who have the least power within their group (Dunn, 2003). This can result in self-hatred, an example of internalized oppression, where women (and men) are unable to challenge the patriarchal system and its male privilege; they may not even see patriarchy as a problem because it is so much a part of the fabric of their life from birth—it is the reality in which all human beings exist (Johnson, 1997).

Stone's (2007) qualitative study identified a number of issues that catalyze HH. These included jealousy, competition, and/or recognition for jobs, control, and power issues and female stereotypes where the women expected their coworkers to behave in traditionally female ways. Behaviors comprising the HH were sarcasm, verbal abuse, public reprimands, sabotage of another's work, taking credit for another's work, exclusion, gossip, whispering, and blaming. Simpson and Cohen (2004), acknowledging that women can be bullies, stated:

> Rather than challenging the masculine hegemony of management, some women—particularly those who employ bullying tactics—may be conforming to the masculine ethic that underpins many management practices. On this basis, while men and women may be involved as perpetrators in bullying situations, and while, irrespective of gender, much bullying involves the abuse of power, such behavior cannot be divorced from gender considerations. (p. 182)

A critical element to patriarchy and oppression is hatred of the very group in which the oppressed is a member. Women's hostility to women is a complex phenomenon that requires discussion.

WOMEN'S HOSTILITY TO WOMEN

Women's hostility to women (WHW) is a perplexing issue complicated by women's anger, sexist beliefs, stereotypes (Cowan, Neighbors, DeLaMoreaux, & Behnke, 1998), and their oppression as a group (Johnson, 1997). When women oppress other women with their hostility to their own gender, they help maintain the patriarchal system (Acher, 1990). WHW occurs when women feel hostility toward other women and hold negative stereotypes of women as a group and therefore reject other women (Cowan et al.). This phenomenon of believing negative stereotypes about one's own group has been called *false consciousness* by Jost and Banaji (1994), and it is a framework that maintains and justifies the status quo of patriarchy.

WHW has its roots in childhood. Tannen's (1990) research with preteen girls' conversations with their friends demonstrated that they become judgmental of other girls who dress in expensive or designer

clothing. Tannen asserted that "appearing better than others is a violation of the girls' egalitarian ethic: People are supposed to stress their
connections and similarity" (p. 217). This ethic is in contrast to boys'
socialization, where displaying their supremacy and boasting is an
advantage in their male friendships. If girls boast and appear better than
their friends, they risk rejection by their peers at a time when affiliation
with their friends is paramount. As a result, girls and women will often
hide their successes and accomplishments to avoid loss of approval from
their friends or the actual loss of friendships. The behavior of concealing
success can later result in women not receiving the recognition deserved,
promotions, and future opportunities.

Loya, Cowan, and Walters (2006) asserted that WHW occurs when
women feel inadequate and dissatisfied with themselves, and project
those negative feelings onto their own gender, in a sense scapegoating
other women. The researchers stated this develops "because socially acceptable prejudices about women already exist. Instead of boosting her
ingroup or derogating outgroups, a woman with a threatened sense of
self may choose to derogate her own group" (p. 9024). This scapegoating
enables her to view other women as equally inadequate as herself,
thereby raising her own self-esteem. A woman's self-esteem was found
to be a critical element in determining the likelihood of that woman's
hostility toward other women (Cowan et al., 1998). For women, one's
self-esteem is often tied to how they view their attractiveness.

Media images of attractive women stimulate WHW because women
compare their own bodies to the bodies and attractiveness of the media
images, resulting in a lowered sense of self and a negative impression of
their own bodies (Loya et al., 2006). Rodin, Silberstein, and Striegel-
Moore (1984) found that women's negative views of their own bodies is
so pervasive as to be the norm. This can result in projecting their discontent on to other women, often resenting them, and stimulating further
hostility toward them. The researchers asserted, however, that the hostility that's generated emanates from devaluing or discounting other wom-
en's attractiveness, not in feeling hostile about the images themselves.
The authors claimed that "women who are more hostile toward women
may make themselves feel better, or at least ... from feeling worse,
when competing with other women who are more favorable on a
dimension traditionally valued in women (e.g., attractiveness) by devaluing or discounting the attributes of the other woman" (p. 581).

Examining Western beauty standards from this perspective has been
argued to represent the oppression of women (Forbes et al., 2007). Jeffreys (2005) stated that beauty standards and practices diminish wom-
en's self-confidence, focus attention on the superficial aspects of
womanhood rather than on a woman's competencies, and reduce
women to sex objects. Forbes and her colleagues argued that women's
dissatisfaction with their bodies reinforces patriarchy, and Jeffreys

indicated that the current beauty standards and practices maintain gender inequality. Forbes et al. also found in their study with women and men that an association existed between sexism, hostility toward women, and the Western standards and practices of what constitutes beauty.

When few women are employed in a male-dominated workplace, they are known as tokens (Kanter, 1977). Kanter discovered that, when women find themselves as tokens, they may disengage in their association with other women, believing that it will improve their standing with their male colleagues. The token woman will come to believe that, to belong with the guys, she needs to detach from the other women to the degree that she begins to incorporate the same prejudices against women as do her male peers. As a female token, her gender becomes particularly salient if she is promoted because the promotion may be due, in part, to her gender. As a result, she is viewed as a competitor by the other women with whom she works, leading to rivalry relationships. Kanter argued that the men with whom the tokens work establish a game of loyalty in which the women are compared to each other on the basis of the amount of loyalty they demonstrate to their male coworkers. One of the aspects of the game is for the women, sometimes unconsciously, to turn against their own gender, collude with the men, and interfere with hiring and promotional practices of other women by criticizing and devaluing them, thereby allowing the men to maintain their dominance.

Harris (1974) found that females were more aggressive to other females than to males. Women tend to use covert aggression in their abuse of other women, such as exclusion and gossip (Mizrahi, 2004). Bjorkqvist, Osterman, and Lagerspetz (1994) identified a variety of aggressive behaviors women use toward each other in addition to exclusion and gossip: negative facial expressions, sharing secrets, spreading rumors, sharing nasty comments about another, and ignoring, to name a few. Both men and women prefer to use covert aggression tactics, with women more likely to use social manipulation than men. Covert aggression by both genders is an attempt to disguise abusive behavior in hopes of preventing retaliation and/or social ostracizing. Likewise, covert aggression was found to be the more prevalent form of aggression in Baron's (Baron et al., 1999) study.

According to Loya, Cowan, and Walters (2006), one catalyst of WHW is any situation that has the power to stimulate negative feelings in women about themselves as women. Heterosexual women who are dependent on men for their social identity tended to devalue other women (Cowan et al., 1998; Henderson & Cunningham, 1993). Cowen and her colleagues also found that women who were hostile to other women tended to be younger, dissatisfied with their personal and sexual lives, less emotionally intimate with their partners, more hostile to men, and were more accepting of interpersonal and sexual violence toward women.

Mizrahi (2004) raised the questions as to whether WHW may constitute gender harassment, a form of sexual harassment, and, if so, whether it can rise to the level of a sexual harassment hostile environment claim. Mizrahi argued that the answers are yes because in many instances women harass and devalue each other because of their gender: "Moreover, female-on-female harassment is often created by sex segregation and discrimination in the workplace, and falls squarely under the coverage of Title VII of the Civil Rights Act of 1964" (p. 1579). Through the Civil Rights Act, employers are prohibited from discriminating, which includes harassment, against any employee on the basis of her or his protected class such as sex, race, color, religion, and national origin (U.S. Equal Employment Opportunity Commission, 1990). She explained the relationship of female-to-female harassment, Title VII, and the superiority of men at work in the following quote:

> Some may argue that Title VII's prohibition of discrimination based on sex was meant to address male supremacy, and that a recognition of female-on-female harassment would be a significant departure from Title VII's goal. However, legal recognition of female-on-female sex harassment does work to combat male supremacy in the workplace. As explained through this chapter the exclusion of women from male-dominated jobs and from positions of authority creates hostile relations among women in the workplace. Holding employers liable for the dynamics that they have created among women shifts the focus back to segregation and thus creates additional incentives for employers to integrate their workplaces and empower female workers. (p. 1620)

Gender harassment is a form of hostile work environment sexual harassment characterized by unwanted behavior that creates a negative work environment and can be psychologically injurious (Fitzgerald & Hesson-McInnis, 1989; Lee, 2001; Piotrkowski, 1998; Yoder and Aniakudo). The hostile work environment classification of sexual harassment is surrounded by ambiguity (Fitzgerald & Ormerod, 1993). Yoder and Aniakudo and others (Schultz, 1998; Weiner & Hurt, 1999) suggested that it is not the behavior alone that determines whether the incidents are hostile, but consideration of the environmental context is required to make the determination. Yoder and Aniakudo posited that "the gender-typing of an occupation, the gender composition of the work groups, and the organizational climate regarding gender all may impact on what is perceived as harassing behavior" (p. 254). The authors stated that these issues are broader than the workplace and reflect societal mores as well.

In the first sexual harassment case that was heard by the United States Supreme Court, *Meritor Savings Bank v. Vinson* in 1986, the court held that a victim could hold an employer liable for a sexual hostile work environment if the conduct the victim was subjected to was because of her sex (*Meritor v. Vinson*, 1986). In 1998 the Supreme Court heard another sexual harassment case, *Oncale v. Sundowner Offshore Services, Inc.,* addressing male-to-male sexual harassment (*Oncale v. Sundowner,* 1998). The court stated that sexual harassment did not need to be the result of sexual desire to constitute sex discrimination/harassment on the basis of one's sex.

Yale law professor Vicki Schultz conceptualized sexual harassment more broadly than many courts and the scholarly literature (1998). Schultz identified sexual harassment as both sexual and nonsexual means to devalue women and ensure they are unsuccessful in male-dominant domains. Her thesis stated that the courts fail sexual harassment victims by not addressing the totality of a woman's experience in the workplace—the subtle and not so subtle ongoing daily discrimination and inequities along with sexual harassment. She asserted that they are one and the same with the intent to hold women from progressing within the organization and their careers.

Since the Oncale ruling, courts and scholars have focused on male-to-male harassment and gay and lesbian harassment, and, according to Mizrahi (2004), "nonsexualized female-on-female harassment remains invisible as well as undertheorized" (p. 1584). Schultz (1998) believed that a major component of sexual harassment evolved from job segregation, which is often based on sex segregation. Sex segregation in the workplace sets the stage for sex stereotyping to occur (Masser & Abrams, 2004; Deaux, 1995). Schultz and Mizrahi asserted that sex segregation creates the dynamics of WHW in the form of harassment, where women are more likely to undermine each other.

Mizrahi (2004) took an additional approach, indicating that WHW is perpetuated by women who are jealous of their female peers who are advancing and have more power than other women—therefore recognizing that WHW is sex-based. Mizrahi posited that an examination of the workplace climate, with attention to the environment and the types of relationship dynamics among the women, would provide needed information to determine if the hostility is sex-based. Mizrahi further explained sex-based harassment in her article:

> In addition, when the reason for the harassment is female-specific, the same "but for" test can be used to determine that the "because of sex" element has been satisfied: If only a woman could be targeted for the harassment, it is by definition sex-based. For example, when a woman harasses a female coworker out of jealousy regarding a female-specific trait, the harassment can be considered sex-based. Recall, too, that sex segregation leads to sex being salient, so that women are more likely to compare themselves to each other along gendered lines than they would be in an integrated environment. (p. 1617)

Mizrahi (2004) stated that courts should address three elements to determine if WHW may constitute female to female harassment: (a) both horizontal and vertical segregation; (b) the relationship between the target and the perpetrator as well as the overall relationships among the women, the role the men play in impacting the women's relationships; and (c) whether the behavior was female to female and/or any other indicators that merit attention such as a general atmosphere of misogyny.

CONCLUSION

Perhaps change is looming in perceptions of strong "masculine" women. Ledet and Henley's study (2000) demonstrated that power was associated with masculine characteristics. The researchers found that women in senior positions within their workplace were seen as masculine in comparison to both women and men in lower positions. This result was viewed in a positive light, indicating that female stereotypes of dependent, soft, and unassertive were not associated with women in senior leadership roles, and therefore may be changing. Examining the results of Ledet and Henley's study, and the research on sexism, stereotypes, and communication, is a critical step in creating a society of equality. Framing these constructs within the patriarchal system of oppression may add a more comprehensive approach to dismantling the patriarchy that has existed for thousands of years (Johnson, 1997) and continues to exert its influence on the double standard between women and men. Changing patriarchy is a challenge that must be stimulated and propelled forward by not only the scholarly research but by organizations who currently support male privilege; and the women and men who are a part of the patriarchal system must know there are alternative paths.

REFERENCES

Abrams, D., Viki, G. T., Masser, B., & Bohner, G. (2003). Perceptions of stranger and acquaintance rape: The role of benevolent and hostile sexism in victim blame and rape proclivity. *Journal of Personality and Social Psychology, 84,* 111–125.

Acher, J. (1990). Hierarchies, jobs, bodies: A theory of gendered organizations. *Gender and Society, 4,* 139–158.

Arliss, L. P. (1991). *Gender communication.* Englewood Cliffs, NJ: Prentice-Hall.

Ashley, J. A. (1976). *Hospitals, paternalism, and the role of the nurse.* Teachers College: Columbia University.

Baron, R. A., Neuman, J. H., & Geddes, D. (1999). Social and personal determinants of workplace aggression: Evidence for the impact of perceived injustice and the type A behavior pattern. *Aggressive Behavior, 25,* 281–296.

Biernat, M., & Kobrynowicz, D. (1997). Gender and race-based standards of competence: Lower minimum standards but higher ability standards for devalued groups. *Journal of Personality and Social Psychology, 72,* 544–557.

Bjorkqvist, K., Osterman, K., & Lagerspetz, K. M. J. (1994). Sex differences in covert aggression among adults. *Aggressive Behavior, 20,* 27–33. Retrieved on January 29, 2006, from EBSCO database.

Burgess, D., & Borgida, E. (1999). Who women are, who women should be: Descriptive and prescriptive gender stereotyping in sex discrimination. *Psychology, Public Policy, and Law, 5*(3), 665–692.

Conway, M., & Vartanian, L. R. (2000). A status account of gender stereotypes: Beyond communality and agency. *Sex Roles, 43*(3/4), 181–199. Retrieved on June 3, 2007, from ProQuest database.

Cowan, G., Neighbors, C., DeLaMoreaux, J., & Behnke, C. (1998). Women's hostility toward women. *Psychology of Women Quarterly, 22,* 267–284. Retrieved on May 3, 2007, from EBSCO database.

Deaux, K. (1995). How basic can you be? The evolution of research on gender stereotypes. *Journal of Social Issues, 51*(1), 11–21. Retrieved on April 16, 2007, from ProQuest database.

Devine, P. (1989). Stereotypes and prejudice: Their automatic and controlled components. *Journal of Personality and Social Psychology, 56,* 5–18. Retrieved on March 28, 2007, from ProQuest database.

Dunn, H. (2003). Horizontal violence among nurses in the operating room. *AORN Journal, 78,* 977–988.

Eagly, A. H. (1987). *Sex differences in social-role interpretation.* Hillsdale, NJ: Lawrence Erlbaum.

Eagly, A. H., & Johnson, B. T. (1990). Gender and leadership style: A meta-analysis. *Psychological Bulletin, 108,* 233–256.

Eagly, A. H., Karau, S. J., & Makhijani, M. G. (1995). Gender and the effectiveness of leaders: A meta-analysis. *Psychological Bulletin, 117,* 125–145.

Eagly, A. H., Makhijani, M. G., & Klonsky, B. G. (1992). Gender and the evaluation of leaders: A meta-analysis. *Psychological Bulletin, 111,* 3–22.

Eagly, A. H., & Mladinic, A. (1994). Are people prejudiced against women? Some answers from research on attitudes, gender stereotypes, and judgments of competence. In W. Stroebe & M. Hewstone (Eds.), *European review of social psychology: Vol. 5* (pp. 1–35). New York: John Wiley.

Ehrenreich, B., & English, D. (1973). *Witches, midwives and nurses: A history of women healers.* Old Westbury, NY: Feminist Press.

Faludi, S. (1992). *Backlash: The undeclared war against American women.* New York: Doubleday.

Fiske, S. T. (1993). Controlling other people: The impact of power on stereotyping. *American Psychologist, 48,* 621–628. Retrieved on March 9, 2007, from ProQuest database.

Fiske, S. T., Bersoff, D. N., Borgida, E., Deaux, K., & Heilman, M. E. (1991). Social science research on trial: Use of sex stereotyping research in *Price Waterhouse v. Hopkins. American Psychologist, 46,* 1049–1060. Retrieved on March 9, 2007, from ProQuest database.

Fiske, S. T., & Glick, P. (1995). Ambivalence and stereotypes cause sexual harassment: A theory with implications for organizational change. *Journal of Social Issues, 51,* 97–116. Retrieved on July 19, 2005, from EBSCO database.

Fiske, S. T., & Stevens, L. E. (1993). What's so special about sex? Gender stereotyping and discrimination. In S. Oskamp & M. Costanzo (Eds.), *Gender issues in contemporary society* (pp. 173–196). Newbury Park, CA: Sage.

Fitzgerald, L. F. (1993). Sexual harassment: Violence against women in the workplace. *American Psychologist, 48,* 1070–1076.

Fitzgerald, L. F., & Hesson-McInnis, M. (1989). The dimensions of sexual harassment: A structural analysis. *Journal of Vocational Behavior, 35*(3), 309–326.

Fitzgerald. L. F., & Ormerod, A. J. (1993). Breaking the silence: The sexual harassment of women in academia and the workplace. In F. L. Denmark & M. S. Paludi (Eds.), *Psychology of women: A handbook of issues and theories.* (pp. 553–581). Westport, CT: Greenwood.

Forbes, G. B., Collinsworth, L. L., Jobe, R. L., Braum, K. D., & Wise, L. M. (2007). Sexism, hostility toward women, and endorsement of beauty ideals and practices: Are beauty ideals associated with oppressive beliefs? *Sex Roles, 56*, 265–273.

Franke, K. M. (1997). What's wrong with sexual harassment? *Stanford Law Review, 49*, 691–772.

Freire, P. (1968). *Pedagogy of the oppressed.* NY: Seabury.

Glick, P. (1991). Trait-based and sex-based discrimination in occupational prestige, occupational salary, and hiring. *Sex Roles, 25*, 351–378.

Glick, P., Diebold, J., Balley-Werner, B., & Zhu, L. (1997). The two faces of Adam: Ambivalent sexism and polarized attitudes toward women. *Personality and Social Psychology Bulletin, 23*, 1323–1334.

Glick, P., & Fiske, S. T. (1996). The ambivalent sexism inventory: Differentiating hostile and benevolent sexism. *Journal of Personality and Social Psychology, 70*, 491–512.

Glick, P., & Fiske, S. T. (1997). Hostile and benevolent sexism: Measuring ambivalent sexist attitudes toward women. *Psychology of Women Quarterly, 21*, 119–135.

Glick P., & Fiske, S. T. (2001). An ambivalent alliance: Hostile and benevolent sexism as complementary justifications for gender inequality. *American Psychologist, 56*, 109–118. Retrieved on May 20, 2007, from EBSCO database.

Glick, P., & Fiske S. T. (2002). Ambivalent responses. *American Psychologist, 57*, 444–446. Retrieved on May 15, 2007, from EBSCO database.

Gutek, B. A. (1985). *Sex in the workplace.* San Francisco: Jossey-Bass.

Gutek, B. A., & Morasch, B. (1982). Sex-rations, sex-role spillover, and sexual harassment of women at work. *Journal of Social Issues, 38*, 55–74.

Harris, M. B. (1974) Mediators between frustration and aggression in a field experiment. *Journal of Experimental Social Psychology, 10*, 561–571.

Harris, M. B. (1994). Gender of subject and target as mediators of aggression. *Journal of Applied Social Psychology, 24*(5), 453–471.

Harris, M. B., & Knight-Bohnhoff, K. (1996). Gender and aggression I: Perceptions of aggression. *Sex Roles, 35*(1/2), 1–25. Retrieved on January 3, 2004, from ProQuest database.

Heim, P. (1995). Getting beyond "she said, he said." *Nursing Administration Quarterly, 19*(2), 6–18.

Henderson, S. N., & Cunningham, J. N. (1993). Women's emotional dependence on men: Scale construction and test of Russianoff's hypothesis. *Sex Roles, 28*, 317–334.

Jeffreys, S. (2005). *Beauty and misogyny: Harmful cultural practices in the West.* New York: Routledge.

Johnson, A. (1997). *The gender knot: Unraveling our patriarchal legacy.* Philadelphia: Temple University.

Jost, J. T., & Banaji, M. (1994). The role of stereotyping in system-justification and the production of false consciousness. *British Journal of Social Psychology, 3,* 1–27.

Infante, D. A. (1981). Trait argumentativeness as a predictor of communicative behavior in situations requiring argument. *Central States Speech Journal, 32,* 265–272.

Infante, D. A. (1985). Inducing women to be more argumentative: Source credibility effects. *Journal of Applied Communication Research, 13,* 33–44.

Infante, D. A. (1987). Aggressiveness. In J. C. McCroskey & J. A. Daly (Eds.), Personality and interpersonal communication (pp. 157–192). Newbury Park, CA: Sage.

Kanter, R. M. (1977). *Men and women of the corporation.* New York: Basics Books.

Ledet, L. M., & Henley, T. B. (2000). Perceptions of women's power as a function of position within an organization. *The Journal of Psychology, 134*(5), 515–526. Retrieved on April 24, 2007, from ProQuest database.

Lee, D. (2001). "He didn't sexually harass me, as in harassed for sex ... he was just horrible": Women's definitions of unwanted male sexual conduct at work. *Women's Studies International Forum, 24*(1), 25–38. Retrieved on June 26, 2005, from ProQuest database.

Lee, D. (2002). Gendered workplace bullying in the restructured UK civil service. *Personnel Review, 31*(1/2), 205–228. Retrieved on June 26, 2005, from ProQuest database.

Lee, M. B., & Saeed, I. (2001). Oppression and horizontal violence: The case of nurses in Pakistan. *Nursing Forum, 36*(1), 15–24. Retrieved on March 23, 2006, from EBSCO database.

Loya, B., Cowan, G., & Walters, C. (2006). The role of social comparison and body consciousness in women's hostility toward women. *Sex Roles, 54,* 575–583.

Masser, B. M., & Abrams, D. (2004). Reinforcing the glass ceiling: The consequences of hostile sexism for female managerial candidates. *Sex Roles, 51*(9/10), 609–615.

Meritor Savings Bank v. Vinson 477 U.S. 57 (1986).

Mizrahi, R. (2004). Hostility to the presence of women: Why women undermine each other in the workplace and the consequences for Title VII. *Yale Law Journal, 113,* 1579–1621.

Nicotera, A. M., & Rancer, A. S. (1994). The influence of sex on self-perceptions and social stereotyping of aggressive communication predispositions. *Western Journal of Communication, 58*(4), 283–307.

Oncale v. Sundowner Offshore Services, 523 U.S. 75 (1998).

Pheterson, G. (1986). Alliances between women: Overcoming internalized oppression and internalized domination. *Signs, 12*(1), 146–160.

Piotrkowski, C. S. (1998). Gender harassment, job satisfaction, and distress among employed white and minority women. *Journal of Occupational Health Psychology, 3*(1), 33–43. Retrieved on April 25, 2004, from ProQuest database.

Price Waterhouse v. Hopkins, 490 U.S. 228 (1989).

Rodin, J., Silberstein, L. R., & Striegel-Moore, R. H. (1984). Women and weight: A normative discontent. In T. B. Sonderegger (Ed.), *Psychology and gender* (pp. 267–307). Lincoln, NE: University of Nebraska Press.

Schultz, V. (1998). Reconstructing sexual harassment. *Yale Law Journal, 107,* 1683–1796.

Sibley, C. G., & Wilson, S. (2004). Differentiating hostile and benevolent sexist attitudes toward positive and negative sexual female subtypes. *Sex Roles, 51,* 687–696.

Simpson, R., & Cohen, C. (2004). Dangerous work: The gendered nature of bullying in the context of higher education. *Gender, Work and Organization, 11*(2), 163–186.

Smith, K. C., Ulch, S. E., Cameron, J. E., Cumberland, J. A., Musgrave, M. A., & Tremblay, N. (1990). Gender-related effects in the perception of anger expression. *Sex Roles, 20*(9/10), 487–499.

Stone, E. A. (2007). *Women and workplace communication: A study of horizontal hostility.* Unpublished master's thesis, Oregon State University, Corvallis, OR.

Stout, K. D., & Kelly, M. J. (1990). Differential treatment based on sex. *Affilia, 5*(2), 60–71.

Stout, K., & McPhail, B. (1998). *Confronting sexism and violence against women: A challenge for social work.* Menlo Park, CA: Addison Wesley Longman.

Tannen, D. (1990). *You just don't understand: Women and men in conversation.* New York: Ballantine Books.

Tannen, D. (1994). *Talking from 9 to 5.* New York: Avon Books.

Troyer, C., & Younts, C. W. (1997). Whose expectations matter? The relative power of first and second order expectations in determining social influence. *The American Journal of Sociology, 103*(3), 692–732. Retrieved on May 25, 2007, from ProQuest database.

Turkel, A. R. (2004). The hand that rocks the cradle rocks the boat: The empowerment of women. *Journal of the American Academy of Psychoanalysis and Dynamic Psychiatry, 32*(1), 41–53.

U.S. Equal Employment Opportunity Commission (1990). *Policy guidance on current issues of sexual harassment.* Retrieved on April 5, 2005, from www.eeoc.gov/policy/docs/currentissues.html.

Wall, H. M., & Barry, A. (1985). Student expectations for male and female instructor behavior. In R. E. Cheatham (Ed.), *Women in higher education: Traditions, transitions and revolutions* (pp. 283–291). St. Louis: Saint Louis University, Metropolitan College, and SAASS, Inc.

Wiener, R. L., & Hurt, L. E. (1999). An interdisciplinary approach to understanding social sexual conduct at work. *Psychology, Public Policy, and Law, 5,* 556–595.

Wood, J. (1994). *Gendered lives: Communication, gender, and culture.* Belmont, CA: Wadsworth.

Wood, W., & Karten, S. J. (1986). Sex differences in interaction style as a product of perceived sex differences in competence. *Journal of Personality and Social Psychology, 50,* 341–347. Retrieved on July 28, 2007, from ProQuest database.

Yoder, J. D., & Aniakudo, P. (1996). When pranks become harassment: The case of African American women firefighters. *Sex Roles, 35*(5/6), 253–270. Retrieved on March 8, 2004, from ProQuest database.

Chapter 2

Lessons from My Father: In My Own Voice

Susan Lehrman

When I was 16 and beginning to think about colleges and majors, I went to my father for advice. My father was a man who appreciated education. He was one of the first college graduates in his extended family and was, at the time, working on an advanced degree. Yet his advice, at least by today's standards, seems sadly outdated. "The plan is for you to go to the local state school, where they have an excellent home economics teaching program. Money is tight and I need to save it to send your brothers away to school. After all, they will be supporting families, while you will have a husband to support you. Plus, you have great interpersonal, family-oriented skills. This is clearly the right path for you."

While my father's advice is sure to set modern teeth on edge, in the mid-1960s it was not that unusual. Although my mother worked part-time to help support our family, she had never been to college, nor had any of my aunts. My father was advanced enough to support the notion of a college education for his two daughters, but his vision was limited to consideration of typical "female" occupations: teaching, social work, or nursing.

Don't get me wrong, these are fine occupations for men or women, and my undergraduate degree in secondary education from our local university is one that I am proud of and one that has informed my life-long love of learning and commitment to the field of education. But who knows what arenas I might have explored if I had not been limited by these early constraints? And it was not just my father who limited my horizons. During high school, although I clearly had excellent math and science skills, I was encouraged to take chorus, acting, and domestic science electives in my junior and senior year rather than advanced science and math courses.

Despite these limitations, I have had an engaging career that I look back on with pride.

I taught high school in Alaska and Australia during my early post-baccalaureate years. I pursued a master's degree in public health, followed by 12 years in hospital management, in my late 20s and 30s. I received my PhD from the University of California at Berkeley in my early 40s. I taught at the college level and then became a higher education administrator in my late 40s and 50s.

As discordant as this career pathway might appear, my internal compass has consistently led me in the direction of using my interpersonal and organizational skills to start new programs and to solve sticky organizational problems.

My first management position was an entry-level job in a hospital. As fate would have it, my boss passed away very suddenly when I had been in the position for a short time. The organization found itself in a tough position. My boss had been spearheading several important projects, and there was no one waiting in the wings to step into his position. After discussing the situation with an individual who was to play an important mentoring role in my life, I went to the president and said that I would be willing to step into my boss's role on an interim basis. His first inclination was, literally, to laugh. I was young and inexperienced and most of the individuals I would be supervising were relatively uneducated older males—a tough group for anyone to control.

In the final analysis, the organization put me into the interim slot, "but only until we find a man who can take on the position." And with the warning, "These guys are going to try to make mincemeat of you, so don't do anything to rock the boat!"

While my father may have been on the wrong track regarding my college education, he left me with a set of values that served me well in this interim leadership position. He hammered home to all his children, "If you accept a job, give 110% and do anything and everything within ethical bounds to make a success of it. I don't care if you have to work 80 hours a week! Never give up!"

With this in mind, I determined that I would have to not only work hard, but be smart. It became clear to me early on that my new department was grossly overstaffed. Although I had been told not to rock the boat, I knew the hospital was experiencing financial difficulties. Another piece of wisdom from my father was to, "Do the right thing, even if it isn't the popular thing."

As natural attrition began to occur in my department, I again turned to my mentor and became convinced that the right thing to do was to reshuffle the workload to accommodate these losses without filling the vacated positions. Observing my actions from afar, seasoned directors from other departments strongly advised me that I was making a terrible mistake. Not only would the individuals I supervised raise a major ruckus, when the next budgetary cycle came around administration would surely require across-the-board labor cuts and I would be placed in the untenable position of having to cut more deeply than my department could bear. Far better, they said, to keep the labor budget padded so I could demonstrate my effectiveness in reducing staff at that time.

While I could see the inherent logic in my peers' recommendations, I could not get my father's voice out of my head. I called together my employees and told them what I intended to do and why. I told them that taking the right road, versus the easy road, would set us apart as a department that would never ask for resources it didn't need and that, in the end, we would all be better off for it. I assured them that I would not ask them to work beyond their capacity, but that together we could work smarter and save resources. To my astonishment, they agreed! As a team we set about to make our department as efficient as possible.

When the predicted time came for across the board cuts, every department but mine was cut by 10%. There was no discussion; the other department heads were simply told to "do it." My department, on the other hand, was rewarded for demonstrating its good stewardship by being allowed to propose a zero-based budget; as long as we could justify what was needed, we could have it. In the end, I was given the job permanently and a number of positions followed with the same organization in which I was asked to tackle difficult situations that required the cooperation of the entire team to succeed.

I learned a number of very valuable lessons from this early management experience that have continued to shape my leadership style to this day: Be transparent with those who work for you and with those you report to. Engage employees at all levels in organizational change. Do the right thing even if it appears the tougher course to follow. Take reasonable risks and do so courageously. Actively seek out mentors, and listen to them carefully, although in the end you have to follow your own intuition.

In my late 30s, I made the difficult decision to pursue a PhD that would eventually take me out of health care and into higher education. When I was 42, I completed my doctoral work, had my first and only child, and along with my husband made the decision to move from San Francisco to upstate New York. I took a 50% pay cut and became "the oldest junior faculty" at a small college teaching in the health MBA program.

While it had been my intention to leave my days as a manager behind me, this was not to be. Just as I was going through the tenure process, a leadership crisis occurred in my academic department. With no one to assume the lead, a critically needed accreditation was in jeopardy. After a failed search for the right candidate, and with much hesitancy, I said I would take the position as long as my colleagues agreed to support me and to work hard to successfully complete the accreditation process. They did, and we were successful.

Not long after this my institution announced its intention of spinning off all of its graduate programs in order to maintain its status as a liberal arts institution. With no one else able or willing to fill the slot, and with many fears about my ability to run a college, I agreed to serve as the founding president of Union Graduate College.

Starting a college, even one that has deep roots in a very old and prestigious undergraduate institution, has been in many ways like starting a new enterprise. The lessons from my first big management position have, however, continued to serve me well.

Pulling together the right team to share my vision of a growing, graduate-only institution, rooted in the liberal arts but deeply tied to the exciting things going on in the local business and professional communities, has been my biggest and most rewarding challenge. Together we have followed my father's injunction to "give 110% and do anything and everything within ethical bounds to make a success of it."

Research shows that women tend to pursue much more circular career paths than men. Indeed, my career path has not conformed to the norm. I have made lateral moves because they were more interesting to me than upward moves. I have accepted jobs that paid much less than prior jobs. In part this may be the result of early implicit or explicit injunctions against aiming high. Ironically, however, being freed from the push to achieve at all costs may have allowed me to follow a personally rewarding but atypical career path.

Perhaps all is well that ends well, but wouldn't it have been so much better if I—if all of us—were encouraged to follow our own dreams but to dream as big and wide as we wanted to? As I mentor young women, I share my father's early injunctions about college to encourage them to confront their own personal, hopefully less explicit but often just as damaging, gender stereotypes. After all, while anyone at any time can ply us with verbiage intended to limit our horizons, it is only when we internalize and accept these stereotypes that we are truly limited.

Chapter 3

Self-Esteem and High-Achieving Women

Tina Stern

INTRODUCTION

The psychology literature is full of empirical studies and theoretical articles on self-esteem, and there is considerable research on women and achievement. Yet, there is relatively little research on the intersection of gender, self-esteem, and achievement, and even less research on the concerns experienced by high-achieving women that may be related to their self-esteem. Over the past 40 years, psychologists have proposed that successful women have characteristics thought to be associated with high self-esteem (Betz & Fitzgerald, 1987; Fitzgerald & Harmon, 2001) and, conversely, that high-achieving women experience self-doubt, success-related fears, and fail to internalize their successes (Horner, 1969; Clance & Imes, 1978). Both hypotheses have, at times, received attention in the professional literature. Vocational development theorists agree that women's achievement is influenced by a complex interaction among various individual characteristics, such as self-esteem, with an array of external and social influences (Betz & Fitzgerald, 1987; Fitzgerald & Harmon, 2001; Gomez et al., 2001; Richie et al., 1997). The purpose of this chapter is to examine literature on the relationship between self-esteem and achievement in women and to learn more about the concerns that high-achieving women experience that are related to their self-esteem.

Research on the relationship among self-esteem and achievement, leadership, and performance has been conducted in diverse disciplines. Counseling psychologists who study career development have examined the role of self-esteem and related characteristics in vocational behavior (Betz, 2001). The disciplines of business management (Pierce & Gardner, 2004) and applied psychology (Judge & Bono, 2001; Schwalbe, Gecas, & Baxter, 1986) have examined the role of self-esteem as it relates to job performance. Personality and social psychologists, along with sociologists, have studied self-esteem as it relates to a wide array of behavioral outcomes including performance (Baumeister, Campbell, Krueger, & Vohs, 2003; Rosenberg, Schooler, Schoenbach, & Rosenberg, 1995), and clinical psychologists have been interested in the relationship between self-esteem and behavioral choices (Baumeister et al.). In the absence of research directly on the topic of women's achievement and self-esteem and self-esteem concerns, this chapter will review and integrate some of the related literature from the areas of vocational development, management, and social psychology. The chapter begins with an examination of some of the literature in the area of vocational development that describes the characteristics of high-achieving women and the role of self-esteem, self-concept, and self-efficacy in their vocational behavior. The chapter continues with a description of some of the research challenges in the study of self-esteem and reviews the literature on self-esteem and performance. This is followed by a description of a theoretical approach to the study of self-esteem that will then be used to review seven qualitative studies of high-achieving women for possible self-esteem–related content.

CHARACTERISTICS RELATED TO WOMEN'S VOCATIONAL BEHAVIOR

Self-Esteem and Self-Efficacy

Vocational development theories have long recognized that traits, such as self-esteem, and other individual characteristics interact with environmental conditions and constraints to influence vocational behavior (Fitzgerald & Harmon, 2001). Self-concept, as distinct from self-esteem, was among the traits considered by early vocational development theorists to be central in the process of career development (Betz, 2001). Early theorists proposed that people developed a vocational self-concept that influenced their choices. In addition to self-concept, some researchers emphasized the importance of self-esteem in career selection (Betz). Betz predicted that people with high self-esteem would make more congruent and fulfilling vocational choices than those with low self-esteem and that they would be more certain about their choices.

Regarding internal characteristics related to success, recent research in the area of vocational behavior has shifted focus away from self-esteem and self-concept as central to the process of vocational choice to an emphasis on the importance of self-efficacy. In contrast to self-esteem, which Betz (2001) defined as a general belief about one's importance and value, she defined self-efficacy as beliefs concerning one's ability to perform a specific behavior or a class of behaviors. Betz has applied the principles of Bandura's work on self-efficacy to the development of a theory of vocational behavior. Betz identified various domains of career self-efficacy, including occupational self-efficacy, task-specific self-efficacy, career decision-making self-efficacy, and self-efficacy and vocational interests. Career self-efficacy is related to outcome expectations, vocational aspirations, academic success, career barriers, vocational interests, occupational congruence, and social support (Phillips & Imhoff, 1997; Fassinger, 2002). The importance of self-efficacy to the vocational choice process has received considerable research support and is an important theoretical advance, particularly for understanding women's vocational behavior (Betz; Fitzgerald & Harmon, 2001). Fassinger (2005) proposed that high self-efficacy is a key ingredient to success for women. Low self-efficacy is "probably the most pervasive and intractable internal barrier to a woman's career success" (Fassinger, 2002, p. 31) as it results in her own underestimation of competencies, talents, and capabilities.

Gender Typing

In addition to self-efficacy, Fassinger (2005) and Phillips and Imhoff (1997) emphasized the critical influence of internalized gender socialization on "vocationally relevant attitudes, beliefs, and personal traits contributing to the self-concept" (Fassinger, 2005, p. 99). Defining characteristics of female gender socialization that influence vocational behavior include nurturance, caretaking, cooperativeness, denial of one's own needs, male-referential self-worth judgments, expectations for marriage and children, and avoidance of cross-typed interests and behaviors (Fassinger, 2005). Such female-typed characteristics manifest themselves in the workplace as a range of "well-documented self-concept problems for women including compromised decision making, self-doubt, low aspirations, underutilization of talents and abilities, lack of confidence, low expectations for success, role conflict, guilt, and inordinate concern over the judgment of others" (Fassinger, 2005, p. 99). An additional consequence of this cycle is that women with weak self-concept will be more likely to blame themselves for external discrimination, which will reduce the likelihood that they will take effective action against it, perpetuating "a cycle of self-doubt and self-denigration" (Fassinger, 2005, p. 99). Gender socialization can also result in depressed entitlement (Fassinger, 2002). Given the numerous negative consequences of strong gender-typing for occupational advancement, it is not surprising that high-achieving women are low in many female-typed characteristics, such as the ones described above, and are high in some traits typically thought of as masculine, such as agency, instrumentality, and autonomy (Betz & Fitzgerald, 1987; Gomez et al., 2001). Traditional female gender-typing disadvantages women for vocational success while masculine-typed traits seem to confer an advantage.

Also related to gender stereotypes and socialization are pressures regarding marriage and motherhood. Expectations related to marriage and motherhood can result in role conflict for working women and can lead to guilt about non-parenting activities. Fassinger (2002) suggested that many women live with contradictory ideas about women's roles. They may have liberal ideologies regarding women working outside the home but maintain traditional attitudes toward women's responsibilities in the home and for the family. Even high-achieving women often expect to perform or assume responsibility for the majority of labor related to home and family (Fassinger, 2002). In addition to the actual responsibilities, spousal views of the woman's employment and gender role attitudes of partners/spouses and other family members are also ways that gender roles influence women's vocational behaviors.

Fear of Success and the Imposter Phenomenon

While there is an intuitive belief that success and self-esteem are strongly related, paradoxically, the opposite belief is also widespread. Reported in both the popular and the psychological literature has been the proposition that successful women have characteristics indicative of low self-esteem. Such reports suggest that they fear success, feel like imposters when they do succeed (Clance & Imes, 1978; Clance & O'Toole, 1987), experience dependency conflicts (Post, 1982), and are self-sabotaging (Post, 1989). The pervasiveness of the belief in women's low self-esteem related to achievement is evidenced even in feminist works like Gloria Steinem's book (1992) *Revolution from Within: A Book of Self-Esteem*, where she writes, "Wherever I traveled, I saw women who were smart, courageous, and valuable, who didn't *think* they were smart, courageous, or valuable—and this was true not only for women who were poor or otherwise doubly discriminated against, but for supposedly privileged and powerful women, too" (p. 3).

Fear of Success (FOS) (Horner, 1969) and the Imposter Phenomenon (IP) (Clance & Imes, 1978) formulate hypothetical constructs that imply that achievement for women is accompanied by self-esteem–related conflicts. Both constructs propose that successful women, more than men, experience self-esteem-related doubts. However, results from studies on these constructs have been contradictory, and researchers have found fault with the constructs themselves (Hyde, 2006; Rollins, 1996; Fried-Buchalter, 1992, 1997). Furthermore, neither construct has received empirical support for its hypotheses that women experience such problems at a rate greater than men (Paludi, 1984; Fried-Buchalter, 1992, 1997).

The premise that underlies both FOS and IP, that women experience problems as a result of success to a greater degree than do men, has not been supported. This premise reflects the widespread belief that women, in general, have lower self-esteem than men (Kling, Hyde, Showers, & Buswell, 1999). Kling and her colleagues conducted a meta-analysis on gender differences in global self-esteem using 216 different samples of more than 97,000 people. While males received a higher self-esteem score on average, the difference between males and females was small and fluctuated with age and ethnicity. The gender difference in self-esteem was very small in children and gradually increased to a moderate size in high school. Gender differences in self-esteem were largest in high school, larger than at any other time of life. For adults between the ages of 23 to 59, the gender difference in self-esteem was almost zero, and the size of the difference continued to decline even further for those over 60 years old. In addition, the meta-analysis found that the gender difference in self-esteem between African-American men and women was also almost zero, suggesting that broad assumptions about women's poorer self-esteem relative to men's is unfounded (Kling et al.).

A final problem with the constructs of FOS and IP is that they focus on internal barriers to women's occupational achievement. Fitzgerald and Harmon (2001) pointed out that discussions of women's career development and career choice have shifted from emphasizing internal barriers to women's success to recognizing the obstacles presented by external, systemic, societal factors, including the effects of gender socialization. Fitzgerald and Harmon's model of women's vocational behavior has removed FOS as an individual influence from their conceptualization because they note that it does little to explain or describe women's behavior.

Other Characteristics and Factors Related to Vocational Behavior

In addition to high self-efficacy and fewer gender-typed constraints and expectations, there is considerable consensus in the recent vocational development literature that women with a strong career orientation have in common a variety of other characteristics and external circumstances (Fassinger, 2002). High-achieving women are likely to have positive self-concepts, have had exposure to role models, have attended all-girl schools or women's colleges, had employed mothers, particularly mothers who enjoyed their work, and had fathers who supported and encouraged their achievements (Crawford & Unger, 2004). In addition, they tend to have strong academic self-concepts, educated parents, taken math courses, and married late (Betz & Fitzgerald, 1987). External or systemic occupational factors that can negatively affect women's achievement include unequal promotion, salary, power, discrimination, hostility, restricted access to information, stereotyping by others, absence of role models, sexual harassment, double standards for performance and behavior, and lack of support for family responsibilities. These negative influences on women's achievement are often compounded when women work in male-dominated fields (Fassinger, 2005; Heilman, Wallen, Fuchs, & Tamkins, 2004).

The next section reviews literature on self-esteem. Researchers have studied self-esteem extensively in a variety of disciplines. The section begins with an examination of some of the complexities in the study of self-esteem. This topic is followed by a discussion of two reviews and one meta-analysis on the relationship between self-esteem and performance, and the section ends with a description of an alternative approach to the study of self-esteem.

SELF-ESTEEM

Researchers agree that the role and importance of self-esteem is heavily influenced by culture (Diener & Diener, 1995); in the United States it has been called a preoccupation (Solomon, 2006), a popular obsession (Koch, 2006), the "holy grail of psychological health" (Crocker & Knight, 2005, p. 200), and "the royal road to happiness and personal fulfillment, and an antidote to a variety of social ills, including unemployment, gang violence, and teenage pregnancy" (Brown & Marshall, 2006, p. 4). Solomon reports that using *self-esteem* as a search term in Google in 2003 resulted in 2,270,000 results. Between January and October of 2001, Baumeister and his colleagues (2003) searched the Psyc-INFO databases for all articles containing the term *self-esteem* in the abstract and found 15,059 articles. Yet despite the widespread interest and belief in self-esteem among some academics and the public, research conclusions about the importance of and behavioral outcomes related to self-esteem have been controversial and a source of debate in the professional literature. Academics who research and study self-esteem disagree about the definition of self-esteem (Mruk, 2006), its nature (Marsh, Craven, & Martin, 2006), its function (Brown & Marshall), and its importance to the individual and to society (Owens & McDavitt, 2006; Crocker & Park, 2004; Pyszczynski, Greenburg, Solomon, Arndt, & Schimel, 2004), whether it produces specific behavioral outcomes (Baumeister et al.), whether it is a basic human need (Koch, 2006), whether having high self-esteem is necessarily positive (Baumeister et al.), and whether people should try to pursue high self-esteem as a goal in itself (Crocker & Park).

Defining Self-Esteem

The first challenge in studying self-esteem is that there is little agreement about what is meant by the term (Brown & Marshall, 2006). Researchers use and define self-esteem in different ways (Mruk, 2006). There are unidimensional and multidimensional approaches to understanding self-esteem (Marsh et al., 2006). A unidimensional use of the term refers to global or trait self-esteem. Global or trait self-esteem refers to the way "people generally feel about themselves" (Brown & Marshall, p. 4) or the overall evaluation of one's worth or importance (Blascovitch & Tomaka, 1991). Global self-esteem has been found to be relatively stable across a person's life span (Brown & Marshall). From a multidimensional perspective, psychologists also study state self-esteem and domain-specific self-esteem (Brown & Marshall). State self-esteem is more changeable than global self-esteem and refers to feelings of self-worth or temporary emotional reactions to various contexts; e.g., feelings that occur after getting a promotion or winning an award. Domain-specific self-esteem refers to self-evaluations of specific abilities and attributes; e.g., occupational self-esteem or academic self-esteem (Brown & Marshall). While the constructs of global, trait, and domain-specific self-esteem are related, they are also distinct, and theorists disagree about which conceptualization is most useful (Brown & Marshall). Brown and Marshall fault researchers for contributing to confusion in the study of self-esteem by not specifying the definition or level of self-esteem they are using in their research. In addition to definitional complications, the nature of self-esteem is also debated; some researchers emphasize the cognitive aspect of self-esteem (a rational assessment of worth; e.g., I am competent), while others focus on the affective component (feeling of liking of oneself; e.g., I feel good about who I am, I feel worthwhile), and some conceptualizations advocate understanding self-esteem as a combination and interaction of both competence and worthiness (Mruk). Finally, to confuse the issue further, there are numerous terms that are similar to but distinct from self esteem, including *self-concept, self-efficacy,* and *life satisfaction.* And there are other terms that are considered to be more or less synonymous with self-esteem, including *self-worth, self-acceptance,* and *self-regard* (Blascovitch & Tomaka).

Self-Esteem and Measurement Challenges

Two methodological weaknesses occur repeatedly in research on self-esteem that make it challenging to study: the use of correlational studies, which makes causal conclusions difficult (Baumeister et al., 2003), and the use of self-report measures. Few of the many thousands of studies published on the topic use the highly rigorous methods that are necessary to establish causal relationships. Although studies may imply that high or low self-esteem is causally related to many behaviors or psychological states, correlational research generally cannot conclude whether level of self-esteem caused a particular outcome (high self-esteem produces professional success), whether the outcome caused the level of self-esteem (professional success results in high self-esteem), or whether a third variable caused both the particular outcome and the level of self-esteem (educational attainment causes high self-esteem and professional success). In fact, the conclusion from substantial research examining the relationship between self-esteem and school performance is that it is more likely that school performance causes changes in self-esteem than the other way around, and many researchers have found that any relationship between self-esteem and school achievement is likely to be a result of a third variable, that is, family background factors (Baumeister et al.).

The use of self-reports in research on self-esteem presents other significant methodological problems. First, most self-esteem measures do not distinguish among "defensive, inflated, narcissistic, and so-called genuine high self-esteem" (Baumeister et al., 2003, p. 5). Some of these types of high self-esteem can be associated with undesirable outcomes like hostility or aggression (Baumeister et al.). Second, people with high self-esteem tend to see all their characteristics in a positive light, and those with low self-esteem tend to be generally negative about many things, not just their self-esteem. "It is hard to distinguish the general negativity from the specific low self-esteem" (Baumeister et al., p. 7). Therefore, self-reports contain a bias, a favorable one for those with high self-esteem and an unfavorable one for those with low self-esteem. Furthermore, as with all self-reports, the responses may or may not be an accurate assessment of a person's characteristics but merely the positive (or negative) self-view of the respondent. When self-esteem is high in the absence of any justification, researchers question whether the high self-esteem is a manifestation of unhealthy narcissism. For example, Baumeister and his colleagues found that while people with high self-esteem believe they are more popular and interpersonally skilled than others, "when rated by peers, teachers or laboratory interaction partners, people with high self-esteem are not liked any better than people with low self-esteem" (p. 20). Therefore, responses on self-report often do not correspond to objective measures.

Notwithstanding the challenges in studying self-esteem, there is considerable research on the topic, and most psychologists agree that it is important, although they may disagree as to the reasons. To better understand the relationship between self-esteem and achievement in women, the following section will examine selected meta-analytic research studies and literature reviews on the relationship between self-esteem and performance.

Self-Esteem and Performance

Judge and Bono (2001) completed a meta-analysis of 81 studies of employed adults that was designed to examine the relationship between each of four traits with job satisfaction and job performance. Judge and Bono were interested in the higher-order construct called core self-evaluation, which they also refer to as positive self-concept, and the four traits they studied indicate a person's core self-evaluation. The four traits studied in this investigation were global self-esteem, generalized self-efficacy, locus of control, and emotional stability/neuroticism. Judge and Bono were investigating whether the components of the core self-evaluation construct had predictive validity for job satisfaction and job performance. For the purposes of this chapter, this discussion will focus on their findings only on the relationship between the trait of self-esteem (or global self-esteem) and job performance.

Judge and Bono (2001) presented theoretical arguments to support their hypotheses that each of the four traits would be related to both job satisfaction and job performance. Specifically, with regard to self-esteem and performance, they cited self-consistency theory as underlying the prediction that individuals with high self-esteem will perform successfully in order to maintain their positive self-image. The meta-analysis concluded that although self-esteem had the strongest positive relationship with job performance from among the variables (.26), the relationship was more complicated than the relationships between the other variables and job performance. These relationships were less clear because of the greater variability in the correlations across the studies on self-esteem and job performance. In fact, more than 10% of the individual studies reported a negative relationship between self-esteem and job performance. They suggested that there are unknown factors that influence the extent to which self-esteem is important to job performance. Baumeister and his colleagues (2003) also found high variability in the relationship between self-esteem and performance in the studies that they reviewed. With regard to the relationship between the other three traits that constitute core self-evaluation and job performance, Judge and Bono found that all three traits had a positive and similar relationship (correlations between .19 and .23) to job performance.

In contrast with Judge and Bono's (2001) investigation of the relationship between global self-esteem and performance, Pierce and Gardner (2004) examined a domain-specific self-esteem, organization-based self-esteem (OBSE). They conducted a review of the literature of the relationship between OBSE and an individual's work and organizational experiences, including performance. They define organization-based self-esteem as "the degree to which an individual believes him/herself to be capable, significant and worthy as an organizational member" (p. 593). Organization-based self-esteem is more changeable than global self-esteem and less changeable than task-specific self-esteem. The purpose of Pierce and Gardner's review was to identify precursors and consequences of OBSE and to examine the role of self-esteem in the work context. Although the authors do not specifically identify the number of articles they included in this review, they identify it as a comprehensive review of over four dozen empirical studies that cover more than a decade of research on the topic. The authors reviewed mainly field studies that relied on cross-sectional data and correlational designs. They included many studies that were conducted in cross-cultural settings.

Looking at the antecedents of OBSE, Pierce and Gardner (2004) found in their review a positive and significant correlation between global self-esteem and OBSE in studies using American samples as well as those with samples from the Middle East, Mexico, and the United Kingdom. They concluded that people high in OBSE are also "high in global self-esteem, positive affectivity, internal locus of control, Protestant work ethic, and need for achievement, and low on negative affectivity and Machiavellianism" (p. 599). Pierce and Gardner also found that high OBSE is related to organizational commitment, improved coping, ethical behavior, altruism and compliance, and lower rates of turnover. With regard to performance, the studies that Pierce and Gardner reviewed found a positive correlation between OBSE and performance that ranged from .21 to .47 on a variety of diverse performance measures such as supervisor ratings or managerial behavior. They concluded that causation is likely to be reciprocal.

Pierce and Gardner (2004) identified organizational conditions that foster OBSE, which included tasks offering a high degree of complexity, self-direction, and control. Opportunities for participation in work groups, the chance to exert influence and participatory leadership are also related to OBSE. These are job characteristics that are likely to be found in positions of responsibility. Exposure to sexism and other forms of discrimination, which women are more likely to experience than men, are related to lower OBSE. In addition, organizational self-esteem is negatively related to stress and job insecurity. In summary, the authors suggest certain external characteristics of a particular position can influence OBSE, which then relates to positive occupational behaviors. High-achieving women are likely to work in conditions that are associated with high OBSE (high complexity, self-direction, and control) and with low OBSE (sexism, discrimination, and stress).

Baumeister and colleagues (2003) reviewed methodologically rigorous studies on self-esteem and its correlates. The purpose of their review was to evaluate whether global self-esteem does, in fact, cause a variety of positive or negative outcomes. They were very selective in the studies they included in this review. They included mainly studies that used objective measures of self-esteem, had large numbers of subjects, or used longitudinal designs that allowed for the evaluation of causality. While they did not identify the exact number of studies they reviewed, they identified their criteria for exclusion; they did not include unpublished studies, studies on the causes of self-esteem, secondary sources, and studies whose outcomes did not have broad social relevance. These criteria resulted in the inclusion of "relatively few" (p. 10) studies. While they examined the relationship between self-esteem and school performance, job and task performance, interpersonal relationships, aggression, violence, delinquency, antisocial behavior, happiness, coping, depression, health, smoking, alcohol and other drugs, sex, and eating, this chapter will describe only their summary of findings that relate self-esteem to job and task performance or to other variables that might also affect job and task performance.

The review by Baumeister and his colleagues (2003) agreed with the conclusions of the above reviews that overall there is a modest, positive correlation between self-esteem and job performance; however, there was considerable variability in the results across studies. The variability, found also in the Judge and Bono review (2001), could be accounted for by the differences in demands and rewards in diverse work settings. They found no studies that could support causal inferences; it is possible that job success causes high self-esteem rather than the other way around. They also examined other performance-related variables, like performance quality and persistence at tasks. They concluded that self-esteem has little or no direct relationship to task performance under challenging or threatening conditions; however, the review supported a relationship between self-esteem and task persistence. They concluded that those with high self-esteem were more likely to persist at tasks, even after failure, than those with low self-esteem. Yet, high self-esteem was also associated with knowing when to quit. They determined that those with high self-esteem "use better self-regulation strategies than people with low self-esteem" (p. 15). Their overall conclusions were that there is a weak relationship between self-esteem and performance, that there is no causal evidence that self-esteem leads to improved job performance, and that most laboratory studies and many field studies show no difference between the performances of people with high and low self-esteem.

Baumeister and his colleagues' conclusions (2003) with regard to the relationship between self-esteem and leadership were similar to their findings about self-esteem and performance: High self-esteem has a

weak relationship to leadership and contributes little when other variables are controlled (like optimism or leadership efficacy). They found
that high self-esteem has a weak but significant association with speaking up in group settings. The strongest relationship was found between
self-esteem and the likelihood of initiating interpersonal contacts and
relationships. However, they point out that initiating behaviors can foster either prosocial or antisocial behaviors. In other words, those with
high self-esteem are overrepresented among both the "perpetrators of
bullying and the people who stand up to bullies and defend victims"
(p. 24). Baumeister and colleagues concluded that self-esteem is related
to initiating behaviors, regardless of whether those behaviors are positive or negative.

Many researchers agree that the main benefits of self-esteem are
emotional (happiness, positive affect, life satisfaction, and less anxiety,
hopelessness, and depression) as well as having positive beliefs about
the self (feeling intelligent, attractive, popular, and self-confident) (Baumeister et al., 2003; Crocker & Knight, 2005). Happiness and life satisfaction have some of the strongest correlations with self-esteem
(Baumeister et al.). In addition, those with high self-esteem show
increased initiative and persistence. Despite these benefits, Baumeister
and colleagues concluded that apart from happiness and good feelings,
the relationships between the other variables in their investigation were
weak to modest and that "self-esteem is thus not a major predictor or
cause of almost anything" (p. 37).

Contingencies of Self-Worth

Despite the conclusions of Baumeister and his colleagues (2003),
Crocker and Park (2004) believe that the desire for self-esteem and its
pursuit underlie much of human behavior. However, they contend that
research and discussions of self-esteem have overemphasized the importance of whether a person's self-esteem is high or low.

The problem with research in this area is not that self-esteem is irrel-
evant but rather that research has focused too much on the level of
trait self-esteem and insufficiently on what people do to demonstrate
to themselves and to others that they have worth and value, and on
the consequences of this pursuit (p. 394).

According to this model, the things that people do to determine that
they are worthy and valuable are of greater significance than the level
of a person's self-esteem (Crocker & Knight, 2005; Crocker & Wolfe,
2001). These behaviors are labeled contingencies of self-worth. For
example, if a person succeeds in a domain on which self-worth is contingent, the person's self-esteem would increase, and failure in a contingent domain would result in a decrease in self-esteem. While global
self-esteem has few specific behavioral correlates, contingencies of

self-worth are somewhat better at predicting behaviors because they influence behavioral regulation. Contingencies of self-worth influence behavior by motivating people to pursue the good feelings associated with success in contingent domains by shaping long-term and short-term goals, by influencing efforts in pursuing those goals, and by affecting reactions to success and failure (Crocker, 2002; Crocker & Knight). Crocker and Knight suggest that contingencies of self-worth influence thoughts and emotions as well as behaviors. They argue that everyone has contingencies of self-worth, but the contingencies on which people's self-esteem is based differ.

While researchers have not agreed on the most common or most important contingencies, Crocker, Luhtanen, Cooper, and Bouvrette (2003) identified seven domains most commonly mentioned in the literature. On the basis of these seven contingencies, they developed an instrument, the Contingencies of Self-Worth Scale (CSWS), to measure contingencies of self-worth in college students. Crocker and her colleagues (2003) do not propose that these are the only or most important contingencies; rather, they are those most often mentioned. They also acknowledge that contingencies may vary depending on culture, gender, age, or other characteristics. The seven domains included in the CSWS are others' approval or regard, physical appearance, competencies, love from family, outdoing others in competition, virtue, and faith. People's successes or failures in the domains that are relevant to their self-esteem result in changes in self-esteem and, in turn, can create both feelings of satisfaction and self-worth, but also vulnerability to depressive symptoms (Crocker, 2002).

Several of these seven domains are dependent on evaluations from external sources and are called external contingencies. The external contingencies of self-worth include others' approval and recognition, physical appearance, love from family, and outdoing others in competition. Competency, faith, and virtue are the internal contingencies of self-worth, which depend less on external influences. Because external contingencies are dependent on responses from other people and are, therefore, under less self-control, they are more likely to be associated with negative outcomes, like depression, neuroticism, and lower self-esteem, than internal contingencies, which are associated with better outcomes (Crocker, 2002; Crocker & Wolfe, 2001; Sanchez & Crocker, 2005; Crocker et al., 2003). For example, if a person's self-worth is based on others' approval, that person is likely to feel a decrease in self-worth after receiving criticism (Crocker, 2006). Though internal contingencies create less psychological vulnerability than external contingencies, whenever self-esteem is contingent, people feel threatened by negative feedback in domains on which their self-esteem depends. For example, if a person's self-esteem is contingent on being a moral person (the internal contingency of virtue), then if that person behaves immorally, that, too, can create a psychological vulnerability to feelings of depression. Therefore, while self-esteem that is based on internal contingencies of self-worth is associated with better outcomes than self-esteem based on external contingencies, both types can be associated with decreases in self-esteem, feelings of depression, or other negative outcomes.

Some researchers suggest that optimal self-esteem is non-contingent self-esteem (Crocker, 2006). Non-contingent self-esteem is self-esteem that is not based on success or failure in particular domains; some researchers think of it as true self-esteem or self-esteem that develops naturally from "autonomous, efficacious action in the context of supportive, authentic relationships" (Crocker & Wolfe, 2001, p. 616). Unfortunately, few people have non-contingent self-esteem and, therefore, attainment of non-contingent self-esteem may be an unrealistic goal (Crocker & Park, 2004; Crocker, 2006; Crocker & Wolfe). It is questionable whether people with truly non-contingent self-esteem actually exist, particularly in the North American culture (Crocker, 2006; Crocker & Wolfe). To avoid the psychological vulnerabilities and other costs of contingent self-esteem, Crocker proposes a shift in goals away from the pursuit of self-esteem altogether and toward goals that are larger than the self, inclusive goals that focus not only on the self but on the good of others (Crocker, 2006). This approach is a paradoxical solution of shifting "away from self-focused, self-centered goals of maintaining and protecting self-esteem, to goals that connect the self to others in an altruistic, compassionate, and meaningful way. These goals keep attention off self-worth, and facilitate the development of authentic relationships that may, in the end, be more sustaining than self-esteem" (Crocker, 2002, p. 148).

SELF-ESTEEM CONCERNS OF HIGH-ACHIEVING WOMEN

Research on high-achieving women and their self-esteem–related concerns is limited. While we know a good deal about high-achieving women in terms of their backgrounds, the important influences on their lives and vocational choices, their career stages and trajectories, the obstacles they have faced, and their coping and leadership styles, research has not focused on their concerns related to self-esteem. The remainder of this chapter will review seven qualitative studies of high-achieving women to illuminate some of the issues and concerns related to self-esteem that were suggested by the participants. Because self-esteem–related concerns were not directly addressed in these studies, I will use Crocker's model of contingencies of self-worth as a framework to understand how women's concerns may reflect contingencies of self-worth, those areas on which their self-esteem is based. In addition to the seven contingencies used in the CSWS (Crocker & Wolfe, 2001;

Crocker et al., 2003), I have added a category of non-contingent self-worth to categorize those comments that are not self-focused but focus on the greater good and the good of others. The studies included in this discussion were chosen because they identify as their purpose the study of women who are high achievers, they used qualitative research methods rather than case studies, biographies, or autobiographies, and they studied diverse groups of women. Each of seven studies will be described and reviewed individually.

Some limitations of this review must be noted. While the purpose of the original studies was not to identify participants' concerns related to self-esteem, illuminating those concerns is one of the intents of this chapter. Absent research that examines this topic directly, I inferred parallels between emergent themes and participants' comments in each qualitative study with Crocker's contingencies of self-worth as described in the CSWS (Crocker et al., 2003). The themes that emerged from the studies were not always a perfect fit with the contingency descriptions, but fitting the themes with the exact contingency was less the objective than to provide some theoretical support for the idea that these concerns may be related to self-esteem and, as such, provide some insight into high-achieving women. Some themes or comments corresponded to a single contingency of self-worth; however, other themes were suggestive of more than one contingency. For example, concerns about taking time off work to have a family may be related to concerns about approval from others, or love from family, or both. In cases where themes may have related to multiple contingencies, they were listed more than once, under each possible contingency. Further, because the respondents in these studies had not been asked to discuss self-esteem, it cannot be assumed that the themes identified by the participants were, in fact, self-esteem contingencies. Said another way, a respondent may have indicated concern about how she is perceived at work, yet that concern is not necessarily one on which her self-esteem is based; there may be other reasons for this concern (Crocker & Wolfe, 2001). In addition, the seven domains of contingent self-worth identified by Crocker and her colleagues (2003) for their measurement instrument were developed for college students, and they are not intended to represent all the contingencies on which people base their self-esteem. Other contingencies, such as power or social identity, have been identified in the literature, and a person's contingencies may differ depending on age as well as culture (Crocker & Wolfe; Crocker et al., 2003). That culture influences the nature, importance, and role of global self-esteem and self-esteem contingencies has been recognized in the literature (Diener & Diener, 1995). Another problem is that because the purpose of these studies was occupational achievement, the respondents may have mentioned only work-related concerns, rather than a broader array of concerns that they may have. Therefore, the effort of this review to identify the participants' self-esteem–related concerns may be limited to identifying only those concerns in a specific domain, occupational self-esteem.

REVIEW OF STUDIES

White, Cox, and Cooper (1992) conducted a qualitative study of 48 women in the United Kingdom who "had achieved extraordinary levels of career success" (p. 5). The women were executives, entrepreneurs, politicians, and senior members of high-status professions. Peers in a prominent women's group for "high-flying women" determined whether a career was considered extraordinarily successful (p. 7), but their criteria were not specified. The purpose of their study was to examine the characteristics and the career trajectory of those who make it to the top. Participants were interviewed for 1 hour, and they were asked about their childhoods, education, work and non-work/family history, and their awareness of organizational power and politics. In addition, participants took three psychometric tests: one on locus of control, one on need for achievement, and one on gender identity. Their scores on these tests were compared to those of women who had low and moderate levels of achievement.

Based on Crocker's contingencies of self-worth (Crocker, 2002), respondents' comments related most often to the contingency of competency. Participants frequently cited competency-related themes, including having a strong belief in their own abilities, having an internal locus of control, recognizing the importance of hard work, being tenacious, wanting to take advantage of opportunities, recognizing the importance of perseverance, being motivated to excel, preferring interesting and challenging work over promotions, recognizing that advancement depended on competence, valuing self-development, and having high standards. Themes related to the contingency of approval or recognition from others included feeling increased self-confidence as a result of feedback from mentors, desiring recognition from others, knowing it was important to "blow their own horn," recognizing the need to "sell" oneself. Related to the contingency of love for family, respondents cited feeling an "energy deficit" related to the complications of managing work and home and worrying about the possible negative impact of family demands on work. Respondents discussed the need to appear professional, which is suggestive of the contingency of self-worth related to appearance. Finally, themes of integrity and honesty at work emerged, which are related to the virtue contingency of self-worth. To summarize, the participants expressed most concerns related to the competency contingency followed by approval or recognition from others and love for family. Concerns related to the contingency of virtue and appearance emerged less often, and concerns related to the faith contingency and the competition contingency were not expressed.

Reddin (1997) completed a qualitative study of six high-achieving women from diverse ethnic backgrounds. Though it is not stated, it appears that this study was conducted in the United States. Reddin defined high achievement as having an advanced degree or career accomplishments. The definition was not further specified. The purpose of Reddin's study was to understand women's achievement and women's career development patterns better. Reddin's results identified several themes and characteristics of high-achieving women, including independence, curiosity, high-achievement motivation, goal-setting, persisting in the face of obstacles, belief in gender equality with regard to women and work, traditional gender attitudes related to familial and social roles, importance of family, and self-doubts despite high achievement and recognition.

Once again, most themes expressed by the participants in Reddin's study corresponded to the competency contingency. Themes related to competency included being determined to find answers, fearing failure, valuing being good at one's job choice, recognizing the importance of career, and emphasizing accomplishments. Respondents in this study expressed concerns related to the self-worth contingency of outdoing others in competition, including being able to solve a problem that others could not solve and fearing not measuring up to others' expectations. Concerns related to the contingency of recognition or approval from others included feeling important, experiencing self-blame related to racism and sexism, and being concerned about taking time off work to have children. Themes related to the love for family contingency included recognizing the importance of family support and the desire of their family's approval of their decisions, being concerned about work/family conflicts, and being concerned about taking time off work to have a family. The importance of using their skills for a good purpose and the desire to make a contribution were themes related to the virtue contingency of self-worth. The desire participants had to enrich their lives, accomplish their goals, and make a contribution could be considered themes suggestive of non-contingent self-esteem. As with the study by Cox and her colleagues (1992), the themes expressed by the participants in Reddin's study relate most often to the self-worth contingency of competency. This was followed by concerns related to competition, recognition, and approval of others, love of family, and virtue contingencies of self-worth. Several themes and comments were reflective of non-contingent self-esteem.

Walton's (1997) research interviewed 11 women who are the heads of colleges in the United Kingdom. Her purpose was to learn more about women "who have reached the highest rung of the British higher education ladder" (p. 70). Her study reviewed the respondents' personal profiles, educational backgrounds, academic career paths, non-academic experiences, the search process, family influence, encouragement, discouraging factors, leadership styles, job satisfaction and stress, salaries, career preparation, and professional development opportunities.

The majority of concerns expressed by the participants in this study related best to the approval and recognition from others contingency of self-worth. Themes and comments that corresponded with this contingency included feeling demands to be an "honorary man" wanting to feel valued and be taken seriously, fearing that other women would feel betrayed by them, feeling apart from the group, feeling manipulated by others because they were female, experiencing pride in their ability to work as a team, fearing negative perceptions of others if a goal was not achieved, and feeling isolated and lonely in the leadership role. Themes related to the competency contingency of self-worth emerged with the next greatest frequency. They included the importance of feeling one has done a good job, feeling satisfied with what one has completed, and recognizing the importance of professional development. Finally, the desire to do something to decrease gender inequity corresponds to the virtue contingency of self-worth.

Marshall (1995) conducted a qualitative study in the United Kingdom of 12 women who had reached senior management and board levels in diverse employment sectors and then left or contemplated leaving employment. The purpose of her study was to consider career management and organizational development issues and explore why women left their positions. Given that the women had left or were contemplating leaving their positions, the participants had more to say about the negative aspects than the positive aspects of the work environment.

The themes and comments related to the contingency of recognition or approval from others represented the vast majority of the concerns. They included experiencing friction and bullying when relating to other people in power, feeling isolated in male-dominated cultures, feeling they were being tested by others, having aggression directed at them, feeling both close to and separated from subordinates, having their effectiveness blocked or undermined, feeling uncertain about how to exert power, being uncertain about relating to other women, and not knowing how to manage in a male-dominated culture. Several of these themes also related to the self-worth contingency of competency. Those that correspond to both categories included feeling concern about having their effectiveness blocked or undermined and feeling uncertain about how to exert power. Additional themes that related to the competency contingency of self-worth include wanting to operate as a change agent and feeling overworked and over-committed. Concern about having their image fit into a male-dominated environment related to the appearance contingency of self-worth.

Gomez and her colleagues (2001) conducted a qualitative research study of 20 notable Latinas in the United States. The participants were chosen by a panel of eight "distinguished Hispanic women who published a biographical directory of 275 notable Latinas in the United States" (p. 288). The purpose of this study was to develop a theoretical framework for career development that extends previous theory to include background and contextual factors particular to the Latina culture. To collect their data, the authors used an in-depth, semi-structured interview and a brief demographic questionnaire. They asked questions about career path, professional stress, external challenges and limitations to achievement, success and failure, background and current influences, family-work interface, cultural identity, career and life satisfaction. The researchers propose a career development theory that conceptualizes interacting spheres of influence that compose the career-life path.

Participants' concerns that related to the competency contingency of self-worth included feeling a strong need to achieve their best in any situation, believing that they must work twice as hard to prove themselves in the face of sexism and racism, having a strong work ethic, possessing high career self-efficacy, believing strongly in their own ability to succeed, and feeling unsuccessful at managing work and family because attending to one resulted in neglecting the other. Concerns related to the contingency of recognition and approval from others included believing that they must work twice as hard to prove themselves in the face of sexism and racism, desiring to prove themselves to others, fearing being perceived as "selling out" to others (only a concern among Mexican-American women), and being concerned about violating the cultural standards of gender roles. Themes related to love for family were frequent. Participants cited feeling loyalty to family, having a collective identity that emphasized family, having a strong cultural identity, being concerned about managing work and family, being concerned about meeting family expectations to marry and conform to traditional gender roles. More themes related to the virtue contingency of self-worth emerged in this study than in the other studies. These themes included having a desire to fulfill a calling or life conviction, being motivated to make a difference and stand up for something, emphasizing social responsibility and service, wanting to make a contribution, feeling responsible toward others in terms of mentoring and being role models, and creating opportunities for others. The desire to make a contribution, to make a difference, to fulfill social responsibilities to others, and to serve as a role model to others also correspond to non-contingent self-esteem, or self-esteem that emphasizes others and making a contribution to something bigger than the self. These findings correspond to research on cultural differences in self-esteem, which suggests that the sources of self-esteem and life satisfaction tend to differ between collectivist and individualistic cultures (Diener & Diener, 1995). The repetition of themes related to love for family and contributing to the good of society emerged more among the Latina women as compared to the women cited in the studies above whose race and ethnicity were unspecified.

Richie and her colleagues (1997) completed a qualitative study in which they interviewed 18 high-achieving African-American and White women (nine African-American women and nine White women) who were closely matched on age, occupation, and geographic location within eight occupational fields. The purpose of their study was to explore critical influences, particularly those related to professional success, on the career development of these women with the ultimate goal of constructing a comprehensive and inclusive theory of women's career development. The researchers used a questionnaire that focused on background influences, stress, coping, and resiliency; self-efficacy and attributional factors; community and social support; external challenges and obstacles; and factors related to individual personality and temperament.

Women in this study exhibited many strengths that did not fit neatly into the contingencies of self-worth yet are worth mentioning. These include persevering when facing challenges, relying on internal standards and judgment, and feeling passion for their work. They expressed few concerns about conflicts between achievement and femininity. In fact, the participants "displayed expressive characteristics (e.g., nurturance, relational orientation, and sensitivity) that contrast with the rugged individualism often depicted in traditionally masculine styles of achievement." Participants reported a strong ability to manage stress and overcome adversity.

Using Crocker's model (2002; Crocker et al., 2003) of contingencies of self-worth, some of the participants' comments could be understood in terms of the competency contingency. These themes include having a strong commitment to their careers, persisting in the face of obstacles, living up to their own standards, worrying about time demands, valuing their own work, and balancing their work and home life. Responses that best matched the contingency related to the importance of the approval and recognition from others included demonstrating nurturance and other expressive characteristics, valuing support from friends and the community, and having a relational orientation. Responses relating to the self-worth contingency for love of family included recognizing the importance of support from partners and from family. A minority of African-American women also reported that faith was important to them. Themes relating to the contingency of virtue included recognizing the importance of the collective rather than just the individual, committing to improving conditions for other women and for African Americans, being motivated to succeed as a way of opening doors for others, seeing the value in giving back to society and the community. Several of these responses are also reflective of non-contingent self-esteem, including thinking of the collective as well as the individual, improving conditions for others, wanting to succeed as a way of helping others, being motivated to give back to society, feeling interconnected with others, and believing that they and their work fit into the larger world. Participants in this study made a high number of virtue and non-contingent responses.

Kawahara, Esnil, and Hsu (2007) conducted a qualitative study on 12 women of Asian descent. This sample purposely included participants to ensure that diverse Asian ethnicities and professions would be represented. All women were leaders and considered to be high achievers on the basis of a variety of criteria. Each participant completed a five-question interview that lasted from 45 minutes to 2.5 hours. The purpose of the study was to gain a greater understanding of Asian-American women leaders.

The authors identified six themes that emerged from the interviews. The themes were knowing oneself and doing something you believe in; having a vision and inspiring others to work on the vision; having a relational and collaborative leadership style; taking on challenges, struggles, and conflicts; having both dominant culture efficacy and biculturalism; and recognizing the importance of support and encouragement. The greatest number of comments corresponded with the virtue contingency of self-worth. These included making choices in accordance with their values, recognizing the importance of things beyond themselves and their own interests, being concerned about others and the community in general, recognizing one's responsibility to others, wanting to be a social activist and be of service, creating equality in the workplace regardless of position or level, having a commitment to social justice, promoting the empowerment of others, and wanting to create a harmonious environment. All the comments related to virtue also match the non-contingent self-esteem in that they go beyond the self, express the desire to help others, and focus on something larger than the self. Several comments corresponded with the contingency of self-worth related to competency. These included recognizing the importance of self-development, being willing to take charge, wanting to learn new skills, being willing to work hard, being willing to become involved in challenges, and being willing to do whatever it takes to achieve the desired outcome. Comments related to the contingency of approval or regard from others included wanting to command people's respect and cooperation, being able to inspire others, desiring to understand others and to be understood by them both within and outside one's community, desiring support and encouragement from others, wanting to present a positive image of Asian-American women, and wanting to show that Asian-American women are competent leaders. Comments relating to the love for family contingency included recognizing the importance of support from family members and partners. Some comments related to ethnicity did not correspond to any of Crocker's (2002) contingencies of self-worth. These included experiences with oppression and prejudice as well as the desire to challenge cultural norms for Asian women. Once again, the number of comments reflective of collectivist values was expressed more frequently by the Asian-American women than by some of the other samples, with the exception of the Latinas.

SUMMARY AND CONCLUSIONS

To gain a better understanding of women's self-esteem and how it relates to achievement, as well as to learn more about self-esteem–related concerns, I've examined research on separate aspects of this topic from a variety of disciplines. I've examined research in the area of women's vocational development, including characteristics associated with high-achieving women. I have explored some of the research on self-esteem as it relates to performance, and I have used the contingencies of self-worth model to explore possible self-esteem–related concerns in seven qualitative studies of high-achieving women.

The research findings on women and achievement seemed to disagree with some of the literature on self-esteem and performance. The review by Baumeister and his colleagues (2003) and Judge and Bono (2001) found modest positive relationships between self-esteem and performance. Pierce and Gardner (2004) found a slightly broader range of correlations, but they reviewed studies on very specific task behaviors. Yet, the literature reviews on high-achieving women concluded that achievement for women is associated with many characteristics related to high self-esteem, including high self-efficacy, instrumentality, and autonomy (Betz & Fitzgerald, 1987; Judge & Bono). One explanation may have to do with the fact that the reviews and meta-analysis examined performance, and the other studies investigated achievement. While performance and achievement are related concepts, they are not identical. Performance may refer to behavior related to a specific task (task performance) or to behavior related to the job (job performance). Achievement refers to broader and more complex responses than performance. Second, the reviews and meta-analysis examined studies that measured self-esteem directly. The studies on women's achievement were not focused directly on self-esteem. Another explanation of the different conclusions drawn from the two types of studies may relate to the purpose of these studies. Applied psychologists may be interested in knowing whether measuring self-esteem will help employers identify employees who will perform well, whereas research in the area of women's career development attempts to identify the complexity of influences on women's achievement. For example, Gomez and her colleagues (2001) describe a career life-path model. This model recognizes the multiple and complex influences on women's achievement and includes not only a variety of personal characteristics like self-esteem, but also factors in the immediate context, like social support and coping skills, aspects of the culture, family, and personal background, as well as sociopolitical conditions. The influences on women's achievement are numerous, interactive, and complex.

The next goal of this chapter was to begin to identify self-esteem–related concerns that high-achieving women experience. To understand the importance and influence of self-esteem, Crocker and Wolfe (2001) suggested that it is essential to look beyond the usual research preoccupation of whether an individual's self-esteem is high or low. They proposed that understanding the basis of a person's self-esteem will yield more useful information than knowing the level of that person's self-esteem. The domains on which our self-esteem is based are called contingencies of self-worth (Crocker & Wolfe). In the absence of research that directly investigates the self-esteem concerns of high-achieving women, the contingencies of self-worth model provided a framework for understanding these concerns. I have used the seven contingencies of self-worth that Crocker and her colleagues identified as those most often mentioned in the literature (2003; Crocker & Wolfe) to examine comments made by participants in seven qualitative studies of high-achieving women. It bears repeating that the seven contingencies used in this analysis are not intended to be exhaustive, nor am I proposing that the comments made by participants reported in these studies match definitively with the contingency with which they have been paired. Further, while the participants' comments reflect their concerns, these concerns are not necessarily contingencies on which their self-esteem is based. Rather, the objective of this review was to begin to explore some concerns expressed by high-achieving women and to put them in a framework that provides theoretical support for understanding how these concerns could potentially be related to their self-esteem.

Crocker and her colleagues (2003) designed a scale to measure contingencies of self-worth based on the seven contingencies most frequently cited in the literature; however, they clearly stated that other contingencies exist. In fact, participants in the seven studies frequently mentioned concerns related to a contingency that was not included on the CSWS—social identity. Social identity has been described as one of several other contingencies on which people's self-worth may be based (Crocker & Wolfe, 2001; Crocker et al., 2003). Many of the studies' participants talked about concerns related to their identities as women, including gender roles and sexism. The participants in the studies with Latinas, African-American women, and Asian-American women described concerns related to their cultural identities as well. Not only were the respondents concerned about the majority culture's expectations for them as women, but also with the gender-role expectations within their cultures or subcultures. In addition to cultural gender expectations, minority women were also concerned about racism and racial discrimination as well as sexism. The addition of social identity as a contingency for self-esteem is relevant for both women and minorities.

Several themes and patterns emerged from among the other concerns expressed by participants in these seven studies. Certain contingencies of self-worth received very few related comments. Study participants mentioned very few concerns that related to two of the four domains of external contingencies, those contingencies most likely to result in psychological vulnerabilities and unhealthy behavior. Participants expressed two or fewer concerns related to the external contingencies of physical appearance and outdoing others in competition. Concern with physical appearance is a female gender-typed response. That participants made few comments related to this contingency may not be surprising given that research suggests that high-achieving women are low in gender-typed behaviors (Betz & Fitzgerald, 1987). However, participants also made few comments related to concerns about competition, a male-typed behavior. The studies' participants did express concerns related to two external contingencies: recognition and approval from others and love for family. The concerns related to recognition and approval from others may be understood in light of research findings that suggest that when women are successful in a male arena, they are less liked, personally denigrated, and treated differently in ways that affect their career outcomes (Heilman et al., 2005). The external contingency related to love from family may be related to the uneven distribution of household responsibilities, the expectation that women assume the majority of household responsibilities, the lack of support for child care in society and the workplace, and the conflict between family and work demands that results from these conditions.

Overall, study participants in the seven qualitative studies expressed a high number of concerns related to internal contingencies. Internal contingencies are contingencies associated with more favorable outcomes because they do not depend on the evaluation of others. Participants expressed concerns related to the internal contingencies of competency and virtue. The greatest number of participants' total comments related to the internal contingency of competency. On the basis of the content and frequency of comments related to this contingency, high-achieving women are concerned about their performance, reaching their goals, and meeting demanding standards. Given their levels of achievement, this is not surprising. Interestingly, women expressed numerous concerns related to virtue. Many of these concerns dealt with wanting to make a contribution and wanting to make things

Study participants' comments categorized by contingencies of self-worth

	Others' approval or regard	Physical appearance	Competency	Love from family	Outdoing others in competition	Virtue	Faith	Non-contingent self-esteem
White, Cox, & Cooper (1992) • 48 women • U.K.	4	1	11	2		1		3
Reddin (1997) • 6 women • U.S.	3		5	4	2	2		
Walton (1997) • 11 women • U.K.	8		3			1		
Marshall (1995) • 12 women • U.K.	9	1	4					
Gomez et al. (2001) • 20 Latinas • U.S.	4		6	5		7		4
Richie et al. (1997) • 9 African-American women • 9 White women • U.S.	3		6	1		4	1	6
Kawahara, Esnil, & Hsu (2007) • 12 Asian-American women • U.S.	6		6	1		9		9
Total comments	37	2	41	13	2	24	1	22

better for other women or members of their ethnic group. Only one concern related to the internal contingency of faith, and this was expressed by an African-American participant. Finally, and importantly, many comments were reflective of non-contingent self-esteem, self-esteem some consider to be optimal. Non-contingent self-esteem is demonstrated when, instead of focusing on the self, a person's focus is outside of the self and on helping others and making a contribution. Latinas, Asian-American women, and the participants in the study with both African-American and White participants cited many more concerns that were reflective of non-contingent self-esteem than did the participants in other studies.

Participants repeated specific concerns across studies that dealt with negotiating the demands of work and family, gaining recognition in the workplace, valuing competence, and having the desire to make a contribution. Despite theoretical disagreements about many aspects of self-esteem and its weak predictive relationship to performance, based on findings from research on women and achievement, high-achieving women possess many characteristics that are suggestive of high self-esteem. These characteristics include high self-efficacy, instrumentality, autonomy, and persistence. Gomez and her colleagues (2001) concluded that a profile for high-achieving, professional women is emerging in the literature that finds them to be passionate, tenacious, high in career self-efficacy and conviction, and to have effective coping skills, internal motivation, career persistence, and high instrumentality.

REFERENCES

Baumeister, R. F., Campbell, J. D., Krueger, J. I., & Vohs, K. D. (2003). Does high self-esteem cause better performance, interpersonal success, happiness, or healthier lifestyles? *Psychological Science in the Public Interest, 4*, 1–44.

Betz, N. (2001). Career self-efficacy. In F. T. L. Leong & A. Barzak (Eds.), *Contemporary models in vocational psychology* (pp. 55–77). Mahwah, NJ: Lawrence Erlbaum.

Betz, N., & Fitzgerald, L. (1987). *The career psychology of women.* Orlando, FL: Academic Press.

Blascovitch, J., & Tomaka, J. (1991). Measures of self-esteem. In J. P. Robinson, P. R. Shaver, & L. W. Wrightsman (Eds.), *Measures of personality and social psychological attitudes* (pp. 115–155). San Diego, CA: Academic Press.

Brown, J. D., & Marshall, M. A. (2006). The three faces of self-esteem. In M. K. Kernis (Ed.), *Self esteem issues and answers* (pp. 4–9). New York: Psychology Press.

Clance, P. R., & Imes, S. (1978). The imposter phenomenon in high achieving women: Dynamics and therapeutic intervention. *Psychotherapy Theory, Research and Practice, 15*, 1–8.

Clance, P. R., & O'Toole, M. A. (1987). The imposter phenomenon: An internal barrier to empowerment and achievement. *Women and Therapy, 6*, 51–64.

Cox, M. J., Owen, M. T., Henderson, V. K., & Margand, N. A. (1992). Prediction of infant-father and infant-mother attachment. *Developmental Psychology, 28,* 474–483.

Crawford, M., & Unger, R. (2004). *Women and gender: A feminist psychology* (4th ed.). Boston: McGraw Hill.

Crocker, J. (2002). Contingencies of self-worth: Implications for self-regulation and psychological vulnerability. *Self and Identity, 1,* 143–149.

Crocker, J. (2006). What is optimal self-esteem? In M. K. Kernis (Ed.), *Self-esteem issues and answers* (pp. 119–124). New York: Psychology Press.

Crocker, J., & Knight, K. M. (2005). Contingencies of self-worth. *Current Directions in Psychological Science, 14,* 200–203.

Crocker, J., Luhtanen, R., Cooper, M. L., & Bouvrette, S. A. (2003). Contingencies of self-worth in college students: Measurement and theory. *Journal of Personality and Social Psychology, 85,* 894–908.

Crocker, J., & Park, L. E. (2004). The costly pursuit of self-esteem. *Psychological Bulletin, 130,* 392–414.

Crocker, J., & Wolfe, C. T. (2001). Contingencies of self-worth. *Psychological Review, 108,* 593–623.

Diener, E., & Diener, M. (1995). Cross-cultural correlates of life satisfaction and self-esteem. *Journal of Personality and Social Psychology, 68,* 653–663.

Fassinger, R. (2002). Hitting the ceiling: Gendered barriers to occupational entry, advancement, and achievement. In L. Diamant & J. A. Lee (Eds.), *Psychology of sex, gender, and jobs* (pp. 21–46). Westport, CT: Praeger.

Fassinger, R. (2005). Theoretical issues in the study of women's career development: Building bridges in a brave new world. In W. B. Walsh & M. L. Savickas (Eds.), *Handbook of vocational psychology: Theory, research, and practice* (3rd ed., pp. 85–126). Mahwah, NJ: Lawrence Erlbaum.

Fitzgerald, L. F., & Harmon, L. W. (2001). Women's career development: A postmodern update. In F. T. L. Leong & A. Barzak (Eds.), *Contemporary models in vocational psychology* (pp. 21–45). Mahwah, NJ: Lawrence Erlbaum.

Fried-Buchalter, S. (1992). Fear of success, fear of failure, and the imposter phenomenon: A factor analytic approach to convergent and discriminant validity. *Journal of Personality Assessment, 58,* 368–379.

Fried-Buchalter, S. (1997). Fear of success, fear of failure, and the imposter phenomenon among male and female marketing managers. *Sex Roles, 37,* 847–859.

Gomez, M. J., Fassinger, R. E., Prosser, J., Cooke, K., Meija, B., & Luna, J. (2001). Voces abriendo caminos (voices forging paths): A qualitative study of the career development of notable Latinas. *Journal of Counseling Psychology, 48,* 286–300.

Heilman, M. E., Wallen, A. S., Fuchs, D., & Tamkins, M. M. (2004). Penalties for success: Reactions to women who succeed at male gender-typed tasks. *Journal of Applied Psychology, 89,* 416–427.

Horner, M. S. (1969). Fail: Bright women. *Psychology Today, 3,* 36.

Hyde, J. S. (2006). *Half the human experience,* 7th ed. Boston, MA: Houghton Mifflin.

Judge, T. A., & Bono, J. E. (2001). Relationship of core self-evaluation traits— self-esteem, generalized self-efficacy, locus of control, and emotional stability—with job satisfaction and job performance: A meta-analysis. *Journal of Applied Psychology, 86,* 80–92.

Kawahara, D. M., Esnil, E. M., & Hsu, J. (2007). Asian American women leaders: The intersection of race, gender, and leadership. In J. L. Chin, B. Lott, J. K. Rice, & J. Sanchez-Hucles (Eds.), *Women and leadership: Transforming visions and diverse voices* (pp. 297–313). Malden, MA: Blackwell.

Kling, K. C., Hyde, J. S., Showers, C. J., & Buswell, B. (1999). Gender differences in self-esteem: A meta-analysis. *Psychological Bulletin, 125,* 470–500.

Koch, E. J. (2006). Examining the role of self-esteem in psychological functioning and well-being. In M. K. Kernis (Ed.), *Self-esteem issues and answers* (pp. 260–266). New York: Psychology Press.

Marsh, H. W., Craven, R. G., & Martin, A. J. (2006). What is the nature of self-esteem? Unidimensional and multidimensional perspectives. In M. K. Kernis (Ed.), *Self esteem issues and answers* (pp. 16–25). New York: Psychology Press.

Marshall, J. (1995). Working at senior management and board levels: Some of the issues for women. *Women in Management Review, 10,* 21–25.

Mruk, C. J. (2006). Defining self-esteem: An often overlooked issue with crucial implications. In M. K. Kernis (Ed.), *Self esteem issues and answers* (pp. 10–15). New York: Psychology Press.

Owens, T. J., & McDavitt, A. R. (2006). The self-esteem motive: Positive and negative consequences for self and society. In M. K. Kernis (Ed.), *Self-esteem issues and answers* (pp. 398–406). New York: Psychology Press.

Paludi, M. A. (1984). Psychometric properties and underlying assumptions of four objective measures of fear of success. *Sex Roles, 10,* 765–781.

Paludi, M. A. (2002). *The psychology of women* (2nd ed.). Upper Saddle River, NJ: Prentice Hall.

Phillips, S. D., & Imhoff, A. R. (1997). Women and career development: A decade of research. *Annual Review of Psychology, 48,* 31–59.

Pierce, J. L., & Gardner, D. G. (2004). Self-esteem within the work and organizational context: A review of the organization-based self-esteem literature. *Journal of Management, 30,* 591–622.

Post, R. D. (1982). Dependency conflicts in high-achieving women: Toward an integration. *Psychotherapy: Theory, Research, and Practice, 19,* 82–87.

Post, R. D. (1989). Self-sabotage among successful women. *Psychotherapy in Private Practice, 6,* 191–205.

Pryszczynski, T., Greenberg, J., Solomon, S., Arndt, J., & Schimel, J. (2004). Why do people need self-esteem? A theoretical and empirical review. *Psychological Bulletin, 130,* 435–468.

Reddin, J. (1997). High-achieving women: Career development patterns. In H. S. Farmer (Ed.), *Diversity and women's career development from adolescence to adulthood* (pp. 95–126). Thousand Oaks, CA: Sage.

Richie, B. S., Fassinger, R. E., Linn, S. G., Johnson, J., Prosser, J., & Robinson, S. (1997). Persistence, connection, and passion: A qualitative study of the career development of highly achieving African American and White women. *Journal of Counseling Psychology, 44,* 133–148.

Rollins, J. H. (1996). *Women's minds women's bodies: The psychology of women in a biosocial context.* Upper Saddle River, NJ: Prentice-Hall.

Rosenberg, M., Schooler, C., Schoenbach, C., & Rosenberg, F. (1995). Global self-esteem and specific self-esteem: Different concepts, different outcomes. *American Sociological Review, 60,* 141–156.

Sanchez, D. T., & Crocker, J. (2005). How investment in gender ideals affects well-being: The role of external contingencies of self-worth. *Psychology of Women Quarterly, 29,* 63–77.

Schwalbe, M. L., Gecas, V., & Baxter, R. (1986). The effects of occupational conditions and individual characteristics on the importance of self-esteem sources in the workplace. *Basic and Applied Social Psychology, 7,* 63–84.

Solomon, S. (2006). Self-esteem is central to human well-being. In M. K. Kernis (Ed.), *Self esteem issues and answers* (pp. 254–259). New York: Psychology Press.

Steinem, G. (1992). *Revolution from within: A book of self-esteem.* Boston, MA: Little, Brown and Company.

Walton, K. D. (1997). UK women at the very top: An American assessment. In H. Eggins (Ed.), *Women as leaders and managers in higher education* (pp. 70–90). Bristol, PA: Open University Press.

White, B., Cox, C., & Cooper, C. (1992). *Women's career development: A study of high flyers.* Cambridge, MA: Blackwell.

Chapter 4

Women in Human Resources: In My Own Voice

Linda Dillon

I have been employed in the human resources field for approximately 27 years. Over the course of these many years, I've held progressively responsible positions within the human resources office, culminating in my current position of director of human resources. I have responsibility for all aspects of human resources, including position classification, staffing and recruitment, payroll and benefits, training, labor relations, and employee services.

Throughout these many years there have been several people who have influenced my life and my decisions both personally and professionally. These people have supported my beliefs, encouraged me when I lost faith in myself, and acted as role models.

My parents from the very beginning were steadfast in their belief in me and my abilities. They always encouraged me to accept new challenges and believe in my own capabilities. I recall that when I was a high school senior and contemplating a college course of study, my parents encouraged me to select a major I was interested in—to select a career I wanted to pursue rather than a career that was traditionally female. Keep in mind that when I was entering college, women were just beginning to pursue careers in law, medicine, accounting, and various sciences. (Previously, women pursed careers in teaching, nursing, library science, and secretarial science if they pursued careers at all.) Thus, the support I received from my parents challenged me to challenge myself.

Their encouragement didn't end once I became a successful human resource professional. I recall two days before my father passed away, he and I were chatting about something minor and he said to me, "Don't defeat yourself. You can do anything you put your mind to." It's just so demonstrative of the steadfast support I was fortunate enough to receive. My parents were outstanding role models for me as well. They instilled in me a strong sense of family, a strong work ethic, and a strong sense of what is fair and ethical.

My husband of 34 years has also been a steadfast supporter. There were often times when I felt overwhelmed trying to balance work and home life. Yet he was there, encouraging me and assisting me along the way.

I was very fortunate recently to have a supervisor who was also very supportive. Not only did he promote me to my current position as director of human resources, he challenged me to do more. Shortly after my appointment, he said, "Linda, this is your time. Make your mark." He provided me the opportunity to make some changes—to introduce new initiatives.

My entrance into the human resources field happened quite by accident. My undergraduate degree is in accounting; however, before I obtained that "perfect" job in accounting, I was offered a promotion to a position in human resources. I accepted the position, thinking it was just a temporary arrangement. What I didn't expect was that the longer I remained in the human resources office, the more I liked the human resources field. So I decided to stay.

We, as women, tend to inexplicably accept the majority of home life responsibilities. As a result, we can be overwhelmed trying to balance home and work life responsibilities. Integrating work and family roles successfully is just about impossible if you don't establish your priorities and have appropriate support and flexibility. Both roles demand your attention and commitment. To me, my family is most important— they are my priority. I could not have juggled climbing the professional career ladder and being a mom without help. My parents were my children's child care during the day. They were the absolute best! On those occasions when one or both of the children were ill, my husband and I would alternate taking time off from work to care for them. I didn't have to concern myself with the quality of their care whether they were healthy or ill.

My supervisors knew how important my family was to me and allowed me to adjust my full-time work schedule to attend various school functions. (I was always very careful to provide as much advance notification to my supervisors as possible.) In return for this flexibility, I would often take work home with me or work extra non-paid hours. In my view, it was only fair. My supervisors provided me opportunities to be a more involved parent at my children's schools. I responded by working harder—clearly a win–win situation. My children are now college graduates and have embarked upon their respective careers, yet I continue to schedule home projects or vacation plans as far in advance as possible. I'll also adjust my schedule to minimize my absence from work. With the use of cell phones, BlackBerries, laptops, and so on, it's easier to keep in touch with the office and attend to the needs of my family.

With regard to integrating work and family, appropriate support may also include hiring a cleaning service or gardening service. When our children were younger, my husband and I had to make a decision regarding the quality of the time we spent with our children. For us, hiring someone to clean our home was a financial sacrifice beneficial to all of us.

Human resources is an increasingly demanding field. It is no longer a clerical payroll function. We are and should continue to be strategic partners with the executive staff and the heads of various operations and legal divisions. Human resources helps balance the needs of the organization to develop and prosper with the needs of our employees to develop and prosper. Both sides need to be successful. As human resources specialists, it's important to enjoy working with people. People are the most interesting part of the job, but they are also the most difficult part of the job. You must demonstrate patience, flexibility, understanding, and perseverance. You must believe that what you do makes a difference. Most importantly, you must be ethical in your decisions and your interactions with people.

As a professional woman in today's workforce, it is fundamental to be secure in who you are as a woman, to know what's most important to you, to allow yourself to be flexible, and to take the time to find the humor in your life. No matter how difficult things get, either at home or in the workplace, always keep in mind that success stops when you do.

Chapter 5

Stress and Health

Paula Lundberg-Love
Donna Lee Faulkner

Sixty-three million women constitute nearly one-half of the United States workforce, an increase of 56% since 1950. Women hold professional and managerial positions as well as jobs in trades traditionally occupied by men. However, with these changes in the workplace women have been exposed to the same occupational hazards as men. One of these hazards is workplace stress. Indeed, data suggest that women report more stress and stress-related illness than men do (Harvard Women's Health Watch, 2000). The purpose of this chapter is to discuss the impact of workplace stress on women's medical and mental health.

When given the opportunity to address the impact of workplace stress on the health and well-being of women, the authors initially envisioned a focus on the relationship between workplace stress and specific medical or psychological disorders. Indeed, we found many studies that investigated the relationship between workplace stress and particular types of disorders. However, after a thorough review of the empirical literature across a number of disciplines, it became apparent that there are various themes that comprise the fabric of the research on the effects of stress in the workplace. For example, there is a body of work that emphasizes the importance of "job control," that is the amount of control over or the degree of autonomy that one has in her job. This line of research investigates the demand-control-support theory of the relationship between jobs and stress and its myriad effects. It is also characterized by various models that seek to assign some quantitative value to the amount of variance that the particular factors in the model contribute to the levels of reported stress. There are also studies that investigate the magnitude of workplace stress in women who have particular types of careers. Finally, much has been learned about the physiological effects of stress, in general, and workplace stress, in particular. Due to the volume of studies that have been published on the effects of workplace stress, this chapter cannot effectively describe the totality of the data in existence. Therefore, we elected primarily to focus on studies that have been published during the past 20 years. Additionally, we chose to organize this chapter with respect to four themes apparent within the body of workplace stress literature, namely, a discussion of the physiological consequences of stress, the effects of stress that have been reported in studies that investigated the demand-control-support model of workplace stress, the effects of stress as it relates to cardiovascular disease, and the effects of workplace stress with respect to particular types of occupations.

THE BIOLOGICAL CONSEQUENCES OF STRESS

Walter Cannon (1929) first demonstrated that the psychophysiological reactions of "fight or flight" could be induced under conditions of fear, pain, hunger, and rage. He observed that environmental threats provoked a general discharge of the sympathetic nervous system (SNS) marked by increases in the release of catecholamines, which prepare the individual to fight or to flee (Cannon, 1932). Hans Selye (1956) subsequently demonstrated that the "stress response" could be elicited via physical, chemical, biological, and psychosocial stimuli. If the stimuli were prolonged, frequent, and/or intensive, stress would lead to physiological damage to the organism. Selye's stress response caused an activation of the pituitary adrenal cortex that resulted in a release of corticosteroids (cortisol and corticosterone). While there have been many differences in the manner in which stress has been defined and measured in the research literature, most contemporary definitions of stress incorporate the following assumptions: Stress is a process that occurs when environmental demands exceed the adaptive capacity of the organism; this process results in biological and/or psychological changes that may have consequences for health; and individual "appraisals" are important in determining responses to stress (Cohen, Kessler, & Gordon, 1998).

When studying the biological consequences of stress, two particular neuroendocrine systems are of interest with respect to their effects on health. These are the sympathetic adrenomedullary (SAM) system and the hypothalamic-pituitary-adrenocortical (HPA) system. Stimulation of the SAM system results in the release of epinephrine (EPI) and norepinephrine (NE), whereas stimulation of the HPA system results in the secretion of cortisol. In response to SNS stimulation, EPI and NE are secreted into the bloodstream, which results in pronounced effects on the cardiovascular system and the release of energy such as glucose and free fatty acids. Cortisol secretion is regulated by the release of adrenocorticotrophic hormone (ACTH) from the anterior pituitary gland, which reaches a peak in the bloodstream after about 30 minutes of acute stress. Release of ACTH stimulates the adrenal cortex to release cortisol. Cortisol influences the metabolism in cells, the distribution of fat and the immune system, and its level is controlled by a feedback system in the hypothalamus and the hippocampus. Furthermore, the stress hormones can be measured in the blood and the urine. Cortisol can even be measured in the saliva. Measurement of these hormones provides a link between an individual's perception of stress and its impact on various health outcomes (Lundberg, 2005).

Many studies have documented the sensitivity of EPI secretion to various types of stressors in the laboratory and stress in natural settings (Frankenhaeuser, 1983; Lundberg, 1984). NE is involved in the regulation of blood pressure and is more sensitive to physical demands and body posture. Consequently, among white-collar workers mainly exposed to mental demands, EPI levels rose about 50% at work as compared to nonwork conditions while NE levels did not. However, among blue-collar workers who were physically active performing manual tasks, the levels of both EPI and NE were increased, EPI about 100% and NE about 50% (Lundberg & Johansson, 2000). Cortisol levels habituate rapidly to regular work conditions and generally do not increase during daily work. Instead, cortisol secretion increases in response to novel conditions, emotional challenge, fear, anxiety, helplessness, and during heavy workloads (Kirschbaum & Hellhammer, 1989; Folkow, 1993). In a study of women who regularly worked more than 50 hours per week, it was found that their cortisol levels were twice as high in the morning compared with women who had a more moderate workload (Lundberg & Hellstrom, 2002). In response to the extreme stress of childbirth, cathecholamine (EPI and NE) levels and cortisol may increase to more than 10 times the levels during pregnancy (Alehagen, Wijma, Lundberg, Melin, & Wijma, 2001).

EPI levels can increase in response to pleasant as well as unpleasant stimuli (Levi, 1972), while cortisol levels seem to be more sensitive to negative emotional conditions (Folkow, 1993; Kristenson, Eriksen, Sluiter, Starke, & Ulsin, 2004). The results of a study of male and female white-collar workers indicated that individuals high in psychological well-being had significantly lower levels of cortisol at work as compared with those who had lower levels of psychological well-being (Lindfors & Lundberg, 2002). However, very low cortisol levels are associated with burnout and post-traumatic stress disorder (PTSD) (Yehuda, Teicher, Trestman, Levengood, & Siever, 1996).

Biological responses to stress have been investigated as a function of gender. In response to performance stress in a laboratory setting, men increased their EPI levels by 50% to 100%, while those of women responded very little or not at all, even though women performed as well or better than the men on the tasks (Frankenhaeuser, 1983). However, in response to a real-life stressor such as an important examination, female students exhibited a significant increase in EPI output, but it was still less than that of their male colleagues (Frankenhaeuser). Lundberg (1996) conducted a series of studies that investigated the effects of a number of variables, such as type of stressor (performance stress versus emotional and interpersonal stress), type of education, gender roles (masculinity, femininity), and sex hormones (testosterone, estrogens) on secretion of stress hormones. Mothers following their child to the hospital had higher levels of EPI than the fathers (Lundberg, de Chateau, Winberg, & Frankenhaeuser, 1981). Women who had chosen a line of male-dominated education had EPI responses to performance stress similar to their male colleagues (Collins & Frankenhaeuser, 1978). Moreover, estrogen replacement therapy (Collins et al., 1982) and high testosterone levels (Lundberg et al., 1983) did not markedly influence women's EPI response during stress. The conclusions of the authors was that gender roles and psychological factors were more important than biological factors in explaining gender-related differences in EPI release during stress.

Although the results of other studies (Frankenhaeuser et al., 1989; Lundberg & Frankenhaeuser, 1999) indicated that men and women at the same occupational level responded in a similar manner to work-related stress, comparisons between male and female white-collar workers showed that women's stress levels tended to remain elevated while men would relax and unwind at the end of the work day (Frankenhaeuser et al.; Lundberg & Frankenhaeuser). The authors speculated that perhaps the gender difference in the stress levels might be caused by the fact that women have a greater unpaid workload as a result of child care and household responsibilities (Lundberg, Mårdberg, & Frankenhaeuser, 1994). Significant correlations also have been obtained for women's physiological stress levels at work and at home in the evening (Frankenhaeuser et al.) and between the number of extra hours of work and EPI levels during the weekend (Lundberg & Palm, 1989).

The secretion of stress hormones has important implications for stress-related health problems. For example, catecholamines have been linked to hypertension, myocardial infarction (MI), and stroke. A model has been proposed that describes how elevated blood pressure could lead to successive thickening of the arterial walls, which could lead to narrowing of the blood vessels, thereby increasing peripheral resistance in the cardiovascular system (Folkow, 1982). Also, elevated blood lipids, increased blood clotting, and the development of atheroscle-rosis, all risk factors for MI, are mediated by levels of catecholamines. Therefore, elevated levels of catecholamines in response to work-related stress can put one at greater risk for cardiovascular disease.

With respect to cortisol, overactivity/dysregulation of the HPA axis has been associated with an array of health problems, including cardio-vascular disease, Type 2 diabetes, cognitive impairment, and reduced immune function, when cortisol levels are high. Because there is a high density of cortisol receptors in the abdomen, elevated cortisol levels result in an accumulation of abdominal fat. Abdominal fat is readily releasable into the bloodstream, which in turn can result in an increase in free fatty acid levels and contribute to cardiovascular disease. High cortisol levels also block the ability of cells to utilize blood glucose, thus resulting in Type 2 diabetes. Additionally, cortisol has anti-inflammatory effects. However, chronically elevated levels of cortisol can impair immune function, and thus increase the risk of infections (Lundberg, 2005). Because cortisol can cross the blood–brain barrier, it can enter the brain and result in the degeneration of neurons in the hippocampus, which manifests itself as memory impairment (Sapolsky, 1996). Finally, in people exposed to chronic psychosocial stress, ele-vated baseline levels of cortisol followed by an attenuated cortisol response have been observed (Kristenson et al., 1998). According to Lundberg (2005),

> countries such as Sweden and Norway have seen a dramatic increase in absenteeism during the past 10 years, particularly among women, due to health problems. These include burnout, depression, muscular pain, headache, gastrointestinal problems, and so on. Most of these disorders have been regarded as stress-related and described as 'medically unex-plained symptoms.' It is possible that the more rapid pace of modern life, increased workload, and continuous adjustment to changes and new demands have contributed to a change between catabolic and anabolic processes.

JOB CONTROL, PHYSICAL HEALTH, AND PSYCHOLOGICAL WELL-BEING

One aspect of working life that has been extensively researched is the degree of control or autonomy that an individual has over her job. It is a crucial feature of the major theoretical approaches to understand-ing the impact of workplace stress (Karasek, 1979; Payne, 1979; Warr, 1987), and it is a central factor of job design theories (Hackman & Old-ham, 1980; Wall, Corbett, Clegg, Jackson, & Martin, 1990). Additionally, in the management literature, the issue of job control is seen as impor-tant for releasing employee potential and improving job performance.

Within the psychological literature the concept of control can be viewed as a characteristic of the environment and a characteristic of the individual. Assembly line work could be viewed as an occupation where an employee lacks control over her job. However, an individual could still view herself as having high control based upon her level of mastery or self-efficacy (Bandura, 1977). Or individuals could be seen as having greater or lesser needs for control (Burger & Cooper, 1979). The major models of job design and stress treat the concept of job control (decision latitude, discretion, autonomy) as characteristics attached to particular job tasks; however, the fact that individuals vary in their perceptions of, or needs for, control, also has implications for the importance of individual differences in these models (Jones & Fletcher, 2003).

The most well-known demand-control-job strain model is that of Karasek (1979), which posits that physical and psychological work-related stress can be predicted from combinations of job demand and job control. Historically, the model has evolved. While many studies focus on the negative impact of jobs that are high in demand and low in control, suggesting that these two variables are additive, other researchers have proposed that the combination of high demand and low control may be interactive such that this particular condition produces greater strain (Terry & Jimmieson, 1999). This is an important distinction because an additive versus an interactive effect has different implications for improving the workplace and reducing stress. If job demand is harmful primarily under conditions of low control, then, theoretically, job strain could be reduced by increasing control without reducing workload (Karasek; Parkes, 1991). Furthermore, Kasl (1996) has observed that some researchers view decision latitude as buffering the effect of job demand such that high demands will be present only in the face of low control, while others regard the interaction as synergistic. Often the design of the studies does not permit one to make such a distinction (Jones & Fletcher, 2003).

The job-strain model has been further developed to include the variable of social support and is often referred to as the iso-strain model (Johnson & Hall, 1988). In this model there are also two alternative hypotheses, an additive model and an interactive one wherein social support acts as a buffer (Van der Doef & Maes, 1999). The job-strain model has been tested using a variety of methods and levels of analysis, including long-term epidemiological studies that have followed subjects over years to predict coronary artery disease and other disease outcomes (Jones & Fletcher, 2003), as well as cross-sectional studies using self-report measures of demand and control to investigate predictors of psychological well-being or other symptoms (Dollard, Winefield, Winefield, & de Jonge, 2000; Fletcher & Jones, 1993).

Nevertheless, the job strain model has been criticized. Researchers have raised concerns regarding the nature and subjectivity of the measurements, the statistical tests used to determine the interaction, a tendency for the core dimensions to be confounded with socioeconomic status, and the fact that the model does not take into account sociocultural issues and individual differences (Ganster & Fusilier, 1989; Jones, Bright, Searle, & Cooper, 1998; Kristenson, 1996; Muntaner & O'Campo, 1993). While it has been criticized for its simplicity and lack of scope, it has stimulated much research on the effects of job control on health.

Another model that investigates the importance of autonomy in job stress is the job characteristics model (JCM). The JCM suggests that there are five core job characteristics: skill variety, task identity, task significance, autonomy, and feedback. The construct of autonomy is concerned with the freedom to decide how to do the job and the opportunity to use one's discretion (Jones & Fletcher, 2003). It is thought that these characteristics in conjunction with experienced meaningfulness, experienced responsibility, and knowledge of results predict work motivation, work effectiveness, and job satisfaction. While this model did not initially suggest a relationship between core job characteristics and health, subsequent researchers added the outcome variable of mental health (Wall, Clegg, & Jackson, 1978; Wall, Kemp, Jackson, & Clegg, 1986).

There also has been criticism of the JCM model particularly because of a bias to utilize cross-sectional studies that rely on self-report measures only (Roberts & Glick, 1981). Moreover, the model posits that job characteristics cause high or low job satisfaction and that self-reports of job characteristics are valid reflections of the objective characteristics of a job. Thus the assumption is that modifying the job tasks to provide greater control will necessarily result in greater motivation of employees because they will perceive themselves as having greater control. But self-reports do not always correspond to the objective characteristics of a job, and perceptions of job characteristics can be manipulated (Sanchez & Levine, 2000; Spector & Jex, 1991). Furthermore, individual differences in one's affective state (positive or negative) can certainly impact the relationship between job characteristics, work effectiveness, and job satisfaction (Champoux, 1991).

Recently, the concepts of job control and Karasek's model have been incorporated into studies in the medical literature that investigate an array of aspects of physical and psychological health and well-being. Where some studies have found a relationship between job strain (high demand and low control), neck pain in salespeople (Skov, Borg, & Orhede, 1996), and adverse outcomes of pregnancy in clerical and commercial workers (Brandt & Nielsen, 1992), the preponderance of this literature focuses on cardiovascular disease (CVD) and its associated risk factors (Jones & Fletcher, 2003).

A review of 36 studies published between 1981 and 1993 concluded that there was a significant relationship between job strain and CVD, job strain and mortality from all causes, and job strain and risk factors for CVD (Schnall, Landsbergis, & Baker, 1994). Other studies have investigated the impact of job strain on risk factors associated with CVD such as high blood pressure and elevated levels of EPI and corti- sol. In a study of nurses (Fox, Dwyer, & Ganster, 1993), it was found that a combination of high demand and low control predicted blood pressure and cortisol levels, while the results of another study using a heterogeneous sample of occupations found no such relationship. Where demands did show any type of relationship, those with lower demands had higher blood pressure (Fletcher & Jones, 1993). However, when one reviews studies that monitored ambulatory blood pressure, a more sensitive measure than blood pressure taken in a clinic, five out of nine studies showed a relationship between control and blood pres- sure (Schnall et al.).

With respect to the impact of job strain on health in general, some researchers have concluded that across different populations, using different measurement methods and job designs, there is substantial support for the hypothesis that the combined effects of high-demand, low-control jobs lead to increased CVD (Van der Doef & Maes, 1998). However, while Schnall et al. (1994) agreed with the preceding conclu- sion, they also considered the separate effects of high-demand and low-control jobs and concluded that although 17 out of 25 studies found significant relationships between job decision latitude and out- come, only eight out of 23 studies demonstrated significant associations between job demand and outcome. Thus, at this point it is not possible to draw an unequivocal conclusion. However, when the effects of job demand and control can be separated, the data suggest that the impact of job control may be greater than job demands. Thus, more research is needed to clarify these relationships.

In the case of the impact of the job-demand and job-control model on psychological well-being, there have been a number of studies. This is due, at least in part, to the fact that while psychological distress is important, in and of itself, it also is a mediating variable whereby work stressors may ultimately lead to illness. According to Jones and Fletcher (2003) there is a "plethora of research indicating that low job control is associated with poor psychological well-being." This is true whether a measure such as the General Health Questionnaire (Gold- berg, 1978) is used or whether specific measures of depression, anxiety, or job satisfaction are employed (Jones & Fletcher, 2003). Results of the studies generally suggest that the combination of high demand and low control are associated with poor psychological well-being, and additive effects are more numerous than moderated effects (Van der Doef & Maes, 1998).

Knowing that people who report low levels of demand and control also experience high levels of distress at work can be important information for employers. However, the data are not strong enough to warrant an assumption that the association is causal, as there are few studies examining the job-demand-control hypothesis and the development of psychiatric illness. However, some studies have found a relationship between low control and symptoms. Occupations associated with lower levels of control have higher levels of depression (Mausner-Dorsch & Eaton, 2000; Muntaner, Tien, Eaton, & Garrison, 1991). In a study of teachers (Cropley, Steptoe, & Joekes, 1999), job strain was linked to "neurotic disorder."

There also are some studies that have investigated the JCM and its relationship to job satisfaction. A meta-analysis of the relationship between job characteristics and job satisfaction in 28 studies found that of all the core job characteristics, autonomy had the strongest relationship to job satisfaction (Loher, Noe, Moeller, & Fitzgerald, 1985). Another meta-analysis looked at perceived control in relation to 19 outcome variables, some of which were health related. A relationship was found between autonomy and emotional distress in addition to absenteeism and physical symptoms (Spector, 1986). Finally, Saavedra and Kwun (2000) have used the JCM to predict affective states and determined that autonomy was associated with enthusiasm and they have suggested that autonomy may relieve job dissatisfaction as well as energize, reinforce, and maintain work behavior. Overall, the bulk of the data suggest that there is evidence to support the hypothesis that job control is an important variable with respect to the development of CVD and reduced psychological well-being.

THE EFFECTS OF WORK STRESS ON RISK FACTORS AND THE DEVELOPMENT OF CORONARY ARTERY DISEASE (CAD)

The physiological responses to stress involve a coordination of activity in a number of bodily systems, including the central nervous system (CNS), the autonomic nervous system (ANS), and the endocrine, cardiovascular, musculoskeletal, gastrointestinal, and immune/inflammatory systems. Current research on the effects of stress on cardiac pathophysiology emphasizes the effects of the CNS and ANS in the development of CAD (Strike & Steptoe, 2004; Rozanski, Blumenthal, & Kaplan, 1999). This activation could predispose one to MI and sudden cardiac death by promoting coronary endothelial dysfunction and immune/inflammatory responses, thus influencing the pathophysiological processes that occur in atherosclerosis. Such processes can increase the vulnerability to clinical cardiac events by triggering lethal arrhythmias through altered neural transmission to the heart (Holmes, Krantz, Rogers, Gottdiener, & Contrada, 2006).

Evidence also exists to support the thesis that several specific components of the physiological responses to stress may promote coronary vasoconstriction, platelet aggregation, or the rupture of plaques in the coronary blood vessels. Mental stress can result in significant arterial blood pressure surges (Rozanski, Bairey, & Krantz, 1988). In people with vulnerable plaques in their arteries, a vascular blood pressure surge may cause a plaque to rupture and lead to coronary thrombosis (blood clots in the coronary arteries). In the presence of atherosclerosis, stress-induced elevations in blood pressure, heart rate, and levels of catecholamines increase the oxygen demand for the heart, which can result in myocardial ischemia (insufficient oxygen levels in the heart tissue). If stress induces coronary vasoconstriction, or a state of blood hypercoagulation caused by increased blood platelet adhesiveness, platelet rupture can trigger the development of small thrombi (blood clots), which can trigger a blood clotting cascade that results in acute coronary occlusion and MI, ischemia, vulnerability to arrhythmias, or sudden death (Muller, Abela, & Nesto, 1994). Data also suggest that mental stress can lead to constriction of arteries in diseased coronary vessels with a damaged endothelium (blood vessel wall) (Yeung, Vekshtein, & Krantz, 1991).

EFFECTS ON BLOOD PRESSURE

While there are a number of risk factors for CAD, including family history, smoking, lack of exercise, and being overweight, two risk factors in particular, namely hypertension and elevated blood lipid levels, have been studied with respect to workplace stress (Shirom, 2003). Blood pressure fluctuates in response to changes in the internal and/or external environment. To discuss blood pressure one needs to understand the difference between systolic and diastolic blood pressure. The maximal pressure of the pulse of blood expelled from the left ventricle of the heart into the aorta is systolic blood pressure, while the minimal pressure exerted when the heart is at rest just before the next heartbeat is termed the diastolic blood pressure (Shirom). As mentioned earlier in this section, blood pressure can be measured when one is seated or when one is ambulatory. The latter is experimentally advantageous because subjects can go about their typical activities while blood pressure can be measured multiple times daily (Pickering, 1993).

Acute diastolic blood pressure reactivity to various stressors has been prospectively linked to an increased incidence of cardiovascular disease, including CAD, stroke, and renal disease (Fredrikson & Matthews, 1990). The results of studies that have investigated ambulatory blood pressure over time have indicated that blood pressure measured at work is higher than all other measures of blood pressure taken during the day independent of the time of day (James & Brown, 1997).

Personality factors such as the Type A personality, which is characterized by impatience, chronic urgency, enhanced competitiveness, aggressive drive, and an inclination toward hostility, can affect blood pressure (Booth-Kewley & Friedman, 1987). Meta-analytic data indicate that individuals with Type A personality show a greater diastolic blood pressure increase in response to daily activities than do people who are not Type A (Lyness, 1993), although the differences were small. Furthermore, in situations involving positive or negative feedback, elements inherent in playing video games, and socially aversive events such as criticism or verbal harassment, Type A individuals were found to have significant increases in blood pressure (Lyness). In a meta-analysis, while the experience of anger was correlated with elevated blood pressure, the effect was small and highly variable (Suls, Wan, & Costa, 1995).

Studies have repeatedly found that during periods of increased work demands blood pressure may be especially high (James, Broege, & Schlussel, 1996). It is possible that chronic exposure to job-related demands may be associated with changes in posture and increased physical activity. However, another pathway leading from chronic stress to elevated blood pressure could be related to one's sense of autonomy and control. In a series of studies that used both job demand and job control appraisals to predict ambulatory blood pressure in a sample of working adults who were followed longitudinally, it was found that low levels of decision latitude and high workload predicted elevated blood pressure at work, at home, and even during sleep (Schwartz, Pickering, & Landsbergis, 1996). Subsequent attempts to replicate this study in working men and women have had mixed results. Sometimes the predicted interaction was confirmed (Fox et al., 1993), and sometimes it was not (Fletcher & Jones, 1993; Kamarck et al., 1998; Weidner, Boughal, Connor, Pieper, & Mendell, 1997). A carefully conducted study of the effects of job strain on ambulatory blood pressure did indicate that situations in which participants perceived as high on control were associated with lower levels of diastolic blood pressure, which suggests that control may protect against acute SNS activation (Kamarck et al.).

In summary, while the effects of chronic stress on hypertension remain inconclusive, and more research is required to clarify this possible relationship, there is considerable support for the hypothesis that short-term stress, such as that associated with critical job events, is implicated in elevated blood pressure (Schwartz, Pickering, & Landsbergis, 1996).

EFFECTS ON BLOOD LIPIDS

Elevated levels of blood lipids, such as triglycerides and cholesterol, particularly low-density lipoprotein (LDL) cholesterol, have been shown to be associated with increased risk of CAD (Brindley, McCann, Niaura, Stoney, & Suarez, 1993; Niaura, Stoney, & Herbert, 1992).

However, levels of serum lipids also have been shown to be influenced by other factors such as heredity, gender, body mass, dietary fat intake, degree of physical activity, and cigarette smoking (Rosenman, 1993). Yet, all of these factors combined still only account for a small fraction of the variability associated with serum lipid levels. As a result researchers have continued to try to determine the impact of psychosocial stress on lipid levels (Dimsdale & Herd, 1982). In a qualitative review of the literature, Niaura et al. (1992), concluded that even though the effect may be inconsistent, there are data that implicate objective or perceived stress as a variable related to elevated concentrations of blood lipids, particularly the types of lipids that are the most atherogenic.

The relationship between cholesterol levels and CAD is graded and continuous (Niaura et al., 1992). For example, the results of the Framingham study revealed that for every 1% reduction in cholesterol levels, there was a 4% reduction in CAD, even after controlling for risk factors such as age, obesity, and blood pressure (NIH Consensus Conference, 1993). Such a dose-response relationship between cholesterol levels and CAD suggests that continuous exposure to psychosocial stress may be implicated as an etiologic factor in the development of coronary heart disease (CHD). The results of studies that investigated the effects of specific types of chronic stress, such as occupational instability and job insecurity, have found elevations of levels of total cholesterol that have persisted for as long as the stressors were present for a time period as long as one or two years (Mattiasson, Lindgarden, Nilsson, & Theorell, 1990; Siegrist, Matschinger, Cremer, & Seidel, 1988). In a quasi-retrospective study of female manufacturing employees, work overload predicted a subsequent elevation of total cholesterol even after controlling for age, obesity, fatigue, emotional reactivity, and burnout (Shirom, Westman, Shamai, & Carel, 1997).

The effects of stress on lipid levels in middle-aged men and women have been studied by Stoney and colleagues (Stoney, Niaura, Bausserman, & Matacin, 1999). They compared the effects of low versus high occupational stress and acute laboratory stress on a battery of lipid and lipoprotein measures. The results indicated that most of the lipid parameters increased significantly in response to both acute and chronic stress. Additionally, Stoney & Niaura et al. (1999) reported the results of an unpublished meta-analysis, which reviewed the results of 101 studies with respect to the effects of chronic stress (greater than 30 days), episodic (1–30 days), or acute stress (no more than 24 hours). Acute and episodic stress were found to have a significant elevation effect on several lipid parameters. Nevertheless, while chronic stress and total cholesterol levels were associated with increases, none of the other lipid parameters provided a significant effect size with respect to chronic stress. Thus the authors concluded that the evidence supported a relationship between acute and episodic stress and lipid reactivity, but that the data were less robust for a relationship between chronic stress and lipid reactivity (Stoney & Niaura et al., 1999). It should be noted, however, that the meta-analysis results could be influenced by the fact that the designation of acute, episodic, and chronic stress were arbitrary, or because there are a small number of studies that investigated chronic stress and its impact on lipid levels (Shirom, 2003).

In a final study that investigated the relationship between lipid levels and acute and chronic stress in 100 men and women, it was found that both types of stress induced both significant and transient elevations of atherogenic lipids that were not attributable to changes in diet, levels of activity, sleep patterns, or changes in plasma volume shifts, which where controlled for statistically (Stoney, Baussermen, Niaura, Marcus, & Flynn, 1999).

THE IMPACT OF WORKPLACE STRESS ON THE HEALTH AND WELL-BEING OF MANAGERIAL WOMEN AND WOMEN IN SPECIFIC OCCUPATIONS

The bulk of the available research with respect to the effects of workplace stress on managerial personnel primarily has been conducted on men. Research investigating the effects of workplace stress on managerial women, a highly educated, motivated, and well-paid group, has only occurred during the past decade (Burke, 2003). Because this group of women is growing in size, we thought that the examination of the impact of workplace stress in managerial women warranted attention. Additionally, there have been some studies that have examined the impact of workplace stress on women in particular occupations, and we will also discuss the results of these studies.

Some researchers have reviewed the literature on stress and health outcomes in women managers and have noted that, while stressors such as role conflict, work overload, and ambiguity are shared by both men and women, women experienced additional stressors unique to them and exhibited different ways of interpreting and coping with them (Offermann & Armitage, 1993; Langan-Fox, 1998; Davidson & Fielden, 1999). The stressors experienced by women managers could be categorized as being in three groups: those from society at large including work–family interface, off-job support, attitudes toward women in management and discrimination; those from organizations such as on-the-job support, sexual harassment, sexual discrimination, tokenism, and old-boys network; and, finally, those from women themselves, which consist of Type A personality, personal control, and self-esteem.

Davidson and Cooper (1992) have proposed a model wherein stressors at work, home, and within the individual act as precursors of a wide range of possible stress outcomes. The results of their research indicated that female managers scored higher on both stressors and stress outcomes than did their male counterparts. Women also reported significantly greater Type A behavior.

A longitudinal study of stress and health outcomes in 311 male senior managers and 172 female senior managers suggested that stress-related illness was more likely to be expressed as physical illness in males, while female managers were more likely to report psychological illness (Jick & Mitz, 1985). Also, Type A behavior predicted cardiovascular risk, poor physical health, and psychological health problems for both men and women, but more so for women. While men scored higher than women on more work stressors, these stressors were only weak or modest predictors of cardiovascular risk, poor physical health, or poor emotional health.

It has been reported that managerial women experience more pressure at work than male managers, while the latter group reported stress from internal sources (Davidson & Cooper, 1986). Women also reported more pressure at home and received little support from their partners (Hochschild, 1989). The women in this study felt isolated at work, exhibited greater symptoms of stress, and tended to exhibit Type A personality. Those women in junior and middle management experienced the highest overall occupational stress levels, although the profiles of male and female managers were different.

Other researchers studied occupational stress in 220 male and 126 female undergraduate business majors. In this sample the female middle and junior level managers reported greater stress levels than the male managers (Davidson, Cooper, & Baldini, 1995). Women also attributed greater stress with respect to gender-related issues such as discrimination, prejudice, and work–home conflict. Finally, the women managers revealed more physical and mental health symptoms than their male counterparts.

Another study examined the stress effects as a function of work and career experiences associated with career advancement in 792 women (Burke & McKeen, 1994). The dependent variables were various aspects of emotional well-being. The authors investigated four groups of predictor variables: (a) individual demographics, (b) organizational demographics, (c) work experiences associated with job and career satisfaction and progress, and (d) work outcomes. Work experiences such as support and encouragement, the absence of strain from conflict, ambiguity, and overload and challenging jobs were consistently and significantly related to self-reported emotional well-being in this sample of managerial women. Additionally, short-term responses to work conditions and work experiences that could affect emotional health also were significantly related to emotional well-being (Burke & McKeen).

With respect to studies on the impact of workplace stress in individuals employed in particular types of occupations, the authors identified some studies that examined workplace stress in supermarket cashiers (Lundberg et al., 1999), men and women in high-ranking positions (Lundberg & Frankenhaeuser, 1999), white-collar teleworkers (Lundberg & Lindfors, 2002), and critical care nurses (Sawatzky, 1996). The remainder of this section will discuss the results of these studies.

Lundberg and colleagues have studied the impact of workplace stress upon various groups of employees in Sweden. In their study of supermarket cashiers, the authors were interested in determining the psychophysiological stress responses as they impacted muscle tension and neck and shoulder pain (Lundberg et al., 1999). The results of the studies suggested a multifactorial etiology of musculoskeletal symptoms wherein physical and psychosocial conditions interact with individual characteristics and behavior. It also is documented that physically monotonous and repetitive work is associated with an increase in lower back, shoulder, and neck pain (Bernard, 1997). However, other studies have indicated that there is a relationship between psychosocial variables in the workplace and musculoskeletal disorders (Johansson, 1994; Moon & Sauter, 1996). Time pressure, lack of influence over one's work, and constant involvement in repetitive tasks of short duration often characterize jobs associated with a high risk for muscular problems. Supermarket cashiers experience time pressure, expectations from the customer and the employer, very little influence over the content of their work, and repetitive physical activity (Lannersten & Harms-Ringdahl, 1990). The results of this study suggested that the stress levels of supermarket cashiers were significantly elevated at work as reflected in the catecholamine levels, blood pressure, electromyographic (EMG) activity, and self-reports. Seventy percent of the cashiers suffering from neck/shoulder pain had higher EMG activity at work and reported more tension after work. Women who described more musculoskeletal pain and kept a diary for 1 week were older, had higher blood pressure, and reported more work stress and psychophysiological symptoms (Lundberg et al., 1999).

Lundberg and Lindfors (2002) studied the psychophysiological reactions to telework in male and female white-collar workers, where teleworkers include individuals who are said to engage in telecommuting, distance work, and remote work. In general such employees typically work outside a traditional workplace and use information technology and telecommunication equipment (Johnston & Nolan, 2000). In this study, psychophysiological data were gathered for 26 healthy, full-time, male and female employees while at the office, engaging in telework at home, and relaxing at home. Blood pressure was significantly higher during work at the office than when teleworking at home. Levels of EPI were significantly elevated in men in the evening after telework at home.

As mentioned in the beginning of this chapter, it is clear that the proportion of women in the labor force is approaching that of men in many industrialized countries. However, data from several countries indicate that, because of unequal division of labor at home, married women who are employed full-time have a greater total workload than their male counterparts (Kahn, 1991). These gender differences have been detected in both blue- and white-collar workers from different parts of the world (Ayree, 1993; Barnett & Brennan, 1997; Beena & Poduval, 1992), thus supporting the hypothesis that there is an interaction between conditions at work and conditions at home that contribute to greater levels of stress in employed women as compared to employed men. Conversely, there also are data indicating that challenging work may serve as a stress buffer (Barnett, Marshall, & Sayer, 1992; Eckenrode & Gore, 1990; Repetti, 1998; Waldron, 1991). Thus, it seems as if workplace stress can result in both health-promoting and health-damaging consequences in women. Lundberg and Frankenhaeuser (1999) conducted a study to determine the effects of physiological and psychological stress responses to work and family situations in full-time female and male manager employees of a large insurance company in Sweden. The results of this study suggested that, while both men and women experienced their positions as stimulating and challenging, the data indicated a more favorable situation for men than for women. Furthermore, women were significantly more stressed by their greater unpaid workload and by a greater responsibility for duties related to home and family. Women had higher levels of NE than men, both during and after work, which the authors suggest was a reflection of the women's greater workload (Lundberg & Frankenhaeuser, 1999). Additionally, women with children at home had significantly higher NE levels after work than did the other participants.

A study of critical care nurses in Canada sought to describe the stressful work experiences, the perceptions of work stressors, and life stress in the lives of these employees (Sawatzky, 1996). Nurses working in intensive care units (ICUs) assume significant responsibility for the management of patient care. Not only is the ICU nurse confronted by impending crises with their patients and their families, but also by the demand for technological excellence (Oehler, Davidson, Starr, & Lee, 1991; Oskins, 1979). The results of this study suggested that patient care–related stressors ranked the highest overall. A sense of lack of control appeared to be a common element among the situations ranked as most stressful. Significant correlations were also obtained for the relationship between perceived life stress and the perceived severity of work stressors as well as between frequency and intensity of stressful work events. The authors concluded that, to address these issues, it is critical to change the perception of powerlessness and inevitability in the ICU, and that one of the best ways to foster a better sense of control is via continuing educational experiences that enhance competence and expertise (Sawatzky, 1996).

RECOMMENDATIONS FOR ENHANCING WOMEN'S HEALTH AND WELL-BEING IN THE WORKPLACE

Given all the information that we have reviewed in this chapter regarding the effects of workplace stress on the health and well-being of women, the authors thought it prudent to offer some recommendations for both organizations and women who are employed. Burke (2003) has identified three levels of prevention: primary, secondary, and tertiary. Primary prevention involves efforts directed at reducing or eliminating the risk factors for workplace stress and/or the sources of stress. Secondary prevention involves helping women manage their responses to the unavoidable demands of work and home, while tertiary prevention directs efforts toward healing women and organizations via appropriate professional care (Burke, 2003). The remaining part of this section will provide some suggestions for the primary, secondary, and tertiary prevention of stress in the workplace.

With respect to primary prevention, organizations could enact policies and procedures to accomplish the following goals:

- Provide flexible work schedules, telecommuting, alternative work schedules, and company assistance with child care and elder care to help women deal with work–home overload issues.
- Develop zero tolerance for inappropriate sexual behavior in the workplace and for sexual harassment, as such problems have been linked to depression, headaches, nausea, and other physiological symptoms (Burke, 2003).
- Ensure that companies institute development and reward systems that promote equitable treatment of all employees with a specific focus on resolving the wage differential between male and female workers.
- Design programs that enhance mentoring and networking to improve social support in the workplace.

Primary prevention suggestions for women employees include but are not limited to:

- Identify the sources of your stress and implement a personal stress management program that could include engagement in regular exercise, daily relaxation interventions, and perhaps intermittent professional counseling "check-ups."
- Utilize developmental opportunities to enhance your experience and use these developmental opportunities as a means of gaining exposure in the organization.
- Recognize the existence of the work–home stress interaction and make suggestions to your employer regarding flexible working arrangements.

- Address your perceptions of stressors because part of primary prevention is changing the stressor. Modifying one's perception of the stressor is the first step in doing that. Optimism and positive self-talk can foster resilience.

Recalling that secondary prevention involves assisting women in managing their responses to stress and tension, organizations can assist women by:

- Creating workplace exercise facilities and options for child care because women have less discretionary time to pursue health club memberships and often need child care to attend an exercise program.
- Create networking groups whose purpose is to facilitate emotional release, a sort of "self-help group therapy."
- Encourage or create opportunities for employees to learn stress management techniques such as diaphragmatic breathing, progressive muscle relaxation, meditation, or yoga.

Because women in the workplace also have a responsibility for secondary prevention, our suggestions for them are similar to those for the employers and include:

- Engage in a regular exercise routine multiple times per week, ideally five days out of seven.
- Engage in a daily stress management technique.
- Talk to others to engage in productive problem-solving as opposed to obsessing and ruminating.

Finally, because tertiary prevention involves symptom management and resolution of the sequelae of workplace stress, organizations should have employee assistance programs that provide appropriate professional care and that recognize the issues of workplace–home stress, which may be more prevalent in women. Such issues can include but are not limited to alcohol abuse, eating disorders, and smoking. Gender-specific interventions may be more successful (Burke, 2003). Women in the workplace need to establish working relationships with physicians, mental health providers, and other trained health care providers to establish a working network for their health and well-being.

REFERENCES

Alehagen, S., Wijma, K., Lundberg, U., Melin, B., & Wijma, B. (2001). Catecholamine and cortisol response to child birth. *International Journal of Behavioral Medicine, 8,* 50–65.

Ayree, S. (1993). Dual earner couples in Singapore: An examination of work and nonwork sources of their experienced burnout. *Human Relations, 46,* 1441–1468.

Bandura, A. (1977). Self-efficacy: Towards a unifying theory of behavioral change. *Psychological Review, 84,* 191–215.

Barnett, R. C., & Brennan, R. T. (1997). Change in job conditions, change in psychological distress, and gender: A longitudinal study of dual-earner couples. *Journal of Organizational Behavior, 18,* 253–274.

Barnett, R. C., Marshall, N. L., & Sayer, A. (1992). Positive-spillover effects from job to home: A closer look. *Women and Health, 19,* 13–14.

Beena, C., & Poduval, P. R. (1992). Gender differences in work stress of executives. *Psychological Studies, 37,* 109–113.

Bernard, B. P. (1997). *Musculoskeletal disorders and workplace factors: A critical review of epidemiologic evidence for work-related musculoskeletal disorders of the neck, upper extremity, and low back.* Washington, DC: U.S. Department of Health and Human Services, Centers for Disease Control, and National Institute of Occupational Safety and Health.

Booth-Kewley, S., & Friedman, H. S. (1987). Psychological predictors of heart disease: A quantitative review. *Psychological Bulletin, 101,* 343–362.

Brandt, L. P. A., & Nielsen, C. V. (1992). Job stress and adverse outcome of pregnancy: A causal link or recall bias? *American Journal of Epidemiology, 135*(3), 302–311.

Brindley, D. N., McCann, B. S., Niaura, R., Stoney, C. M., & Suarez, E. C. (1993). Stress and lipoprotein metabolism: Modulators and mechanisms. *Metabolism, 42,* 3–15.

Burger, J. M., & Cooper, H. M. (1979). The desirability of control. *Motivation and Emotion, 3,* 381–393.

Burke, R. J. (2003). Work experiences, stress and health among managerial women: Research and practice. In M. J. Schabracq, J. A. M. Winnubst, & C. L. Cooper (Eds.), *The handbook of work and health psychology* (pp. 259–278). New York: John Wiley & Sons.

Burke, R. J., & McKeen, C. A. (1994). Work and career experiences and emotional well-being of managerial and professional women. *Stress Medicine, 10,* 65–57.

Cannon, W. B. (1929). *Bodily changes in pain, hunger, fear and rage.* Boston, MA: Branford.

Cannon, W. B. (1932). *Wisdom of the body.* New York: W. W. Norton.

Champoux, J. E. (1991). A multivariate test of the job characteristics theory of work motivation. *Journal of Organizational Behaviour, 12,* 431–436.

Cohen, S., Kessler, R. C., & Gordon, L. U. (1998). *Measuring stress: A guide for health and social scientists.* New York: Oxford University Press.

Collins, A., & Frankenhaeuser, M. (1978). Stress responses in male and female engineering students. *Journal of Human Stress. 4,* 43–48.

Collins, A., Hanson, U., Eneroth, P., Hagenfeldt, K., Lundberg, U., & Frankenhaeuser, M. (1982). Psychophysiological stress responses in postmenopausal women before and after hormone replacement therapy. *Human Neurobiology, 1,* 153–159.

Cropley, M., Steptoe, A., & Joekes, K. (1999). Job strain and psychiatric morbidity. *Psychological Medicine, 29,* 1411–1416.

Davidson, M. J., & Cooper, C. L. (1986). Executive women under pressure. *International Review of Applied Psychology, 35,* 301–326.

Davidson, M. J., & Cooper, C. L. (1992). *Shattering the glass ceiling: The woman manager.* London: Paul Chapman.

Davidson, M. J., Cooper, C. L., & Baldini, V. (1995). Occupational stress in female and male graduate managers. *Stress Medicine, 11,* 157–175.

Davidson, M. J., & Fielden, S. (1999). Stress and the working woman. In G. N. Powell (Ed.), *Handbook of gender and work* (pp. 413–426). Thousand Oaks, CA: Sage.

Dimsdale, J. E., & Herd, J. A. (1982). Variability of plasma lipids in response to emotional arousal. *Psychosomatic Medicine, 44,* 413–427.

Dollard, M. F., Winefield, H. R., Winefield, A. H., & de Jonge, J. (2000). Psychosocial job strain and productivity in human service workers: A test of the demand-control-support model. *Journal of Occupational and Organizational Psychology, 73*(4), 501–510.

Eckenrode, J., & Gore, S. (Eds.). (1990). *Stress between work and family.* New York: Plenum.

Fletcher, B. C., & Jones, F. (1993). A refutation of Karasek's demand-discretion model of occupational stress with a wide range of dependent measures. *Journal of Organizational Behaviour, 14,* 319–330.

Folkow, B. (1993). Physiological organization of neurohormonal responses to psychosocial stimuli. *Physiological Reviews, 62,* 347–504.

Folkow, B. (1982). Mental "stress" and hypertension: Evidence from animal and experimental studies. *Integrative Psychological and Behavioral Science, 26,* 305–308.

Fox, M. L., Dwyer, D. J., & Ganster, D. C. (1993). Effects of stressful job demands and control on physiological and attitudinal outcomes in a hospital setting. *Academy of Management Journal, 36,* 289–318.

Frankenhaeuser, M. (1983). The sympathetic-adrenal and the pituitary-adrenal response to challenge. In T. M. Dembroski, T. H. Smidt, & G. Blumchen (Eds.), *Biobehavioral bases of coronary heart disease* (pp. 91–105). New York: Karger.

Frankenhaeuser, M., Lundberg, U., Fredrikson, M., Belin, B., Tuomisto, M., Myrsten, A. L., Hedman, M., Bergman-Losman, B., & Wallin, L. (1989). Stress on and off the job as related to sex and occupational status in white-collar workers. *Journal of Organizational Behavior, 10,* 321–346.

Fredrikson, M., & Matthews, K. A. (1990). Cardiovascular responses to behavioral stress and hypertension: A meta-analytic review. *Annals of Behavioral Medicine, 12,* 30–39.

Ganster, D. C., & Fusilier, M. R. (1989). Control in the workplace. In C. L. Cooper & I. Robertson (Eds.), *International review of industrial and organizational psychology.* Chichester: John Wiley & Sons.

Goldberg, D. (1978). *Manual of the general health questionnaire.* Windsor: NFER.

Hackman, J. R., & Oldham, G. R. (1980). *Work redesign.* London: Addison-Wesley.

Harvard Health Publications (2000). Women, work and stress. *Harvard Women's Health Watch, 8*(1), 1–2.

Holmes, S. D., Krantz, D. S., Rogers, H., Gottdiener, J., & Contrada, R. J. (2006). Mental stress and coronary artery disease: A multidisciplinary guide. *Progress in Cardiovascular Diseases, 49*(2), 106–122.

Hochschild, A. R. (1989). *The second shift: Working parents and the revolution at home.* New York: Avon Books.

James, G. D., & Brown, D. E. (1997). The biological stress response and lifestyle: Catecholamines and blood pressure. *Annual Review of Anthropology, 26,* 313–353.

James, G. D., Broege, P. A., & Schlussel, Y. R. (1996). Assessing cardiovascular risk and stress-related blood pressure variability in young women employed in wage jobs. *American Journal of Human Biology, 8*, 743–749.

Jick, T. D., & Mitz, L. F. (1985). Sex differences in work stress. *Academy of Management Review, 10*, 408–420.

Johansson, J. (1994). *Psychosocial factors at work and their relation to musculoskeletal symptoms.* Unpublished doctoral dissertation, Department of Psychology, Göteborg University, Göteborg, Sweden.

Johnson, J. V., & Hall, E. M. (1988). Job strain, workplace social support and cardiovascular disease: A cross-sectional study of a random sample of the working population. *American Journal of Public Health, 78*, 1336–1442.

Johnston, P., & Nolan, J. (2000). eWork2000: Status-report on new ways to work in the information society. Brussels: CEC, DG Information Society.

Jones, F., Bright, J. E. H., Searle, B., & Cooper, L. (1998). Modeling occupational stress and health: The impact of the demand-control model on academic research and on workplace practice. *Stress Medicine, 14*, 231.

Jones, F., & Fletcher, B. C. (2003). Job control, physical health and psychological well-being. In M. J. Schabracq, J. A. M. Winnubst, & C. L. Cooper (Eds.), *The handbook of work and health psychology* (pp. 121–142). New York: John Wiley & Sons.

Kahn, R. L. (1991). The forms of women's work. In M. Frankenhaeuser, U. Lundberg, & M. A. Chesney (Eds.), *Women, work and health: Stress and opportunities* (pp. 65–83). New York: Plenum Press.

Kamarck, T. W., Schiffman, S. M., Smithline, L., Goodie, J. L., Paty, J. A., Gnys, M., & Jong, J. Y. K. (1998). Effects of task strain, social conflict, and emotional activation on ambulatory cardiovascular activity: Daily consequences of recurring stress in a multiethnic adult sample. *Health Psychology, 17*, 17–29.

Karasek, R. A. (1979). Job demands, job decision latitude and mental strain: Implications for job design. *Administrative Science Quarterly, 24*, 285–308.

Kasl, S. V. (1996). The influence of work environment on cardiovascular health: A historical, conceptual, and methodological perspective. *Journal of Occupational Health Psychology, 1*, 42–56.

Kirschbaum, C., & Hellhammer, D. H. (1989). Salivary cortisol and psychobiological research: An overview. *Neuropsychobiology, 22*, 150–169.

Kristenson, T. S. (1996). Job stress and cardiovascular disease: A theoretical critical review. *Journal of Occupational Health Psychology, 1*(3), 246–260.

Kristenson, M., Eriksen, H. R., Sluiter, J. K., Starke, D., & Ursin, H. (2004). Psychobiological mechanisms of socioeconomic differences in health. *Social Science Medicine, 58*, 1511–1522.

Kristenson, M., Orth-Gomér, K., Kucienskiene, Z., Bergdahl, B., Calcauskas, H., Balnyiene, I., & Olsson, A. G. (1998). Attenuated cortisol response to a standardized stress test in Lithuanian vs. Swedish men: The LiVicordia study. *International Journal of Behavioral Medicine, 5*, 17–30.

Langan-Fox, J. (1998). Women's careers and occupational stress. In C. L. Cooper & I. T. Robertson (Eds.), *International review of industrial and organizational Psychology* (pp. 273–304). New York: John Wiley & Sons.

Lannersten, L., & Harms-Ringdahl, K. (1990). Neck and shoulder muscle activity during work with different cash register systems. *Ergonomics, 33*, 49–65.

Levi, L. (1972). Stress and distress to psychosocial stimuli. *Acta Medica Scandinavia Supplement*, 528.

Lindfors, P., & Lundberg, U. (2002). Is low cortisol release an indicator of positive health? *Stress Health, 18*, 153–160.

Loher, B. T., Noe, R. A., Moeller, N. L., & Fitzgerald, M. P. (1985). A meta-analysis of the relation of job characteristics to job satisfaction. *Journal of Applied Psychology, 70*(2), 280–289.

Lundberg, U. (1984). Human psychobiology in Scandinavia: II: Psychoneuroendocrinology-human stress and coping processes. *Scandinavian Journal of Psychology, 25*, 214–226.

Lundberg, U. (1996). The influence of paid and unpaid work on the psychophysiological stress responses of men and women. *Journal of Occupational Health Psychology, 1*, 117–130.

Lundberg, U. (2005). Stress hormones in health and illness: The roles of work and gender. *Psychoneuroendocrinology, 30*(10), 1017–1021.

Lundberg, U., de Chateau, P., Winberg, J., & Frankenhaeuser, M. (1981). Catecholamine and cortisol excretion patterns in three year old children and their parents. *Journal of Human Stress, 7*, 3–11.

Lundberg, U., Dohns, I. E., Melin, B., Sandsjö, L., Palmerud, G., Kadefors, R., Ekström, M., & Parr, D. (1999). Psychophysiological stress responses, muscle tension, neck and shoulder pain among supermarket cashiers. *Journal of Occupational Psychology, 4*(3), 245–255.

Lundberg, U., & Frankenhaeuser, M. (1999). Stress and workload of men and women in high ranking positions. *Journal of Occupational Health Psychology, 4*, 142–151.

Lundberg, U., Hanson, U., Andersson, K., Eneroth, P., Frankenhaeuser, M., & Hagenfeldt, K. (1983). Hirsute women with elevated androgen levels: Psychological characteristics, steroid hormones and catecholamines. *Journal of Psychosomatics, Obstetrics and Gynaecology, 2*(2), 86–93.

Lundberg, U., & Hellstrom (2002). Workload and morning salivary cortisol in women. *Work Stress, 16*, 356–363.

Lundberg, U., & Johansson, J. (2000). Stress and health risks in repetitive work and supervisory monitoring work. In R. Backs & W. Boucsein (Eds.), *Engineering psychophysiology: Issues and applications* (pp. 339–359). New Jersey: Lawrence Erlbaum Associates.

Lundberg, U., & Lindfors, P. (2002). Psychophysiological reactions to telework in female and male white-collar workers. *Journal of Occupational Health Psychology, 7*(4), 354–364.

Lundberg, U., Mårdberg, B., & Frankenhaeuser, M. (1994). The total workload of male and female white collar workers as related to age, occupational level and number of children. *Scandinavian Journal of Psychology, 35*, 315–327.

Lundberg, U., & Palm, K. (1989). Total workload and catecholamine excretion of families with preschool children. *Work Stress, 3*, 255–260.

Lyness, S. A. (1993). Predictors of differences between Type A and B individuals in heart rate and blood pressure reactivity. *Psychological Bulletin, 114*, 266–295.

Mattiasson, L., Lindgarden, F., Nilsson, J. A., & Theorell, T. (1990). Threat of unemployment and cardiovascular risk factors: Longitudinal study of quality of sleep and serum cholesterol concentrations in men threatened with redundancy. *British Medical Journal, 301,* 461–466.

Mausner-Dorsch, H., & Eaton, W. W. (2000). Psychosocial work environment and depression: Epidemiologic assessment of the demand-control model. *American Journal of Public Health, 90*(11), 1765–1770.

Moon, S. D., & Sauter, S. L. (Eds.). (1996). *Psychosocial aspects of musculoskeletal disorders in office work.* London: Taylor & Francis.

Muller, J. E., Abela, G. S., & Nesto, R. W. (1994). Triggers, risk factors and vulnerable plaques: The lexicon of a new frontier. *Journal of the American College of Cardiology, 23,* 809–813.

Muntaner, C., & O'Campo, P. J. (1993). A critical appraisal of the demand/control model of the psychosocial work environment: Epistemological, social, and class considerations. *Social Science and Medicine, 36*(11), 1509–1517.

Muntaner, C., Tien, A. Y., Eaton, W. W., & Garrison, R. (1991). Occupational characteristics and the occurrence of psychotic disorders. *Social Psychiatry and Psychiatric Epidemiology, 26*(6), 273–280.

Niaura, R., Stoney, C. M., & Herbert, P. N. (1992). Lipids in psychological research: The last decade. *Biological Psychology, 34,* 1–34.

NIH Consensus Conference (1993). Triglycerides, high density lipoprotein and coronary disease. *Journal of the American Medical Association, 269,* 505–510.

Oehler, J. M., Davidson, M. G., Starr, L. E., & Lee D. A. (1991). Burnout, job stress, anxiety, and perceived social support in neonatal nurses. *Heart & Lung, 20,* 500–505.

Offermann, L. R., & Armitage, M. A. (1993). Stress and the woman manager: Sources, health outcomes and interventions. In E. A. Faegenson (Ed.), *Women in management: Trend, issues and challenges in managerial diversity* (pp. 131–161). Newbury Park, CA: Sage.

Oskins, S. (1979). Identification of situational stressors and coping methods by intensive care nurses. *Heart & Lung, 8,* 953–960.

Parkes, K. R. (1991). Locus of control as a moderator: An explanation for additive versus interactive findings in the demand-discretion model of work stress? *British Journal of Psychology, 82,* 291–312.

Payne, R. L. (1979). Demands, supports, constraints and psychological health. In C. Mackay & T. Cox (Eds.), *Response to stress: Occupational Aspects.* London: IPC.

Pickering, T. G. (1993). Applications of ambulatory blood pressure monitoring in behavioral medicine. *Annals of Behavioral Medicine, 15,* 26–32.

Repetti, R. (1998). Multiple roles. In E. A. Blechman & K. D. Brownell (Eds.), *Behavioral medicine and women: A comprehensive handbook* (pp. 162–168). New York: Guilford Press.

Roberts, K. H., & Glick, W. (1981). The job characteristics approach to job design: A critical review. *Journal of Applied Psychology, 66*(2), 193–217.

Rosenman, R. H. (1993). Psychological influences on the variability of plasma cholesterol. *Homeostasis in Health and Disease, 34,* 129–136.

Rozanski, A., Bairey, C. N., & Krantz, D. S. (1988). Mental stress and the induction of silent myocardial infarction. *New England Journal of Medicine, 318,* 1005–1012.

Rozanski, A., Blumenthal, J. A., & Kaplan, J. (1999). Impact of psychological factors on the pathogenesis of cardiovascular disease and implications for therapy. *Circulation, 99,* 2192–2217.

Saavedra, R., & Kwun, S. K. (2000). Affective states in job characteristics theory. *Journal of Organizational Behavior, 21*(5), 131–146.

Sanchez, J. I., & Levine, E. L. (2000). Accuracy or consequential validity: Which is the better standard for job analysis data? *Journal of Organizational Behavior, 21*, 809–818.

Sapolsky, R. (1996). Why stress is bad for your brain. *Science, 273*, 749–750.

Sawatzky, J. V. (1996). Stress in critical care nurses: Actual and perceived. *Heart & Lung, 25*, 409–417.

Schnall, P. L., Landsbergis, P. A., & Baker, D. (1994). Job strain and cardiovascular health. *Annual Review of Public Health, 15*, 361–411.

Schwartz, J. E., Pickering, T. G., & Landsbergis, P. A. (1996). Work-related stress and blood pressure: Current theoretical models and considerations from a behavioral medicine perspective. *Journal of Occupational Health Psychology, 1*, 287–310.

Selye, H. (1956). *The stress of life.* New York: McGraw-Hill.

Shirom, A. (2003). The effects of work stress on health. In M. J. Schabracq, J. A. M. Winnubst, & G. L. Cooper (Eds.), *The handbook of work and health psychology* (pp. 63–82). New York: John Wiley & Sons.

Shirom, A., Westman, M., Shamai, O., & Carel, R. S. (1997). Effects of workload and burnout on cholesterol and triglyceride levels: The moderating effects of emotional reactivity among male and female employees. *Journal of Occupational Health Psychology, 2*(4), 275–288.

Siegrist, J., Matschinger, H., Cremer, P., & Seidel, D. (1988). Atherogenic risk in men suffering from occupational stress. *Atherosclerosis, 69*, 211–218.

Skov, T., Borg, V., & Orhede, E. (1996). Psychosocial and physical risk factors for musculoskeletal disorders of the neck, shoulders, and lower back in salespeople. *Occupational and Environmental Medicine, 53*(5), 351–356.

Spector, P. E. (1986). Perceived control by employees: A meta-analysis of studies concerning autonomy and participation at work. *Human Relations, 39*(11), 1005–1116.

Spector, P. E., & Jex, S. M. (1991). Relations of job characteristics from multiple data sources with employee affect, absence, turnover intentions, and health. *Journal of Applied Psychology, 76*(1), 46–53.

Stoney, C. M., Bausserman, L., Niaura, R., Marcus, B., & Flynn, M. (1999). Lipid reactivity to stress: II. Biological and behavioral influences. *Health Psychology, 18*, 251–261.

Stoney, C. M., Niaura, R., Bausserman, L., & Matacin, M. (1999). Lipid reactivity to stress: I. Comparison of chronic and acute stress responses in middle-aged airline pilots. *Health Psychology, 18*, 241–250.

Strike, P. C., & Steptoe, A. (2004). Psychosocial factors in the development of coronary artery disease. *Progress in Cardiovascular Disease, 46*, 337–347.

Suls, J., Wan, C. K., & Costa, Jr., P. T. (1995). Relationship of trait anger to resting blood pressure: A meta-analysis. *Health Psychology, 14*, 444–456.

Terry, D. J., & Jimmieson, N. L. (1999). Work control and employee well-being: A decade review. *International Review of Industrial and Organizational Psychology, 14*, 95–148.

Van der Doef, M., & Maes, S. (1998). The job demand-control (-support) model and physical outcomes: A review of the strain and buffer hypotheses. *Psychology and Health, 13*, 909–936.

Van der Doef, M., & Maes, S. (1999). The job demand-control (-support) model and psychological well-being: A review of 20 years of empirical research. *Work and Stress, 13*(2), 87–114.

Waldron, I. (1991). Effects of labour force participation on sex differences in mortality and morbidity. In M. Frankenhaeuser, U. Lundberg, & M. Chesney (Eds.), *Women, work and health: Stress opportunities* (pp. 17–38). New York: Plenum.

Wall, T. D., Clegg, C. W., & Jackson, P. R. (1978). An evaluation of the job characteristics model. *Journal of Occupational Psychology, 51*, 183–196.

Wall, T. D., Corbett, J. M., Clegg, C. W., Jackson, P. R., & Martin, R. (1990). Advanced manufacturing technology and work design: Towards a theoretical framework. *Journal of Organizational Behavior, 11*, 201–219.

Wall, T. D., Kemp, N. J., Jackson, P. R., & Clegg, C. W. (1986). Outcomes of autonomous work groups: A long term field experiment. *Academy of Management Journal, 29*, 280–304.

Warr, P. (1987). *Work, unemployment and mental health.* Oxford: Oxford University Press.

Weidner, G., Boughal, T., Connor, S. L., Pieper, C., & Mendell, N. R. (1997). Relationship of job strain to standard coronary risk factors and psychological characteristics in women and men of the family heart study. *Health Psychology, 16*, 239–247.

Yehuda, R., Teicher, M. H., Trestman, R. A., Levengood, R. A., & Siever, L. J. (1996). Cortisol regulation in posttraumatic stress disorder and major depression: A chronobiological analysis. *Biological Psychiatry, 40*, 79–88.

Yeung, A. C., Vekshtein, V. I., & Krantz, D. S. (1991). The effect of atherosclerosis on the vasomotor response of coronary arteries to mental stress. *New England Journal of Medicine, 325*, 1551–1556.

Chapter 6

Preparing to Be Employed: In My Own Voice

Christa White

I am currently an undergraduate at a small, private college in upstate New York. It's my senior year and I've found myself in the middle of what seems like a quarter-life crisis at the age of 21. After spending eight years away from home at boarding school and college, it's now time to figure out what I'll do with my life after the institutionalized structure that I've become so used to is finally taken away. Still unsure of myself, I do hope for more than the words of George Orwell in *1984* when O'Brien states, "If you want a picture of the future, imagine a boot stamping on a human face—forever." Although I feel lost in translation, I hope for and imagine the best outcome possible; one that reflects my hard work—academically, socially, and athletically—and expands the image of myself in terms of the reality of all that I am capable of.

I've always been entirely independent; it never seemed early enough to get away from home and do things on my own. At four years old I didn't understand why I hadn't yet been placed in the school system. When I was six, I decided that I should go to sleep-away summer camp. At 11, I needed to go on a term abroad for school, and then at the end of my middle school career, I decided that I needed to go to boarding school for high school. It was all over from there; I was away from home, in charge of my own schedule and setting responsibilities for myself. At boarding school I mastered time management and learned how to form mature yet close relationships with my teachers, coaches, advisors, and peers. Although I wasn't stable financially, the school, in cooperation with my friends who fought for me to stay at the institution, made it possible for me to graduate regardless. After being given so many opportunities at boarding school in terms of classes, extracurriculars, and the social environment, my expectations for college were almost impossibly high.

It's not to say that I've been disappointed with my college years. I've had a great sense of social support that has specifically come from my swim team. Especially as an incoming freshman, the team was a necessary distraction from the temporary depression that had overcome me as a result from starting a new life in a new place; I no longer had the best friends who let me live with them when I wasn't able to afford boarding life for senior year, nor did I have the comfort of dorm parents or the general comforts of a familiar environment. I thought that because I was able to approach new situations rather easily that the transition to college would barely even phase me. However, I soon learned that my adjustment had affected me more than I had thought would be the case.

When swim practice started only a few weeks after classes began, it allowed me to regain a sense of schedule and time management. I finally had a healthy alternative to the constant party scene that so many of the incoming freshmen took advantage of almost daily. The training allowed me to mentally focus on something specific and that was not all that I missed about my high school days of security. I quickly grasped onto a routine that included classes and sports practice. I furthermore felt as though I had found one adult, my coach, with whom I could talk freely about my new experiences as a freshman in college. He was one person who understood my sarcasm and personality in general. When this connection formed, as well as those connections with the members on the team, I started to feel as though I would be OK in a new place.

I had gone from positive to distraught, and finally leveled off at hopeful by the end of my first term at college. Four years later, the most special part of my college experience has been my athletic life. I have learned what it means to balance work and training and to work with a team to accomplish goals such as winning conference meets multiple times or making national qualifying consideration times. I've learned to work for others and not only for myself. I've found myself on a team for which I would sacrifice myself; I have gone beyond my comfort limits for something that is more important than the individual; and in turn I have found that my own successes stem from realizing the importance of working for a team. I have learned that I thrive most in a competitive, fast-paced environment where my efforts are relied on by others. This has been valuable to learn about myself, not only for efforts in the pool but also for where my personal best can be found most evident in my academic as well as social life.

I've had some obstacles along the way, of course, regardless of how well athletics has treated me during these years. I've been frustrated with certain aspects of the academic life. One professor once told my psychology class on the first day that not all of us would get A's. I wondered how she knew that on the first day. It turns out that she made sure that there was always a perfect bell curve with every grading period so that she would not be addressed by superiors for being too easy or too hard. It seemed more important that she appear legitimate in the eyes of the administration rather than to work with each student to ensure success. I found it frustrating that a professor whom I initially entrusted to provide me with a valuable learning experience spent more time missing class herself and setting rules to disallow any possible cheating that could take place. My teachers in high school seemed to have more faith in me as a student than this particular college professor.

Another setback in my academic experiences has been the lack of courses available specifically in the department of my major, psychology. Finding that I was nearly done with the requirements for my major during the middle of my third year, I wondered where I would spend my time for the remainder of my college credits. An understaffed department was unable to offer courses that had been previously set up as electives, and as a result there was a slim selection of courses. One professor who has graciously worked with me along the way suggested that I take on a program in the graduate school that had to do with human resources. I was thrilled that such an opportunity was available; it seemed as though I would be able to graduate having an added benefit to give me an edge upon graduation—both because I would have added experience in a particular study and because I would be more confident about entering the workforce in an area that I would specifically desire. However, the school administration soon turned me down, with hardly an explanation. They were sorry that I didn't understand, and would I please stop inquiring about the situation. This was one of the most upsetting setbacks during my academic experience because it seemed as though I was being denied a valuable opportunity for no justifiable reason.

However, despite these obstacles in my academic life, I have had a few professors in my college career who have helped me learn a little bit of what I want out of life after college. In terms of work, it seems that it's becoming less of a man's world than it used to be. Women are now receiving more benefits than before, thanks to research that shows that successful integration of work and family life benefits both the employee as well as the employer than if such benefits were otherwise not offered.

For example, direct services offered by companies are important factors in the workforce. On-site health services and fitness centers would ensure a healthy experience for me and therefore a more successful work experience. Culture change strategies where there is training for managers and others to help deal with work and life conflicts, as well as the focus of quality work and not quantity, also seem to be important factors to consider as a young woman attempting to enter the workforce for the first time. Although I'm not yet at the place of marriage and family, it's important that companies understand information-based strategies in terms of giving information to employees about child care, and so on, and further accommodating childbirth leave and child-care options. Again, although this does not directly and immediately concern me, it's important to me that companies are accommodating and understanding in these ways, because it shows the value that they place on their employees. If companies understand the importance of work and life integration, it seems that we are all in the right place.

Chapter 7

Mental Health Impact of Sexual Harassment

Susan Fineran
James Gruber

Over the last 25 years, scholars from a variety of disciplines (e.g., psychology, social work, women's studies) and a wide range of nations have documented the devastating impact of sexual harassment on the health and well-being of girls and women. This chapter provides an overview of the literature and research on one aspect of the harm of sexual harassment: its effect on women's and girls' mental health. We begin the chapter with a brief explanation of the laws that cover sexual harassment for both the workplace (Title VII) and educational environments (Title IX). Given that sexual harassment was first introduced as a form of employment discrimination, the chapter will begin by summarizing the research on the mental health effects of workplace harassment and then move on to harassment in university and K–12 education environments.

Title VII of the Civil Rights Act of 1964 (42 U.S.C. § 2000e-2(a)) provides the principal framework prohibiting discrimination on the basis of race, color, religion, national origin, and sex. In 1980 the Equal Employment Opportunity Commission (EEOC) defined sexual harassment as a form of sex discrimination and issued specific guidelines to prohibit it. Six years later, the U.S. Supreme Court further refined the law by specifying two categories of sexual harassment: *hostile environment* and *quid pro quo* (EEOC, 2000). Hostile environment is applicable when the behavior of one or more people (not only a supervisor) causes the workplace to become sexually abusive, intimidating, or offensive and interferes with an employee's job. Quid pro quo applies when a person in a power position (e.g., a supervisor) makes decisions that affect an employee's job, on the basis of whether the employee complies with his or her sexual demands.

Title VII set the stage for Title IX, which was signed into law in 1972 and states: "No person in the United States shall, on the basis of sex, be excluded from participation in, or denied the benefits of, or be subjected to discrimination under any educational program or activity receiving federal assistance" (Title IX of the Education Amendments of 1972 to the Civil Rights Act of 1964). Using language that is similar to Title VII, the U.S. Department of Education defines sexual harassment under Title IX as

> unwelcome sexual advances, requests for sexual favors, and other verbal, nonverbal, or physical conduct of a sexual nature by an employee, by another student, or by a third party, that is sufficiently severe, persistent, or pervasive to limit a student's ability to participate in or benefit from an education program or activity, or to create a hostile or abusive educational environment. (Department of Education, 1997, p. 12038)

Both Title VII and Title IX protect women and men from sex discrimination in education and the workplace. However, although sex discrimination can occur to either males or females, sexual harassment has had the distinction of being more problematic to women and girls.

SEXUAL HARASSMENT OF WORKING WOMEN

Sexual harassment is a common phenomenon among working women in America. Every year at least 40% of employed women experience some form of this unwanted and uninvited sexual attention. A review of research across cultures found that it is also a frequent problem for women around the world and has similar effects (DeSouza & Solberg, 2003). It appears, however, that Nordic countries, which actively promote programs and policies to reduce gender inequality, have lower rates of sexual harassment. Compared to American blue- and white-collar workers, Danish and Finnish women with similar jobs not only experienced less sexual harassment but fewer adverse job and health outcomes as well (Kauppinen & Gruber, 1993). The factors that *cause* sexual harassment, including profiles of the targets (e.g., non-married, young), the types of jobs that have high rates of harassment (e.g., male-traditional occupations), the ways in which women cope with harassment, and the negative consequent health outcomes appear to be fairly universal across cultures (Gruber, Smith, & Kauppinen, 1996; DeSouza & Solberg).

To date, the most ambitious studies of working women (and men) have been conducted by the Merit Systems Protection Board of the U.S.

federal government (USMSPB). Their three national surveys of federal employees (1981, 1987, 1995) provide some of the best data on the extent and impact of sexual harassment. Also, their survey items have been adapted by a number of researchers for studies of other public sector employees (e.g., MacIntyre, 1982; Stringer-Moore, 1982) as well as by foreign scholars (e.g., Canadian Human Rights Commission, 1983; Hogbacka, Kandolin, Haavio-Mannila, & Kauppinen, 1987). The overall rate of harassment of women in the USMSPB samples remained fairly constant across the three surveys (over 40%), as did the incidence of most of the individual categories (e.g., sexual teasing, looks and gestures, pressure for sexual favors). One finding that has been replicated by a large number of studies across time and cultures is that less severe forms of harassment, such as sexual remarks or sexually offensive looks or gestures, are much more common than more severe (and more harmful) forms, such as sexual touching or pressure for sexual favors.

The Merit Systems surveys also provided evidence of commonly found coping strategies. Most women dealt with the harasser/harassment by ignoring the behavior, avoiding the harasser, or asking him to stop. Women infrequently reported the behavior through formal channels or directly confronted the harasser. Women stated that direct or confrontational responses were used less often either because the more common coping responses were effective in resolving the problem or because the women feared the consequences (e.g., retaliation, job loss) of more assertive action (USMSPB, 1995: Table 11). As other research has confirmed, women's fear that assertive action would make things worse is well founded (Hesson-McInnis & Fitzgerald, 1992).

The job and health impacts of sexual harassment have been well documented over the last quarter century for a variety of occupations, workplace settings, and educational environments. Some of the earliest research studies found that targets of harassment experienced low life satisfaction and self-esteem (Gruber & Bjorn, 1982), anxiety, anger, and helplessness (Crull, 1982; Gutek, 1985), and depression (Hamilton, Alagna, King, & Lloyd, 1987), as well as a number of job-related outcomes. Similar adverse health outcomes have been found outside the United States. Canadian and European women experienced psychosomatic symptoms, depression, an inability to concentrate, and heightened job dissatisfaction as a result of harassment (Canadian Human Rights Commission, 1983; Hogbacka et al., 1987). A comparative study of working women found that Americans suffered greater psychological stress and had poorer self-images than either their Scandinavian or former Soviet (Russian and Estonian) counterparts as a result of harassment (Kauppinen & Gruber, 1993).

These and other adverse outcomes have been found in more recent research. An oft-cited study by **Louise Fitzgerald** and her colleagues on two samples (workers at a utility company and university staff) found that targets of harassment in both samples had lower life satisfaction, poorer mental health, and more symptoms of post-traumatic stress disorder (PTSD) than other women did (Schneider, Swan, & Fitzgerald, 1997). Additionally, their analyses revealed that even low levels of (or low exposure to) sexual harassment produced negative health outcomes or, in their own words, "harassment apparently does not have to be particularly egregious to result in negative consequences" (p. 412). Indicators of mental stress that were used by Richman and her colleagues—excessive drinking (both drinking as an escape and drinking to intoxication) and prescription drug use were significant outcomes of sexual harassment among university staff members (Richman et al., 1999). Negative body image and eating disorders were also found to be a consequence of sexual harassment among college students (Harned, 2000).

Though women's self-reports of depression and stress symptoms resembling post-traumatic stress syndrome (PTSS) have appeared frequently in the research literature, the clinical dimensions of these problems were not formally documented until the mid-1990s. Researchers at the Medical University of South Carolina developed survey items for PTSS using Diagnostic Statistical Manual III-Revised (DSM-III-R) criteria in a national sample of more than 3,000 women. When compared to women who had not experienced harassment, victims—in particular, those whose experiences met EEOC criteria—were at an increased risk of PTSD and/or depression (Dansky & Kilpatrick, 1997). The relationships between harassment and PTSD were explored further by Avina and O'Donohue (2002). They argued that a number of harassing experiences can fit the DSM-IV criteria as probable causes because they pose a threat to physical integrity—specifically, by threatening the target's financial well-being, threatening her physical boundaries, and/or threatening the victim's control over situations that she should be able to control (p. 73).

SEXUAL HARASSMENT ON COLLEGE CAMPUSES

Hall and Sandler (1982) gave a name to a problem that thousands of women experienced during college—"the chilly climate." They used narratives and interviews to reveal the marginalization and maltreatment of women, and the consequent suffering they experienced. The publication of *The Lecherous Professor* by Billie Dzeich and Linda Weiner in 1984 brought national attention to the problem. Several years later Michele Paludi expanded our understanding of the problem in *Ivory Power: The Sexual Harassment of Women on Campus* (1991). All three publications presented sexual harassment as a widespread, endemic problem caused by male professors with an inflated sense of entitlement who routinely groped, propositioned, and verbally abused their female colleagues and students. Paludi's book was ground-breaking insofar as it examined the problem of sexual harassment from a variety of perspectives. Its chapters included measurement issues, the confluence of racism and sexism, the effects of coping responses of harassment targets, profiles of male perpetrators, and institutional strategies for preventing and remediating harassment. A chapter by Mary Koss on the psychological impact of harassment told of the stress caused not only by the harassment—diminished self-confidence, anxiety, psychosomatic ailments, among others—but also of the problems women faced when they told others about their treatment. Women who complained were doubly victimized: first, by the harassment itself, and then by stigmatization by their peers and retaliation by their harassers.

Louise Fitzgerald and her colleagues first used their Sexual Experiences Questionnaire (SEQ) on samples of students and staff at two universities (Fitzgerald et al., 1988). They found high levels of harassment (over 50%) for women in both groups. Most targets experienced *gender harassment*. Approximately 5% of each group had been sexually bribed. Harassment by professors was frequent among women undergraduate (49%) and graduate (53%) students on a large campus studied by Cortina, Swan, Fitzgerald, and Waldo (1998). Harassment rates were especially high among lesbian and bisexual women (81%). More recent studies that used the SEQ have found similar results. Fifty-six percent of the women students in a study by Huerta, Cortina, Pang, Torges, & Magley (2006) experienced harassment from faculty, staff, or peers during the last year. Harassment targets experienced significant levels of psychological stress, more health problems (including symptoms of eating disorders), and less academic satisfaction.

THE HARM OF SEXUAL HARASSMENT

Though it is clear that sexual harassment causes adverse health outcomes in women (and men as well), the question remains as to which victims experience greater harm than others. Though much early research compared victims and non-victims, recent studies have focused on a variety of factors that may either increase or buffer the effects of harassment. We present four.

Severity of Sexual Harassing Experiences

While research models of sexual harassment have become more sophisticated over the years, even some of the earliest studies examined harassment severity as an issue apart from simply whether or not someone had been a target (Gruber & Bjorn, 1982; USMSPB, 1981). Severity is related to frequency insofar as some experiences *become* harassing while others become *more severe* through repeated exposures. Some experiences have a very low threshold and are harassing with one exposure (sexual bribery, sexual assault), while others with a higher threshold become more severe as a result of repetition and/or contextual factors (e.g., acts by a supervisor versus a peer). In addition to frequency, Gruber (1992) argued that there were at least four other factors that affected severity: source of the harassment (e.g., supervisor versus coworkers), directness (whether the harassment was personal or "environmental"), averseness or offensiveness, and threat. Some experiences are severe (e.g., sexual assault, sexual bribery) because they are highly offensive, threatening, and single out the victim. Others are less severe (e.g., a woman who hears sexually degrading comments about a female coworker) because they are indirect or environmental and offensive, and arguably less threatening because the comments are not about her.

USMSPB (1981) divided their seven categories into "most severe," "severe," and "less severe" and found that more severe harassment was associated with the respondents' "emotional and physical condition" becoming worse. The frequency of harassment was also significantly associated with adverse psychological outcomes in a more recent study. Schneider et al. (1997) tabulated how often respondents had been harassed, regardless of the type of harassment, and found that higher frequencies as measured by the SEQ significantly predicted life satisfaction, mental health, and PTSD symptoms. A strong relationship between harassment severity and PTSD was found among college students as well (McDermot, Haaga, & Kirk, 2000). Rather than use a simple frequency measure, they divided the SEQ categories into "severe" and "mild" forms and found that victims of the former had higher scores on all three PTSD subscales (re-experiencing the harassment, avoidance and numbing, and hypervigilance).

Male Domination

Research over the last quarter century provides compelling evidence that women in nontraditional jobs experience more frequent and severe harassment than other working women. Part of the reason for this, as Kanter (1977) has demonstrated, is because of highly skewed sex ratios. In addition, there is a significant minority of occupations where a skewed gender imbalance (numerical dominance) is coupled with occupational roles and norms that reinforce traditional, sexist masculine values and perspectives (normative dominance). A survey of military personnel found that more than two-thirds of the women had been harassed (Bastian, Lancaster, & Reyst, 1996). Similarly, women working in other male-dominated occupations like policing and firefighting have significantly higher rates of harassment than their counterparts in other public sector jobs (Brown, Campbell, & Fife-Schaw, 1995; LA Commission on Women, 1992).

Similar problems have been found for women in nontraditional fields on college campuses (e.g., Paludi, 1991). Women students and faculty in nontraditional fields (e.g., physical and natural science, computer science, engineering) experience more frequent harassment and are subjected to a wider range of sexist behavior (e.g., lower evaluations, poorer mentoring, limited access to training opportunities) than their peers in other departments.

The health outcomes for women in these situations are fairly predictable given the higher levels of harassment they experience. Female targets of harassment in the military reported decreased satisfaction with health and recorded problems with emotional and physical health, even when the experiences were somewhat infrequent (Magley, Waldo, Drasgow, & Fitzgerald, 1999). Because women in male-dominant work settings are often treated as "outsiders" and endure ostracism and isolation, they lose the potential buffering or protective effects of social support and collegiality that other women use to moderate the psychological harms of sexual harassment. The organizational hierarchy also poses a potential problem because women's superiors—typically men—may not understand or sympathize with the plight of female subordinates. And, the leadership of an organization has a significant impact on its gender climate and the tolerance of sexual harassment (Niebuhr, 1997; Pryor, LaVite, & Stoller, 1995).

Work Structure and Processes

Sociological research over the last half century has demonstrated the adverse effects of work structure and processes on the health, well-being, and job attitudes of women and men (Blauner, 1964; Kohn, 1990; Miller, 1980). Kauppinen and Gruber (1993) were among the first to show that work structure and processes were a significant cause of sexual harassment and, correspondingly, of psychological distress. Likewise, Mueller, DeCoster, and Estes (2001) found that centralized decision making, a lack of formal policies that protect employee rights, and rigid organizational structures that provided little job mobility predicted sexual harassment above and beyond "gender climate" variables that are used in a number of studies. In a related vein, Kauppinen and Patoluoto (2005) found that bullying was frequently found in workplaces where the pace of work had increased and/or the structure of work had become more hierarchical.

Personal and Situational Factors

Not all women are harmed in the same way by similar types of harassment. There are a number of "Who, what, and when?" issues that influence the impact of harassment. To begin with, women may have one or more "personal resources" that enable them to cope with sexual harassment. Those with high self-esteem, high life satisfaction, and/or high job status (Gruber & Bjorn, 1986) or a feminist orientation (Gruber & Smith, 1995) are more apt to respond assertively to their harassers than other women. Also, women who have social support, either in the workplace through positive collegial relationships or outside of work through networks of family and friends, are able to buffer some of the potentially damaging effects of harassment to their well-being. Kauppinen and Gruber (1993), for instance, found that friendly, cooperative relationships with coworkers protected women in nontraditional jobs from some of the psychological distress that troubled other women. More recently, Rederstorff, Buchanan, and Settles (2007) found that a feminist orientation buffered White sexually harassed college students from post-traumatic stress. However, this was not the case for African-American students.

Conventional wisdom suggests that women should deal with harassment by confronting the harasser or reporting him to their superiors. The implied assumption is that women who don't take such action have personality problems. While having significant personal resources may encourage women to respond assertively to their harassers, these strategies have a low "success" rate. A number of studies have documented the fact that responding assertively (confronting the harasser or reporting his behavior) often makes matters worse by prompting more harassment and/or retaliation (Fitzgerald, Swan, & Fischer, 1995). So, while providing emotional and social support to targets of sexual harassment is highly commendable, we should be cautious in urging them to take matters into their own hands. There are numerous contingencies that affect the outcomes of harassment situations (e.g., organizational policies, attitudes of supervisors, procedures for investigating and resolving complaints) that may either undermine women's attempts to stop the harassment or help them resolve the problem.

SEXUAL HARASSMENT AND K–12 STUDENTS

Unlike the body of research that has accumulated over the past 25 years regarding workplace sexual harassment and its impact on adults, sexual harassment in K–12 schools has a shorter (15 year) history. Many of the behaviors identified as sexual harassment in the school environment are also identified as noxious forms of stress or sexual violence and contribute to the psychological and health distress of both school employees and students alike. It is also important to note that these behaviors may also rise to the level of impermissible employment or education discrimination as determined under Title VII or Title IX. For this reason, studies examining the impact of sexual harassment are important to provide scientific evidence to school administrators, policy makers, and the courts who may be considering complex problems regarding mental and physical health issues for both children and adults.

Researchers, for the most part, have not examined the effects of sexual harassment on adult personnel employed in K–12 school environments, and, unlike the body of research regarding mental and physical health outcomes for adults in various types of work environments, only a few studies have examined mental and physical health outcomes for children in schools. This is especially the case for young (K–6) students. Most of the information on sexual harassment experiences and outcomes has come from a small number of case studies that have garnered media attention and/or been litigated. Because of this, our discussion focuses on middle and high school students.

Sexual harassment that occurs in schools is primarily peer to peer, although the American Association of University Women (AAUW) (1993, 2001) estimated that 1 in 4 girls and 1 in 10 boys has been harassed by school personnel (teacher, coach, school bus driver, etc.). Lee, Croninger, Linn, and Chen (1996), in a re-analysis of the 1993 AAUW, found that 16% of students had been harassed by a teacher (girls, 20%; boys, 8%) and 44% by other school personnel (girls, 48%; boys, 37%). However, unlike studies on adult women where degree of threat or harm has been examined on the basis of how much power a harasser has over his target, no studies have examined differential effects of adult-to-student as opposed to student-to-student harassment.

The most comprehensive reports on school sexual harassment were conducted by the American Association of University Women (AAUW) in 1993 and repeated with similar results in 2001. Their most recent report, *Hostile Hallways* (2001), found that 81% of students in U.S. schools had experienced peer sexual harassment (83% female, 79% male). Other studies on sexual harassment report similar figures: Between 50% and 88% of the students were victims (Fineran & Bennett, 1999; Fineran & Bolen, 2006; Permanent Commission on the Status of Women (PCSW), 1995; Roscoe, Strouse, & Goodwin, 1994; Stratton & Backes, 1997; Trigg & Wittenstrom, 1996).

Sexual harassment research to date has primarily focused on prevalence and situational factors (type of behavior, when and where it occurs, student responses to it, etc.). Except for the AAUW (1993, 2001) studies, which used a stratified random sampling technique to select a representative sample of the U.S. student population, and the PCSW (1995) study, where the findings can be generalized to the Connecticut student population, the remainder of the studies used convenience samples that constrain findings to individual schools.

Peer sexual harassment may include unwanted or unwelcome behaviors such as making sexual comments, jokes, gestures, or looks; showing sexual pictures, photographs, illustrations, messages, or notes; writing sexual messages or graffiti on bathroom walls or locker rooms; spreading sexual rumors; calling someone gay or lesbian in a malicious manner; spying on someone dressing or showering at school;

"flashing" or "mooning" someone; touching, grabbing, or pinching in a sexual way; pulling at clothing in a sexual way; intentionally brushing against someone in a sexual way; pulling clothing off or down; blocking or cornering in a sexual way; and forcing a kiss or other unwelcome sexual behavior other than kissing (AAUW, 1993, 2001). Sexual harassment may also include "spiking" or pulling down someone's pants, "snuggies" or pulling underwear up at the waist so it goes in between the buttocks, and or being listed in "slam books," which identify student's names and have derogatory sexual comments written about them by other students (Strauss & Espeland, 1992).

The AAUW (1993, 2001) reports indicated that over 50% of male and female students experienced sexual comments, jokes, gestures, or looks. Over 30% of boys and girls experienced being touched, grabbed, pinched, or brushed up against in a sexual way from schoolmates. In a study by Fineran and Bennett (1999), unwanted sexual attention, including pressure for dates and sex, was reported by approximately 43% of girls and 30% of boys, while in the PCSW (1995) studies, 25% of girls and 5% of boys reported unwanted sexual attention. Gender differences in victimization are common; girls report experiencing sexual harassment more frequently than boys, and boys perpetrate sexual harassment more frequently than girls (AAUW, 1993, 2001; DeSouza & Ribeiro, 2005; Fineran & Bennett, 1999; Fineran & Bolen, 2006; Hand & Sanchez, 2000; PCSW, 1995; Stratton & Backes, 1997; Trigg & Wittenstrom, 1996).

Mental Health Outcomes

A few of the studies inquired about mental and physical health symptoms and students self-reported the following: loss of appetite, loss of interest in their usual activities, nightmares or disturbed sleep, feelings of isolation from friends and family, and feeling sad, nervous, or angry (AAUW, 1993, 2001; PCSW, 1995; Stein, Marshall, & Tropp, 1993; Stratton & Backes, 1997; Trigg & Wittenstrom, 1996). Students also noted feeling afraid, upset, or threatened by the sexual harassment (AAUW, 1993, 2001; Duffy, Wareham, & Walsh, 2004; Fineran & Bennett, 1999; Fineran & Bolen, 2006; PCSW, 1995; Stein et al., 1993).

Duffy, Wareham, and Walsh (2004) found that girls felt the negative impact of sexual harassment victimization more than boys. Specifically, girls felt more embarrassed, afraid, self-conscious, and they talked less in class. These behaviors translate into lowered self-confidence, concentration, classroom participation, and leadership potential. Most school sexual harassment studies derived detailed descriptions of harassment situations by asking respondents to provide information on an experience that was particularly upsetting. These descriptions reveal that girls not only experience a wider range of harassing behaviors more frequently than boys, they also consistently answer that they found these behaviors to be more threatening or upsetting (AAUW, 1993; PCSW, 1995; Fineran & Bennett, 1999; Fineran & Bolen, 2006; Duffy et al., 2004; Trigg & Wittenstrom, 1996). Similarly, Lee et al. (1996) also found that girls were more severely harassed than boys and had a higher probability of experiencing more psychological problems (i.e., trouble sleeping or loss of appetite) than boys. Hand and Sanchez (2000) also conducted a re-analysis of the 1993 AAUW data and found that girls who experienced physical sexual harassment had more negative educational outcomes than boys. In addition, their analysis showed that "girls experience qualitatively more severe, physically intrusive, and intimidating forms of harassment than do boys" and that the "deleterious effects of physical sexual harassment were stronger for girls than boys, *across all of the measured outcomes*" [emphasis added] (p. 740).

Several recent studies conducted by Gruber and Fineran used a variety of scales to measure psychological outcomes of the impact of sexual harassment on students. In one study comparing middle school and high school girls, six outcomes (self-esteem, mental and physical health, trauma symptoms, life satisfaction, and substance abuse) were compared (Gruber & Fineran, 2005). Study results showed high school girls experienced more sexual harassment and had poorer health outcomes than their middle school peers.

In another study comparing bullying and sexual harassment victimization (Gruber & Fineran, 2007), girls were particularly harmed by both forms of victimization. Twice as many psychological outcomes for bullying and sexual harassment were statistically significant for girls compared with boys. Additionally, an analysis of data on 8th graders showed sexual harassment impacted the mental health of girls more negatively than boys, and girls reported more trauma symptoms than boys (Fineran & Gruber, 2004). On the basis of the few outcome studies conducted on adolescents, many of the symptoms reported by students due to peer sexual harassment resemble symptoms experienced by women subjected to sexual harassment in the workplace.

Mental Health and Sexual Minority Students

Compared to the published material on gender, the research on the mental and physical health risks of sexual minority students is sparse because most studies to date have not asked for this type of information. A study by Fineran (2001) found that sexual minority students experienced sexual harassment more frequently than heterosexual students. Specifically, sexual minority girls experienced significantly more sexual harassment than heterosexual girls for the following behaviors: being called sexually offensive names, having rumors told about them, being called gay or lesbian in a derogatory way, receiving sexually offensive photos or messages, being touched or grabbed in a sexual way, being pressured for a date, and being sexually assaulted.

Studies conducted by Gruber and Fineran (2006, 2005) have also shed some light on the experience of sexual minority youth. They found that in both high school and middle school, lesbian girls experienced more sexual harassment and ridicule than their heterosexual peers. In another study comparing bullying and sexual harassment, gay and lesbian students experienced more bullying (79% vs. 50%) and sexual harassment (71% vs. 32%) (Gruber & Fineran, 2007).

Although there have been no large-scale studies examining the psychological impact of sexual harassment on student mental health, there have been some statewide statistics gathered on general student populations. An annual school survey, *The Massachusetts Youth Risk Behavior Survey* (Massachusetts Department of Education, 2007), found that sexual minority students when compared to their heterosexual peers had higher suicide rates, were more apt to skip school because they felt unsafe, had been threatened with or injured by a weapon at school, and experienced more dating violence and nonconsensual sex. A recent report (2005) by the Gay, Lesbian and Straight Education Network on Michigan schools revealed that two-thirds of students in their sample were harassed because they were, or appeared to be, gay or lesbian. More than 80% of these students reported hearing derogatory homophobic comments.

Supporting this very negative picture, Fineran and Gruber (2004) found in a study of 8th graders that gay/lesbian/bisexual students who experienced sexual harassment had poorer mental health and more trauma symptoms in contrast to their heterosexual peers. In addition, sexual minority students and heterosexual girls reported being significantly more upset and threatened by peer sexual harassment victimization than boys, and lesbian girls experienced significantly more sexual harassment than gay boys and heterosexual students (Fineran, 2001).

The fact that sexual minority students appear to experience a significantly higher frequency of sexual harassment than their heterosexual peers reinforces concerns regarding increased mental health risks to sexual minority youth in schools. Sexual minority students feel unsafe in schools where they are experiencing more sexually harassing behaviors than their straight peers, including the experience of physical violence. Current research, however, continues to suggest that girls are most threatened by these behaviors and that more attention should be directed at the overall hostile environments of schools for both of these at-risk populations—sexual minority students and heterosexual girls.

Turning our attention to younger elementary students (K–6) or students with disabilities, we find that little research has been conducted on these populations and there is no conclusive information regarding sexual harassment victimization and mental health outcomes. One small pilot study consisting of 26 students with disabilities (Rousso & Wehmeyer 2001) found that students were sexually harassed in public places and girls were more likely to be the target of non-disabled male peers. Fineran (2002) reported that high school students with disabilities experienced sexually harassing behaviors more frequently than non-disabled students, while a study of 8th graders found that disabled and able students have similar levels of sexual harassment victimization, but disabled students experienced more negative mental health outcomes as a result of these experiences (Fineran & Gruber, 2004). No other studies have been conducted on this issue with this population.

Large-scale survey research exploring sexual harassment has not been conducted on populations of younger children in the same way that junior high and high school students have been studied. Most of the elementary school examples are single cases that have garnered media attention and/or been litigated (Stein, 2007). Many elementary school administrators struggle with naming the range of behaviors that young children experience as sexual harassment and frequently reframe these behaviors as teasing and bullying (Stein, 1999). Generally, however, victims tend not to be identified in the press and so their stories do not become as familiar as those who are identified as perpetrators and defended. In summary, the lack of data on this very young population makes it difficult to say how sexual harassment affects the mental health of children who are at an impressionable age.

SEXUAL HARASSMENT AND STUDENTS WHO WORK

While the adverse effects of sexual harassment on mental health have been documented for adults who have experienced sexual harassment in the workplace, little attention has been given to students who work while attending school.

A preliminary study by Fineran and Gruber (2005) of 260 New England girls looked at the frequency and the outcomes of sexual harassment among those who worked while attending high school. In addition to comparing the health outcome differences between girls who had and had not been harassed, the study also compared the health outcomes of the harassed teens to published data on health outcomes among adults.

Most of the teens who worked were under age 18 (72%) and were employed mostly in two broad categories of the formal wage economy: restaurant service jobs (44%) and retail sales (36%). More than 52% of the teens reported that they had experienced some form of sexual harassment during the past year at their jobs. More than half (56%) of the perpetrators were coworkers, while supervisors and vendors/customers accounted equally for the remainder. A large majority of the perpetrators were older than the teens, with nearly half (46%) described as older than 30.

When the teens were compared to a study of working adults by Richman et al. (1999), the results were compelling. The teens reported experiencing significantly higher levels of unwanted sexual attention (38%) than women in all three of Richman's samples (service workers, 15%; clerical staff, 14%; and employed college students, 10%). The percentages for sexual coercion in Richman's three samples—5% of service workers, 3% of clerical workers, and 1% of college student workers— are comparable to the study on teens. This suggests that the teens experienced more harassment than adults because teens are working part time while Richman et al. (1999) collected data from women working full time.

Results also showed sexually harassed teens experienced greater work stress and lower satisfaction with both supervisors and co-workers, and they were more apt to avoid work or to think about leaving their jobs. Also, they were more apt to miss school and less able to focus on school. However, their psychological and physical well-being were not negatively impacted by workplace harassment. Findings from the teen study contrast with the considerable research literature cited earlier in this chapter that finds that workplace sexual harassment is a source of low self-esteem, psychological distress, and health problems for adult women. It appears that workplace harassment for teens does not produce the level and range of negative outcomes that have been found in studies of adult women. This may be because of the smaller role that work plays in teens' busy lives. Only a fraction of girls indicated their jobs were important to their identities.

Though research has found that sexual harassment at school has detrimental effects on the psychological and physical health of girls, findings from Fineran and Gruber (2005) suggest that the overall mental health and health risks of workplace sexual harassment for teens are fairly modest. However, teens' work experiences may have an impact on school. Teens who were sexually harassed at work did not find school as exciting or engaging as other classmates. These findings may be alarming because students who are avoiding school, daydreaming in class, and receiving lower grades may find their full career potential threatened or at the very least impeded. Additionally, although the overall mental health risks of workplace sexual harassment for teens may be low, this may not accurately reflect health risks involving physical safety. Sexual harassment consists of many behaviors, some of which are described as acts of sexual assault (Fineran, 2002). Redefining sexual harassment as sexual violence and educating girls about workplace violence may be an important precaution for schools, for communities where teens are employed, and for parents to initiate.

CONCLUSION

Millions of women and girls experience sexual harassment as a daily part of their work and school lives, and those who are targeted experience a multitude of consequences that negatively impact their mental health. A number of factors concerning sexual harassment appear to be consistent globally: age of targets, types of occupations where harassment occurs, ways women cope, and psychological reactions to harassment. Less severe harassment behaviors (i.e., sexual remarks or sexually offensive looks or gestures) appear to be much more common than more severe behaviors (i.e., sexual touching or pressure for sexual favors), and low levels of (or low exposure to) sexual harassment produce negative reactions.

Mental health outcomes appear to be similar across age groups for both students and employees alike. Students who experience sexual harassment in schools and universities have similar outcomes as women who experience sexual harassment on the job. Overall, research overwhelmingly demonstrates that sexual harassment has a major impact on women and girls' psychological well-being and mental health, and that schools, universities, and the workplace have responsibility for making these environments safe and nondiscriminatory.

REFERENCES

American Association of University Women Educational Foundation (1993). *Hostile hallways: The AAUW survey on sexual harassment in America's school* (Research Rep. No. 923012). Washington, DC: Harris/Scholastic Research.

American Association of University Women Educational Foundation (2001). *Hostile hallways: Bullying, teasing and sexual harassment in school.* Washington, DC.

Avina, C., & O'Donohue, W. (2002). Sexual harassment and PTSD: Is sexual harassment diagnosable trauma? *Journal of Traumatic Stress, 15,* 69–75.

Bastian, L., Lancaster, A., & Reyst, H. (1996). *The Department of Defense 1995 sexual harassment survey.* Arlington, VA: Defense Manpower Data Center.

Blauner, R. (1964). *Alienation and freedom.* Chicago: University of Chicago Press.

Bowen, G., & Richman, J. (1995). *The school success profile.* Chapel Hill: University of North Carolina at Chapel Hill.

Brown, J., Campbell, E., & Fife-Schaw, C. (1995). Adverse effects experienced by police officers following exposure to sex discrimination and sexual harassment. *Stress Medicine, 11,* 221–228.

Canadian Human Rights Commission (1983). *Unwanted sexual attention and sexual harassment.* Montreal: Minister of Supply and Services of Canada.

Commission on the Status of Women (1992). *Report on the City of Los Angeles 1992 sexual harassment survey.* Los Angeles, CA: The City of Los Angeles.

Cortina, L., Swan, S., Fitzgerald, L., & Waldo, C. (1998). Sexual harassment and assault: Chilling the climate for women in academia. *Psychology of Women Quarterly, 22,* 419–441.

Crull, P. (1982). Stress effects of sexual harassment on the job: Implications for counseling. *American Journal of Orthopsychiatry, 52,* 539–543.

Dansky, B. S., & Kilpatrick, D. G. (1997). Effects of sexual harassment. In W. O'Donohue (Ed.), *Sexual harassment: Theory, research, and treatment* (pp. 152–174). Needham Heights, MA: Allyn & Bacon.

Department of Education, Office for Civil Rights (March 13, 1997). Sexual harassment guidance: Harassment of students by school employees, other students, or third parties. *Federal Register, 62*(49), 12034–12051.

DeSouza, E. R., & Ribeiro, J. (2005). Bullying and sexual harassment among Brazilian high school students. *Journal of Interpersonal Violence, 20*(9), 1018–1038.

DeSouza, E. R., & Solberg, J. (2003) Incidence and dimensions of sexual harassment across cultures. In M. Paludi, & C. Paludi (Eds.), *Academic and workplace sexual harassment: A handbook of cultural, social science, management, and legal perspectives* (pp. 3–30). Westport, CT: Praeger.

Duffy, J., Wareham, S., & Walsh, M. (2004). Psychological consequences for high school students of having been sexually harassed. *Sex Roles, 50*(11–12), 811–821.

Dyregrov, A., & Yule, W. (1995, November). *Screening measures: The development of the UNICEF screening battery.* Presented at the annual meeting of the International Society of Traumatic Stress Studies, Boston, Massachusetts.

Dzeich, B., & Weiner, L. (1984). *The lecherous professor: Sexual harassment on campus.* Boston: Beacon Press.

Equal Employment Opportunity Commission (1980). *Guidelines on discrimination because of sex,* 29 C.F.R. § 1604.11.

Fineran, S. (2001). Sexual minority students and peer sexual harassment in high school. *Journal of School Social Work 11*(2), 50–69.

Fineran, S. (2002a). Adolescents at work: Gender issues and sexual harassment. *Violence Against Women, 8,* 953–967.

Fineran, S. (2002b). *Sexual harassment and students with disabilities.* Paper presented at the Society for the Study of Social Problems, Washington, DC.

Fineran, S., & Bennett, L. (1999). Gender and power issues of peer sexual harassment among teenagers. *Journal of Interpersonal Violence, 14*(6), 626–641.

Fineran, S., & Bolen, R. M. (2006). Risk factors for peer sexual harassment in schools. *Journal of Interpersonal Violence, 21,* 1169–1190.

Fineran, S., & Gruber, J. E. (2004, January). *The impact of sexual harassment victimization on the mental and physical health and coping responses of 8th grade students.* Paper presented at the 8th Annual Conference Society for Social Work and Research, New Orleans, LA.

Fineran, S., & Gruber, J. E. (2005, August). *Sexual harassment of working teens.* Paper presented at the International Coalition Against Sexual Harassment Conference, Philadelphia, PA.

Fineran, S., & Gruber, J. E. (2006, January). *Bullying and sexual harassment: A comparison of the effects on victimization on the mental and physical health and coping responses of students in junior high and high school.* Paper presented at the 11th Annual Conference Society for Social Work and Research, San Antonio, TX.

Fitzgerald, L. F., Shullman, S., Baily, N., Richards, M., Swecker, J., Gold, Y., Ormerod, A. J., & Weitzman, L. (1988). The incidence and dimensions of sexual harassment in academia and the workplace. *Journal of Vocational Behavior, 32,* 152–175.

Fitzgerald, L., Swan, S., & Fischer, K. (1995). Why didn't she just report him? The psychological and legal implications of women's responses to sexual harassment. *Journal of Social Issues, 51,* 117–138.

Gay, Lesbian, and Straight Education Network (2005). *National school climate survey.* New York.

Gruber, J. E. (1992). A typology of personal and environmental sexual harassment research and policy implications for the 90's. *Sex Roles, 26*(11/12), 447–464.

Gruber, J. E. (1998). The impact of male work environments and organizational policies on women's experiences of sexual harassment. *Gender & Society, 12,* 301–320.

Gruber, J. E., & Bjorn, L. (1982). Blue collar blues: the sexual harassment of women autoworkers. *Work and Occupations, 9,* 271–298.

Gruber, J. E., & Bjorn, L. (1986). Women's responses to sexual harassment: An analysis of sociocultural, organizational, and personal resource models. *Social Science Quarterly, 67,* 814–826.

Gruber, J. E., & Fineran, S. (2004, August). *Sexual harassment and bullying: Mental health implications for adolescents.* Paper presented at the Society for the Study of Social Problems, San Francisco, CA.

Gruber, J. E., & Fineran, S. (2005, August). *The impact of bullying on health and academic outcomes of middle and high school girls.* Paper presented at the Society for the Study of Social Problems, Philadelphia, PA.

Gruber, J. E., & Fineran, S. (2007, August). *Teens and trouble: A comparison of the health and school-related effects of bullying and sexual harassment among middle and high school students.* Paper presented at the Society for the Study of Social Problems, New York, NY.

Gruber, J. E., & Smith, M. (1995). Women's responses to sexual harassment. *Basic and Applied Social Psychology, 17,* 543–562.

Gruber, J. E., Smith, M., & Kauppinen, K. (1996). Sexual harassment types and severity: Linking research and policy. In M. Stockdale (Ed.), *Sexual harassment in the workplace: Perspectives, frontiers, and response strategies* (pp. 151–173). Thousand Oaks, CA: Sage.

Gutek, B. A. (1985). *Sex and the workplace.* San Francisco, CA: Jossey-Bass.

Hall, R., & Sandler, B. (1982). *The classroom climate: A chilly one for women?* Washington, DC: Association of American Colleges, Project on the Status and Education of Women.

Hamilton, J., Alagna, S., King, L., & Lloyd, C. (1987). The emotional consequences of gender-based abuse in the workplace: New counseling programs for sex discrimination. *Women and Therapy, 6,* 155–182.

Hand, J. Z., & Sanchez, L. (2000). Badgering or bantering? Gender differences in experience of, and reactions to, sexual harassment among U.S. high school students. *Gender & Society, 14*(6), 718–746.

Hanisch, K. A., & Hulin, C. L. (1991). General attitudes and organizational withdrawal: An evaluation of a causal model. *Journal of Vocational Behavior, 39,* 110–128.

Harned, M. (2000). An examination of the relationships among women's experiences of sexual harassment, body image, and eating disturbances. *Psychology of Women Quarterly, 24,* 336–348.

Hesson-McInnis, H., & Fitzgerald, L. (1992). *Modeling sexual harassment.* Paper presented at the APA/NIOSH Conference on Stress in the 90's. Washington, DC.

Hogbacka, R., Kandolin, I., Haavio-Mannila, E., & Kauppinen, K. (1987). *Sexual harassment in the workplace: Results of a survey of Finns.* Helsinki: Ministry of Social Affairs: Equality Reports, Series E.

Huerta, M., Cortina, L., Pang, J., Torges, C., & Magley, V. (2006). Sex and power in the academy: Modeling sexual harassment in the lives of college women. *Personality and Social Psychology Bulletin, 32,* 616–628.

Kanter, R. (1977). *Men and women of the corporation.* New York: Basic Books.

Kauppinen, K., & Gruber, J. (1993). The antecedents and outcomes of women-unfriendly behavior. *Psychology of Women Quarterly, 17,* 431–456.

Kauppinen, K., & Patoluoto, S. (2005). Sexual harassment and violence toward police women in Finland. In J. Gruber & P. Morgan (Eds.), *In the company of men: Male dominance & sexual harassment* (pp. 195–214). Boston: Northeastern University Press.

Kohn, M. (1990). Unresolved issues in the relationship between work and personality. In K. Erikson and S. Vallas (Eds.), *The nature of work* (pp. 36–68). New Haven, CT: Yale University Press.

Lee, V. E., Croninger, R. G., Linn, E., & Chen, X. (1996). The culture of sexual harassment in secondary schools. *American Educational Research Journal, 33*(2), 383–417.

MacIntyre, D. (1982). *Sexual harassment in government: The situation in Florida and the nation.* Tallahassee: Florida State University.

MacKinnon, C. (1979). *The sexual harassment of working women.* New Haven, CT: Yale University Press.

Magley, V., Waldo, C., Drasgow, F., & Fitzgerald, L. (1999). The impact of sexual harassment on military personnel: Is it the same for women and men? *Military Psychology, 11,* 283–302.

Massachusetts Department of Education (2007). *2005 Massachusetts youth risk behavior survey results.* Boston, MA.

McDermot, J., Haaga, D., & Kirk, L. (2000). An evaluation of stress symptoms associated with academic sexual harassment. *Journal of Traumatic Stress, 13,* 397–411.

Miller, J. (1980). Individual and occupational determinants of job satisfaction. *Sociology of Work and Occupations, 7,* 337–366.

Mueller, C., DeCoster, S., & Estes, B. (2001). Sexual harassment in the workplace. *Work and Occupations, 28,* 411–426.

Murnen, S. K., & Smolak, L. (2000). The experience of sexual harassment among grade-school students: Early socialization of female subordination? *Sex Roles 43*(1–2), 1–17.

Niebuhr, R. (1997). Sexual harassment in the military. In W. O'Donohue (Ed.), *Sexual harassment: Theory, research, and treatment* (pp. 250–262). Boston: Allyn & Bacon.

Paludi, M. (1991). *Ivory power: Sexual harassment on campus.* Albany, NY: SUNY Press.

Permanent Commission on the Status of Women (1995). *In our own backyard: Sexual harassment in Connecticut's public high schools.* Hartford, CT.

Pryor, J., LaVite, C., & Stoller, L. (1995). A social psychological analysis of sexual harassment: The person/situation interaction. *Journal of Vocational Behavior 42,* 68–81.

Rederstorff, J., Buchanan, N., & Settles, I. (2007). The moderating roles of race and gender-role attitudes in the relationship between sexual harassment and psychological well-being. *Psychology of Women Quarterly, 31,* 50–61.

Richman, J. A., Rospenda, K. M., Nawyn, S. J., Flaherty, J. A., Fendrich, M., Drum, M. L., & Johnson, T. P. (1999). Sexual harassment and generalized workplace abuse among university employees: Prevalence and mental health correlates. *American Journal of Public Health, 89,* 358–363.

Richman, J., Rospenda, K., Nawyn, S., & Flaherty, J. (1997). Workplace harassment and the self-medication of distress. *Contemporary Drug Problems, 24,* 179–200.

Roscoe, B., Strouse, J. S., & Goodwin, M. P. (1994). Correlates of attitudes toward sexual harassment among early adolescents. *Sex Roles, 31*(9/19), 559–577.

Rousso, H., & Wehmeyer, M. L. (2001). *Double jeopardy: Addressing gender equity in special education.* Albany, NY: SUNY Press.

Schneider, K. T., Swan, S., & Fitzgerald, L. F. (1997). Job related and psychological effects of sexual harassment in the workplace: Empirical evidence from two organizations. *Journal of Applied Psychology, 82,* 401–415.

Stein, N. (1999). *Classrooms and courtrooms: Facing sexual harassment in K-12 schools.* New York: The Teachers Press.

Stein, N. (2007). Locating a secret problem: Sexual violence in elementary and secondary schools. In L. O'Toole, J. Schiffman, & M. Edwards (Eds.), *Gender violence: Interdisciplinary perspectives* (pp. 323–332). New York: New York University Press.

Stein, N., Marshall, N. L., & Tropp, L. R. (1993). *Secrets in public: Sexual harassment in our schools.* Wellesley, MA: Wellesley College Center for Research on Women.

Stratton, S., & Backes, J. (1997, February/March). Sexual harassment in North Dakota public schools: A study of eight high schools. *The High School Journal, 80,* 163–172.

Stringer-Moore, D. (1982). *Sexual harassment in the Seattle city workforce.* Seattle: Office for Women's Rights.

Strauss, S., & Espeland, P. (1992). *Sexual harassment and teens.* Minneapolis: Free Spirit Publishing.

Title VII, Civil Rights Act of 1964, 42 U.S.C. x 2000e (1994).

Trigg, M., & Wittenstrom, K. (1996). That's the way the world goes: Sexual harassment and New Jersey teenagers. *Initiatives, Special Issue: Sexual harassment, 57*(2) 55–65.

U.S. Equal Employment Opportunity Commission. (2000). Guidelines on discrimination because of sex. *Federal Register, 45,* 74676–74677.

U.S. Merit Systems Protection Board (1981). *Sexual harassment of federal workers: Is it a problem?* Washington, DC: United States Government Printing Office.

U.S. Merit Systems Protection Board (1987). *Sexual harassment of federal workers: An update.* Washington DC: U.S. Government Printing Office.

U.S. Merit Systems Protection Board (1995). *Sexual harassment of federal workers: Trends progress and continuing challenges.* Washington, DC: United States Government Printing Office.

Williams, J., Fitzgerald, L., & Drasgow, F. (1999). The effects of organizational practices on sexual harassment and individual outcomes in the military. *Military Psychology, 11,* 303–328.

Chapter 8

Religion and Women at Work

Michael B. Mathias

In 2002 the U.S. Conference of Catholic Bishops' Committee on Women in Society and in the Church (USCCB) undertook a project to examine the relationship between women's spirituality and their employment outside the home. The committee invited dioceses to convene focus groups on the topic, and between the fall of 2002 and the spring of 2004 focus groups involving more than 800 women were conducted by 36 arch/dioceses. Based on the feedback from these initial focus groups, the committee identified several themes that it wanted to explore more in depth and then conducted another round of focus groups in 14 arch/dioceses. The women in these focus groups described a strong, often intense, relationship between their faith and their work. They see spirituality as a unifying factor that permeates all of life, and they resist compartmentalization in their lives. Many of these women spoke of their work as a vocation, a call from God. These women see their work as an extension of their spiritual lives. Most of the focus group participants reported that helping and serving people is the most satisfying aspect of their work. They reported that their faith exhibits itself in the workplace in a number of different ways. Many of them expressed a desire to "model Christ"—that is, to set a good example by treating others as Christ would. A lot of them reported that their faith helps them deal with difficult situations at work, including interpersonal issues with colleagues and ethical challenges. Many of these women said that they witness to their faith in the workplace. While some find their workplace to be conducive to their spiritual life, others indicated that expressions of faith are discouraged in their workplace. They sometimes see fundamental tensions between Christian ideals and the realities of business life.

In its follow-up study, the committee asked focus group participants to discuss in greater detail workplace experiences that they think are unique to women. Many participants said that relationships in the workplace are more important to women than men. They believe women are more supportive of one another, exhibit more empathy and compassion, and are less competitive. Women, in their view, tend to be better communicators than men. They maintain that women try harder to create a cooperative workplace and that women generally are more concerned to make the world a better place through their work.

This study provides a good picture of how women in this particular faith tradition think about and experience spirituality in the workplace, and its findings are generally confirmed by solid research in the behavioral and social sciences. The study's findings also hint at some of the challenges that religious women face in the workplace as a result of their spiritual orientation. Importantly—and at long last, some might say—it acknowledges and explores the distinctive ways that women think about and experience religion and work, and the relationship between the two. This chapter explores all of these themes in greater depth.

The first part of this chapter examines the fundamental ways that women attempt to integrate faith and work, particularly in light of feminine conceptions of identity, religion, and work. In most cases, religion is a healthy, vital part of an individual's identity, and successfully integrating faith and work has a number of benefits. However, the second part of this chapter shows that the common policy of separating spirituality from the workplace leads many religious employees to compartmentalize their religious and work lives. The fragmented sense of identity that results leads to significant psychological and moral strain. The view that the workplace is primarily a secular sphere is reinforced by federal law governing religion in the workplace. Part three discusses Title VII of the Civil Rights Act, which prohibits religious discrimination in the workplace. Although Title VII requires employers to reasonably accommodate the religious beliefs and practices of employees, a series of court decisions have significantly limited the employer's duty. The final part of this chapter compares and contrasts two organizational approaches to religion in the workplace.

Before proceeding, there is an important matter of conceptual clarity to be addressed. To this point, the terms *religion* and *spirituality* have been used interchangeably, but many Americans see a great difference between the two. Spirituality is regarded as highly personal yet inclusive in that it embraces all ways of experiencing the sacred. Religion is regarded as institutional, dogmatic, inflexible, and divisive. As Spilka, Hood, Hunsberger, and Gorsuch (2003) explain, in this usage "spirituality is about a person's beliefs, values, and behavior, while religiousness is about the person's involvement with a religious tradition and institution."[1] So, spirituality is more psychological and religion more sociological. Given this bifurcation, a person can be spiritual without being religious, though being religious invariably involves being spiritual. Roof (1993) dubs the baby boomers "a generation of seekers," and says "these intense seekers prefer to think of themselves as 'spiritual' rather than as 'religious.'" Rayburn and Richmond (2002) report that women more often distinguish between religion and spirituality, and more often see themselves as more spiritual than religious, than men do.

As Hicks (2003) points out, authors of management literature more frequently talk about spirituality than about religion in the workplace.[2] Mitroff and Denton (1999) claim that there are good empirical reasons for this approach. In their recent book, *A Spiritual Audit of Corporate America*, they report that the respondents to their survey generally differentiated strongly between religion and spirituality.

> They viewed religion as a highly inappropriate topic and form of expression in the workplace. Conversely, spirituality was viewed as highly appropriate. Religion was largely viewed as formal and organized. It was also viewed as being dogmatic, intolerant, and dividing people more than bringing them together. In contrast, spirituality was largely viewed as informal and personal, that is, pertaining mainly to individuals. It was also viewed as universal, nondenominational, broadly inclusive, and tolerant, and as the basic feeling of being connected with one's complete self, others, and the entire universe. (p. xvi)

Roughly 60% of those surveyed and interviewed had a positive view of spirituality and a negative view of religion. Mitroff and Denton argue it is appropriate (and strongly advisable) to foster spirituality in the workplace, but agree that "any and all expression of religion in the workplace is highly inappropriate." To the extent that Mitroff and Denton's argument for accommodating spirituality in the workplace seems to entail that religion also should be accommodated, this position, it will later be argued, appears to be inconsistent. This chapter will focus primarily on the experience of those women who would self-identify as religious (and, by implication, spiritual). But most of the discussion here is highly relevant to women who would identify themselves as spiritual but not religious. When the distinction is relevant, this will be noted.

INTEGRATED FAITH AND WORK

America is a deeply religious nation. As Prothero (2006) explains,

> In the United States, religion matters. In overwhelming numbers, Americans believe in God, pray, and contribute their time and money to

churches, synagogues, mosques, and temples. As much as race, gender, ethnicity, or region, religious commitments make individual Americans who they are. The significance of religion is not confined, however, to self-identity and the private sphere. In the United States, religion is as public as it is pervasive, as political as it is personal. And so it has been for a long, long time. (p. 1)

According to a recent poll, roughly 9 in 10 Americans profess a belief in God or a universal spirit (Gallup, 2007). Nearly the same percentage says religion is either very important (57%) or fairly important (27%) (Gallup, 2006). About two-thirds of Americans (63%) report that they are members of a church or synagogue, and 43% report attending religious services at least once a week or almost every week (Gallup, 2006). International comparisons indicate that the United States is one of the most religious nations in the West (Spilka et al., 2003, 149f). Moreover, in *A New Religious America* (2001), Diana Eck has demonstrated that the United States is among the most religiously diverse countries on the globe. Today the United States is home to more than 2,000 different faiths and denominations, and more than 500,000 churches, mosques, synagogues, and temples.

As Prothero suggests, many Americans regard their religion as a very public matter. For the devout, religion provides the overarching framework that orients them in the world and provides them with motivation and direction for living. As Hill and Pargament (2003) explain, "religion and spirituality are not a set of beliefs and practices divorced from everyday life, to be applied only at special occasions; instead, religion and spirituality are ways of life to be sought, experienced, fostered, and sustained consistently" (p. 68). Nasr's (1993) account of Islam nicely illustrates the point in the context of this particular faith tradition:

> In the Islamic perspective, religion is not seen as a part of life or a special kind of activity along with art, thought, commerce, social discourse, politics, and the like. Rather, it is the matrix and worldview within which these and all other human activities, efforts, creations, and thoughts take place or should take place. (p. 439)

Despite the widespread notion that religion is intimately related to all aspects of life, sociologists agree that the process of differentiation dominates modern societies. As Fenn (2001) describes it, differentiation is "the process by which areas of social life become separated from each other and operate under their own, independent auspices" (p. 11). As a result of this process, Fenn explains, each separate sphere becomes relatively autonomous of the others in setting its own internal standards, setting its goals and policies, and determining its own identity and belief system. Through this process, religion has been separated from the sphere of economic life and other facets of so-called public life. Thus, according to one of the grand narratives in the sociology of religion,

> Abandoned to the impersonal structures of impersonal institutions, modern men and women find themselves trapped in an iron cage of rationalized bureaucracy, which can supply neither meaning nor significance. Homeless, alienated, and anomic minds can now find purpose and value only in the realm of personal and private life. Religion, once part of the public realm, correspondingly shrinks in scope, and can work its enchantments—if at all—only in a severely delimited sphere. It becomes, in other words, a "privatized" means by which a declining number of people cope with the dislocations and restrictions of public life. (Woodhead, 2001, p. 76)

The so-called Religious Right—represented by organizations such as the Christian Coalition and the Moral Majority—has mobilized in an effort to combat this process of differentiation in American society, and, over the past three decades, it has emerged as a powerful political and social force.[3] While the evangelical movement's initial efforts were primarily directed at giving greater voice to religion—specifically, Christianity—in political matters, it has increasingly directed its efforts toward the workplace. As a result of this, and a number of other contributing factors, there has been a sharp increase in interest in religion in the workplace, and a large body of literature devoted to the topic has emerged over the past decade.[4]

Another factor driving this trend is the increased participation of women in the U.S. labor force.[5] Women not only exhibit a greater affinity for religion than men, but they also experience faith differently than men. As the USCCB study noted at the outset indicates, religious women tend to see spirituality as infusing all they do, including their jobs. So, as women enter the workforce, they tend to bring their faith with them.

Those who are religious—men and women alike—have a fundamental desire to integrate their religious lives and their work lives. (Indeed, to the extent that one considers religion as an overarching framework in one's life, the dichotomy between religious life and work life makes little sense.) In *God and Mammon in America* (1994) sociologist Robert Wuthnow examined the relationship between religious commitment and economic behavior in the United States.[6] Wuthnow found that a considerable portion of the American workforce thinks about how to relate their faith to their work and discusses their faith with others at work. When asked how much they had thought during the past year about "how to link your faith more directly with your work," 33% of working Americans said they had thought about this a great deal or a fair amount. Among persons who said they were members of a church or synagogue, this proportion rose to 46%, and among persons who attended religious services every week, it was 60%. Based upon these findings, Wuthnow inferred two things: Many American workers are interested in making their faith relevant to their work; and, because the proportions are lower than one would expect given the religiosity of Americans, "many people have learned to compartmentalize [their faith and work]." On the whole, approximately one-third of working Americans claimed to have discussed their faith with someone at work during the past year. Among members of churches or synagogues, this proportion rose to 47%, and among those who attend religious services every week, it was 58%. Wuthnow determined that women are more likely than men to engage in discussions about faith at work.

Religious individuals seek to relate their faith to their work in a number of fundamental ways. First, religion imbues work with meaning and purpose. Many religious workers emphasize the non-instrumental value of their work; first and foremost, they see their work as service to others. In addition, by emphasizing transcendence of the self, religion encourages workers to view the workplace as a communal setting. Religious workers often report closer connections to coworkers, and, again, tend to call attention to the non-instrumental value of work relations. Moreover, religion provides guidance in relating work to other aspects of life, such as family. Religious workers also find their faith to be a powerful resource for managing stress. Religion may also provide the moral grounding needed to address ethical challenges that arise at work. Ultimately, many religious individuals see work as an opportunity for spiritual growth and self-actualization. This section proposes that, in light of feminine understandings of identity, religion, and work, as well as the unique circumstances of working women, there is good reason to believe that the desire to experience and express spirituality in the context of work and the workplace will be particularly strong in religious women.

The evidence is clear and well established: Women are generally more religious than men on a wide range of measures (Spilka et al., 2003; Walter & Davie, 1998; Francis, 1997; Beit-Hallahmi & Argyle, 1996; Cornwall, 1989). Findings demonstrate both stronger beliefs and higher levels of religious activity on the part of women. Donelson (1999) reports that, "relative to men, women attend worship services more often, pray more often, report more intense religious experiences, regard religion more favorably, feel closer to God, are more likely to express need for a religious dimension in their daily lives, and are more involved in religious social activities." An extensive study by Wilson and Sherkat (1994) found that women are less likely to become apostates than are men, though women apostates are also less likely to return to the fold than are men. A number of theories have been proposed to explain why women tend to be more religious than men, but as of yet little empirical research has been undertaken to test these hypotheses.[7]

Many observers see women's extensive participation in religion as paradoxical. All of the major religious traditions—including Buddhism, Christianity, Hinduism, Islam, and Judaism—have historically placed women in a subordinate position to men (Reinke, 1995). Their teachings have traditionally been interpreted to support the doctrine of "separate spheres."[8] Despite the mass entry of women into the U.S. labor force in the late 20th century, it is clear that these teachings still influence some women: "To the extent that a woman is religious, she is likely to maintain established sex roles in marriage, to continue to be a homemaker and mother, and not to work outside the home" (Spilka et al., 2003, p. 188). Not surprisingly, Wuthnow (1994) found this to be true particularly for women associated with more conservative religious traditions. These teachings can be the source of guilt and frustration for religious women that enter the workforce. Willits and Crider (1988) found that, for females in the workforce, increased adolescent religious participation is negatively associated with job satisfaction. (Note that they found no relation between *current* religious participation and job satisfaction.) They write, "Since the primary socialization on gender roles takes place during childhood and adolescence ... religious women may see employment for pay as an intrusion on their perceived God-given roles of wife, mother and keeper of the home." Bridges and Spilka (1992) write about the potential negative effects of religion on the mental health of women. Through the patriarchal organization of sex roles, these religions may offer negative meanings to women, reducing their sense of personal control and lowering their self-esteem.

Hence, scholars like Ozorak (1996) have asked why women disproportionately invest in an institution that systematically devalues them. She suggests that the answer might lie in recent work showing that women and men experience God and faith differently. "For women, the emphasis commonly seems to be on personal relationships with a loving God and with others in the religious community," says Ozorak, "while men are more likely to focus on God's power and judgment, and on their own spiritual discipline." These differences, she notes, are reminiscent of the two voices of morality contrasted by Gilligan (1982): the feminine voice of relationship and the masculine voice of individuation.[9] Regarding the women in her study, Ozorak writes,

> It is striking that the women in this sample, almost without exception, emphasized the centrality of caring and community to their religious experience and insisted on a view of God as a friend and confidant rather than as a cosmic ruler or judge. This offers a possible explanation for the paradox proposed earlier.... Most of the women in this study recognized that by social standards, organized religion does not treat them as well as it might.... But in absolute terms, they do not see themselves as

disenfranchised. The power of connection and relationship, most essential to their own views of the faith experience, is available to them in
abundance. (p. 27)

Woodhead (2001) sees in findings like this evidence of the feminization
of religion, which involves a "shift of weight towards the relational in
religion" (p. 78). Women in particular (but increasingly men as well)
have come to regard and value religion primarily in terms of its ability
to sustain and validate various forms of relationship. When the recent
history of religion is reconceptualized from a feminist perspective,
Woodhead argues, "religion can be seen as far from the private matter
that has so often been assumed." Indeed, the narrative of modern religious history presented earlier, according to which religion has become
a matter of purely private significance, makes no sense from this perspective because the sharp line between "private" and "public"
spheres of life that is central to this narrative is drawn from a masculine point of view. Women tend not to see themselves as "unencum-
bered" or "separate" selves but as being "radically situated" in a rich
network of relations with others (Miller, 1976; Chodorow, 1978; Gilligan, 1982).[10] Religious women report that spirituality is pervasive in
these relations, and, hence, the notion that a sharp boundary can be
drawn between one's religious life and other aspects of one's life, such
as one's work life, is inconsistent with their experience. Consider representative comments from two participants in the USCCB study mentioned at the outset: One woman said, "Categorizing where spirituality
lies can be artificial; it penetrates all we do"; another put it this way,
"Spirituality is intertwined in everything."

This feminine, relational understanding of religion encourages the
sacralization of everyday life, including work life. Ozorak (1996)
reports that the women in her study repeatedly mentioned service to
others as an integral part of religious practice, and many of these
women see work as an important venue for this service.[11] One of her
subjects, a Unitarian woman, said, "Going to church is nice, but I really
feel religious when I am working. I enjoy working with dying people.
So, I really feel like that my God's work on earth is to do that kind of
stuff." Another subject, a Methodist businesswoman, expressed it this
way, "I have the power to make a difference, to be the hands that
work for Jesus." Ozorak concluded that these women "experience
God's power not just in God's goodness to them but in the work they
feel God empowers them to do for others ... they feel better about
themselves in part because they believe that their own behavior and
capabilities change for the better." For these women, work is construed
as a form of religious expression. They regard their work as important
and valuable in light of their religious views, and this strong sense of
purpose promotes their self-esteem.

The desire to find meaning and purpose in one's work is common to men and women, but Ruthellen Josselson's longitudinal study (1996) of how women construct their identities over a lifetime suggests that this desire may be particularly acute for women. Josselson found that "unlike many men, few women defined themselves as 'a manager' or 'a teacher.' Occupation may be what she 'does' for many hours of her life, but is seldom what she feels she 'is.'" While the women in her study were generally disinclined to define themselves in terms of their occupation, she reports that "more than half the women I have interviewed define themselves in an important spiritual way.... For many of these women, [spiritual development] is an even more consuming quest than occupational self-definition." For the women in her study, the degree to which occupational endeavors were assigned prominence in their identity was a function of whether they perceived their work to have a meaningful impact on the lives of others. In an otherwise diverse group, "nearly all located meaning—and identity—in their work relative to the impact they felt they had in the lives of others." When these women felt stymied by the inflexibility or indifference of their organizations, and, consequently, believed that they were not getting anything of worth accomplished, they came to feel great dissatisfaction with their jobs. Josselson acknowledges that men may also become very disappointed with their jobs, but she suggests that women, who are less likely to define themselves by their work, experience this sort of dissatisfaction more intensely and for different reasons.

> I think that because these women bring a deep sense that they are choosing to work, that they are a first generation pioneering high-status roles for women, they demand more from what they are doing. Unlike men, they don't see themselves, in most cases, of "having" to work in order to "have" an identity at all.... These women don't seem to value themselves based on their income level.... They work in hopes of self-realization and a feeling of effectiveness. When this is thwarted, the whole enterprise of employment is open to question. (p. 195)[12]

All of this may be especially true for religious women because They see their faith as more fundamental to their identity than their occupation, they see their work as serving a higher purpose, and they may feel that their choice to enter the workforce conflicts with the traditional teachings of their faith.

Those who are religious feel deeper connections not only to their work but also to their fellow workers. Religion connects individuals to one another and promotes sociality (Spilka et al., 2003, p. 18f). It fosters a sense of community and a sense of belonging to something larger than oneself. Scholars from many fields have noted that employees—both the religious and non-religious—increasingly see the workplace as a communal center (Conger, 1994). This is due, in part, to the fact that Americans spend a lot of time there. Indeed, according to Galinsky et al. (2005), one-third of all U.S. employees can be viewed as being chronically overworked.[13] "As more Americans spend more time 'at work,'" writes Poarch, "work gradually becomes less of a one-dimensional activity and assumes more of the concerns and activities of both private (family) and public (social and political) life" (cited in Putnam, 2000, p. 86). Religious concerns and activities should certainly be added to this list. Partly because Americans are spending more time at work, participation in traditional forms of social association, including church, has diminished significantly in recent decades (Putnam).[14] In the past, civic organizations offered support and provided a place for people to contribute and establish connections. But as involvement in these organizations has declined, people have brought their need for community (and spirituality) to work. As Nash and McLennan (2001) say, "For many businesspeople, the corporation is the closest thing that they have to community after the family."

As indicated, an influential line of research in psychology has found that women in general have a more communal orientation than men. To the extent that this is true, the increased presence of women in the workplace is likely to encourage the notion of "company as community." In fact, it opens the prospect of a revolutionary change in the nature of work and the workplace. Fenn (2001) nicely summarizes the idea:

> As women enter the labor force in increasing numbers, the very relatedness of people to one another will make it increasingly difficult for corporations and bureaucracies to separate domains such as education and the family, the neighborhood and the community, from the spheres of work and politics. In fact, the increased presence of women in the areas formerly dominated by men may intensify pressures to put back together areas of social life that the Western world has torn apart.... As the world of work becomes feminized, relationships on the job will become connected to wider possibilities, networks of relationships, and universes of meaning. (p. 11)

The relational conception of religion common to women further promotes the transformation of work and work relations. Traditionally, work and work relations have been regarded as having primarily (or only) instrumental value—that is, work provides the means to life, but not the meaning of life. But when work and work relations are sacralized, they are seen as having significant non-instrumental value. Work, as explained above, becomes an expression of one's deepest principles, and the workplace is a venue for self-actualization, which one pursues by helping and serving others in the workplace community and the community at large.

In addition to bestowing deeper significance to work and work relations, many women report that religion constructively helps integrate work in their broader lives. By offering a conception of the nature and purpose of life generally, religion offers adherents motivation and direction for living. It identifies and prioritizes activities that are truly worthwhile and important. Hence, religion provides followers with a mechanism for balancing career pursuits with other activities. A sacral perspective, Nash and McLennan (2001) suggest, "is a way of preventing oneself from getting too caught up in a corporate mindset that throws the individual out of balance, a state neither personally rewarding nor ultimately effective" (p. 23). Consider the comments of one of their interviewees, a woman struggling with career decisions that would affect her family life:

> I really get carried away with work. I need to put my priorities in balance, and I think a deeper spiritual life will help me do that. You can't wait until it's all over to decide what's really important. My religious belief helps me keep the important things in mind. (p. 25)

The need to find balance in one's life is especially pressing for working women. As Gutek (1993) makes clear, employed women face more stressors, on average, than men, due to gender-asymmetric change in work and family roles. Employed women face a wide variety of stressors owing to the major commitments of time and energy associated with the roles of spouse, parent, and worker.

In addition to the strain that comes from juggling multiple roles in life, there are the day-to-day stresses associated with work. Numerous surveys and studies indicate that occupational pressures are by far the leading source of stress for American adults and that these pressures have steadily increased over the past few decades. For example, according to surveys cited by the National Institute for Occupational Safety and Health (NIOSH, p. 4f), 40% of workers report that their job is "very or extremely stressful," and one-fourth of employees view their jobs as the number one stressor in their lives. Galinsky et al. (2005) found that, while men work longer hours, take less vacation time, and tend to have jobs with characteristics leading to more stress, women report having more demanding jobs and feeling more stress. Women face a variety of unique stressors in the workplace, related to: the social isolation that can result from entering a male-dominated workplace or field; a sense of being undervalued in their efforts or contributions; challenges to their competency rooted in false stereotypes; sexual discrimination and harassment; and, as mentioned above, work/family conflicts. Many women report that religion plays an important role in stress management.

Religious commitment has been tied to positive methods of coping.[15] As Silverman and Pargament (1990) explain,

> People do not face stressful situations without resources. They rely on a system of beliefs, practices, and relationships which affects how they deal

with difficult situations. In the coping process, this orienting system is translated into concrete situation-specific appraisals, activities, and goals. Religion is part of this general orienting system. (p. 2)

Spilka et al. (2003, p. 483f) indicate that three needs underlie people's attempts to cope: a need for meaning, based on a desire to make sense of life events; a need to maintain one's sense of control over life events; and a need to maintain one's sense of self-esteem. Religion is responsive to all of these needs, and, hence, provides many possible ways of coping with the stresses of life. Moreover, studies show that religion plays a significant role, not only in coping with major negative life events—such as death, divorce, or job loss—but also in a person's experience with minor stressors on a day-to-day basis (Spilka et al., p. 494). Wuthnow (1994) found that those who regularly attend religious services face the same sorts of psychological, emotional, interpersonal, and ethical problems as other workers, but religious people are more likely than non-religious people to engage in two types of activities that alleviate job-related stress. Some of these are "religious-specific" activities (activities such as praying, meditating, or seeking help from a member of the clergy) and others are "religion-related" activities (activities such as talking with friends and family, or seeing a therapist, which are encouraged by religious involvement but do not necessarily occur in a religious setting).[16]

Studies have consistently found that religious coping is more common among women, Blacks, the poor, and the elderly (Pargament, 1997). Pargament notes two characteristics of these groups to explain these findings. First, these groups report higher levels of personal religiousness than others—for them, religion has become a larger part of their orienting system. Second, these groups tend to have less access to secular resources and power in our society; so, religion may be one of the few resources accessible to members of these groups. A number of recent studies have linked these general findings to the experience of women in the workplace. Bacchus and Holley (2004) found that professional Black women utilize spirituality—particularly prayer, meditation, and inspirational readings—to gain personal strength, inner peace, and guidance and to reflect on and reappraise stressful situations in the workplace. Sullivan (2006) determined that the primary role for faith in the workplace for very low income, urban mothers centered on coping with the stresses of low-wage service sector work. Two-thirds of the women in her study reported that they connected their faith with their daily lives, despite the fact that few attended church regularly. In Sullivan's words: "These mothers found their faith to be a powerful tool in helping them calm down and deal productively with rude customers or difficult bosses or coworkers. Faith helped them carry out unpleasant tasks and complete the work that had to be accomplished" (p. 106).

One source of stress in the workplace involves ethical problems, and the workplace is rife with such challenges. Indeed, a number of surveys indicate the widespread perception that there is a crisis in business ethics. In a survey conducted by the Gallup Organization for Wuthnow (1994), 86% of the public said corruption in business is a serious or extremely serious problem in American society. Daniel Yankelovich has even claimed that the main force driving the current search for spiritual growth in America is declining confidence in the ethics of business leaders (cited in Nash & McLennan, 2001, p. 31).[17] Nash and McLennan report that "people feel the need for a personal recovery of moral grounding and membership in a moral community." Religion plainly satisfies both needs, and one would expect adherents to turn to the moral tenets of their religion for guidance and support when facing ethical predicaments at work. One would also expect to find a positive relation between religious commitment and ethical conduct.

Wuthnow (1994) found that religious commitment deters ethically questionable behavior in the workplace, but not much. While religious people are somewhat more likely to avoid activities such as bending the rules, lying, arriving late, taking time off that they shouldn't, using office equipment for themselves, and charging illegitimate expenses than are nonreligious people, "what is also obvious," Wuthnow says, "is that the differences between religious and nonreligious people on these items are not great." This finding is generally consistent with the analysis of Spilka et al. (2006). Based on their review of nearly a century's worth of studies, they conclude that, although religious people say that they are more ethical than others, religion in fact has little or no impact in reducing dishonesty and cheating among religious persons.

Wuthnow (1994) attributes these findings to the powerful countervailing influence of workplace culture and secular society more generally.

> If religion often has only a small impact on how people think about ethics and how they conduct themselves at work, an important reason is that the workplace itself has come to provide its own understanding of ethics, and even more than that, its own well-established procedures that sometimes obviate the need for ethics at all. Both of these developments are characteristics of postindustrial society. (p. 88)

Wuthnow is describing the general effect that the process of differentiation has had on the ethical climate of the American workplace. In the economic sphere, ethics has come to be understood in terms of economic logic—honesty, for example, is "right" because it generally pays to be honest. "In this perspective, ethics becomes a kind of autonomous system that can be understood entirely within the framework of the workplace," Wuthnow explains, "rather than needing any external validation or grounding in an ultimate or transcendent sense of reality." But when conduct is justified in terms of economic logic, it may become too easy to argue that it is permissible to do whatever is in one's own (or one's firm's) self-interest.

These findings imply that religious workers have compartmentalized their thinking about ethics: Ethics is understood one way in a work context but in another way in nonwork contexts. This shapes Wuthnow's general conclusion about the relationship between faith and work in America today:

> Religious commitment plays a more important role in guiding work than has generally been acknowledged in the scholarly literature on this subject, especially the literature that instructs us to think about work strictly from a market or organizational orientation. But I also suggest that prevailing cultural assumptions have weakened the influence of religious commitment in the workplace. We have come to think of religion—at least implicitly—as a way of making ourselves feel better and have largely abandoned the idea that religion can guide our behavior, except to discourage activities considered blatantly immoral. (p. 39)

Religious conviction makes workers feel better by contributing meaning to their work; however, Wuthnow believes this therapeutic function may be one of the few roles it still can play in a secular society. The "prevailing cultural assumptions" create a major obstacle for the seamless integration of faith and work. Before moving on to discuss these difficulties, it is important to note that those who do successfully link their faith and work generally experience positive benefits for doing so.

Validating earlier research, Wuthnow (1994) found that individuals with higher levels of religious commitment also have higher levels of job satisfaction.[18] Although those who are religious value their relationship to God more than their work, they also value their work more in absolute terms than those who are not religious. Several lines of empirical research provide support for the connection between religious commitment and job satisfaction: (a) People reportedly experience less conflict with, derive greater satisfaction and meaning from, and invest more time, care, and energy into those aspects of their lives they view as sacred; (b) religious motivation appears to have positive psychological implications; (c) measures of intrinsic religiousness have been tied to positive methods of coping (Hill & Pargament, 2003, p. 68). Spilka et al. (2003) suggest that the greater attachment to religion on the part of women implies that religion is likely to possess more utility for women than for men.[19] "Because the preponderance of evidence generally indicates a positive association between spirituality or religion and the health and well-being of women," Williams-Nickelson (2006, p. 186) writes, "spiritual self-care strategies such as meditation (or prayer for women of faith) may be useful."

COMPARTMENTALIZING RELIGIONS AND WORK LIVES

Henry Ford asked, "Why is it that I always get the whole person when all I really want is a pair of hands?" (cited in Pollard, 1996, p. 25). Many of today's business organizations still reflect Ford's attitude, particularly when it comes to the religious and, more broadly, spiritual dimensions of employees' identity. According to convention, religious and spiritual concerns are personal matters that have nothing to do with work. Moreover, they can lead to animosity and division. So, employees are encouraged to check their faith at the door when they go to work. A recent *Fortune* magazine article referred to spiritual expression in the workplace as "the last taboo in corporate America" (Gunther, 2001, p. 58). This conventional view is defended in terms of the private-public distinction and is advanced by the process of differentiation. But whether or not business organizations want whole persons, whole persons report for work. To the extent that prevailing cultural norms discourage religion in the workplace, it is not surprising that many religious workers report less-than-satisfactory connections between religion and work in their lives.

A theme that consistently emerges in empirical studies of religion and spirituality in the workplace involves the strong sense of fragmentation that religious and spiritual workers experience in their lives. As noted earlier, Wuthnow (1994) concluded from his comprehensive study that "many people have learned to compartmentalize [their faith and work]" (p. 55). Mitroff and Denton (1999) report that their interviewees "realized that they had to separate and compartmentalize significant parts of themselves at work" (p. 38), and Nash and McLennan's (2001) subjects "express feelings of radical disconnection between Sunday services and Monday morning activities, describing a sense of living in two worlds that never touch each other" (p. 6f). Those with strong religious convictions clearly sense that they cannot express them at work and, as Nash and McLennan put it, "They are left feeling as if they live out a spiritual schizophrenia" (p. 213). Obviously, they wish this were not the case. As Mitroff and Denton explain:

> People do not want to compartmentalize or fragment their lives. The search for meaning, purpose, wholeness, and integration is a constant, never-ending task. It is also a constant, never-ending struggle. To confine this search to one day a week or after hours violates people's sense of integrity, of being whole persons. In short, the soul is not something one leaves at home. People want to have their souls acknowledged wherever they go, precisely because their souls accompany them everywhere. They especially want to be acknowledged as whole persons in the workplace, where they spend the majority of their waking time. (p. xvf.)

Nash and McLennan likewise conclude that businesspeople of faith are seeking a greater degree of integration of faith and work.

Despite their clear desire to live their faith in the workplace, these studies have found that religious and spiritual workers are extremely hesitant to act on it. They fear being marginalized, ridiculed, taken advantage of, or even punished. Mitroff and Denton (1999) refer to this as the Faustian dilemma: "On the one hand, [the employees, managers, and executives to whom they spoke] wished fervently that they could express more of themselves in the workplace, but they were afraid to do so. Indeed, many of those to whom [they] talked were terrified to do so" (p. 7). Nash and McLennan's subjects came up against the same problem:

> This split [between the religious and work-related dimensions of one's identity] poses significant psychological and moral uncertainty.... [Those who are religious] struggle with how they can act on, articulate, and symbolize Christian spirituality within a secular social context. To disguise faith seems inauthentic, but taking it out of the closet may provoke conflict or accusations of being inappropriate. (2001, p. 7)

Mitroff and Denton point out that "almost the entire set of respondents [in their study] was unable to mention at least one organization that they regarded as a role model in fostering spirituality" (p. 44). This is an indictment of the business community at large.

As indicated, many employees cope with this dilemma by compartmentalizing their lives. These workers resign themselves to the fact that they will not realize their full potential at work. This can exact a considerable toll: "The individual," Wolfteich (2002) writes, "lives with a hollow feeling that one's everyday life lacks meaning—or at least meaning that is strongly affirmed by one's religious tradition" (p. 144). These employees work without the engagement that comes from feeling that they are fully bringing themselves to what they are doing, and this sense of alienation from their work brings great disappointment. Part one of this chapter indicated that feminine conceptions of identity, religion, and work suggest that religious women will have a particularly strong desire to resist fragmentation in their lives. But, clearly, prevailing cultural norms governing spirituality in the workplace have made it immensely difficult for religious women to maintain a cohesive sense of identity.

Commentators fault not only business leaders but also religious leaders for their failure to provide constructive models of faith in the contemporary workplace. This is a central theme in Nash and McLennan (2001) and Wolfteich (2002). Despite surging interest in spirituality in the workplace, the church has largely failed to respond. The inadequacy of the clergy's response is exemplified in a quote from one of Nash and McLennan's subjects: "I see many tensions between my Christian beliefs and what I do at work, and I feel deeply responsible to be a 'good Christian' in my daily life. But my pastor is the last person I'd discuss this with" (p. 3). Based upon their research, Nash and McLennan concluded that "businesspeople and clergy live in two worlds" (p. 128). These two groups have conflicting attitudes about the nature and value of business in general. Moreover, businesspeople perceive that members of the clergy have little understanding of the day-to-day life of a businessperson. (Most members of the clergy that were interviewed confirmed that this perception is accurate.) Wolfteich argues that the Roman Catholic Church has failed to adequately address the complexity of women's work in particular. For example, the church has not offered up female role models whose lives indicate that work can be a spiritual path.

> This paling of work in the lives of great women in the [Roman Catholic] tradition encourages contemporary women to compartmentalize their working lives from their faith. Work seems irrelevant to faith, or uncomfortably dissonant with the values women learn in church. The reality is that women find themselves in new, demanding social and economic roles with little guidance about how to fit these new roles into traditional religious frameworks that, however, remain important sources of identity and community. No wonder women describe an experience of fragmentation. No wonder many compartmentalize these two seemingly unrelated areas of life; compartmentalization is a useful strategy for living with dissonance. (p. 143f.)

So, religious businesspeople in general—and women in particular—do not receive helpful guidance or support from either their work or religious organizations, and they are left to navigate these complex issues of identity and meaning on their own.

PART III

As it has been interpreted by the courts, federal law addressing religion in the workplace tends to reinforce the conventional view that religion is a private matter and the workplace is a secular sphere. Title VII of the 1964 Civil Rights Act (42 U.S.C. § 2000e et seq.) prohibits religious discrimination in private and public employment.[20] The Act also requires employers to reasonably accommodate the religious beliefs and practices of an employee, unless doing so would create an undue hardship on the employer's business (42 U.S.C. § 2000e(j)). Under the Act, the term *religion* includes "all aspects of religious observance and practice, as well as belief." But the Equal Employment Opportunity Commission's (EEOC) Guidelines interpret *religion* more liberally: Religious beliefs include "moral or ethical beliefs as to what is right or wrong which are sincerely held with the strength of traditional religious views" (29 C.F.R. § 1605.1).

According to the EEOC (2007), between 1997 and 2006, complaints under Title VII alleging religion-based discrimination jumped nearly 50% (from 1,707 complaints in 1997 to 2,541 in 2006). During this same period, charges alleging race-based discrimination dropped almost 7% (from 29,199 to 27,238); sex-based discrimination charges dropped about 6% (from 24,728 to 23,247); and discrimination charges filed under the Americans with Disabilities Act dropped around 14% (from 18,108 to 15,575).

Some religious discrimination claims arising under Title VII involve simple or ordinary discrimination. This occurs when a person is denied an employment opportunity because an employer makes a negative judgment based on her religion.[21] Also, an employer's policies and practices may not favor one religion over another. For example, it would be unlawful for a company to refuse to hire a Muslim simply because she is a Muslim, or for it to allow Christian employees to display religious articles or messages in their workspace while prohibiting Hindu employees from doing the same.

While Title VII permits religious expression by employees and their supervisors, it prohibits harassment. *Quid pro quo* harassment occurs when an employee is required, explicitly or implicitly, to acquiesce to the religious beliefs or practices of a superior in order to obtain a job benefit. A more common form of harassment involves a supervisor or coworker creating a hostile work environment. Like in cases of sexual or racial harassment, whether a particular employee's work environment is "hostile" for purposes of religious discrimination depends on the totality of the circumstances, including the frequency of the allegedly harassing conduct, the severity of the conduct (whether it is humiliating or physically threatening), and whether the conduct unreasonably interferes with the employee's work performance. If, for example, Christian workers inspired by their recent viewing of Mel Gibson's *The Passion of the Christ* repeatedly taunt a Jewish colleague, making working conditions very unpleasant, the worker has suffered religious harassment. If, after she has complained, nothing is done to stop the abuse, the employer may be implicated.[22]

A third type of religious discrimination occurs when an employer fails to properly accommodate an employee's religious beliefs or practices. In these cases, an employee establishes a prima facie case of religious discrimination by showing that: the employee has a bona fide religious belief that conflicts with an employment requirement; the employee informed the employer of this belief; and the employee was disciplined for failing to comply with the requirement.[23] After this prima facie showing, the employer then must demonstrate that it offered a reasonable accommodation or that any reasonable accommodation would have resulted in an undue hardship to the employer. Common employee accommodation requests involve holy day observances (such as when a Sabbatarian requests Saturdays or Sundays off, or a Roman

Catholic requests Good Friday off), religious garb requirements (such as when a Muslim woman wears a headscarf or a Jewish man wears a yarmulke), and religious grooming requirements (such as when a Rastafarian wears dreadlocks or a Sikh wears a mustache and beard). But accommodation claims may also involve religious speech issues (such as when a "pro-life" Christian wears a button with a photograph of an aborted fetus[24]), issues related to specific job-related duties (such as when a pharmacist refuses on religious grounds to speak to any customers unless they are pre-screened by another employee to ensure that they are not seeking birth control[25]), or issues related to union membership (such as when an employee refuses to affiliate herself with a labor organization because of religious beliefs[26]).

The Supreme Court has interpreted the key provisions of Title VII's accommodation requirement very narrowly, and in so doing it has significantly limited the employer's obligation to accommodate employees' religious beliefs and practices. In *Trans World Airlines v. Hardison* (432 U.S. 63 (1977)), the Court determined that anything more than a *de minimis* cost—that is, a nominal or negligible cost—to an employer constitutes an "undue hardship" for purposes of the accommodation requirement. Undue hardship also may be shown if accommodating the employee would require an employer to violate a statute or regulation.[27] The Court held in *Ansonia Board of Education v. Philbrook* (479 U.S. 60 (1986)) that an employer can satisfy its duty to accommodate by offering *any* reasonable accommodation. This means that the employer does not have to provide the accommodation preferred by the employee, so long as the employer's proposed accommodation effectively eliminates the religious conflict and does not disadvantage the individual's employment opportunities.

Based upon her review of recent cases involving religious accommodation claims under Title VII, Smith (2004) concluded:

> The safeguards provided for employee religious practices have been so restricted by court decisions that an employee who requests a religious accommodation must rely more on an employer's generosity and goodwill than on statutory protection. In case after case, employers have chosen to deny employees' requests for accommodation by citing some trivial difficulty, perhaps even a "potential" hardship, as undue; in other words, requiring more than a *de minimis* cost. (p. 64)

There does, however, remain a category of very-low-to-no-cost accommodations that employers are typically required to provide, including exemptions from dress codes and grooming rules, scheduling changes that can be accomplished without overtime pay and without infringing on the rights of other employees, and approved absences for occasional religious holidays. Moreover, some lower federal courts appear to have deviated from the restrictive doctrine that flows from *Hardison* and

Philbrook by writing opinions favoring the employee's position.[28] This
has left the judicial landscape somewhat unsettled, as the line between
the trivial costs that do constitute undue hardship and the even more
trivial costs that do not remains unclear.

The Supreme Court's constrictive readings of Title VII's accommodation requirement have been sharply criticized by those who favor more
extensive religious freedom in the workplace. The Workplace Religious
Freedom Act (WRFA), which has been introduced in every Congress since
1997, aims to strengthen the existing requirements imposed on employers
to accommodate the religious practices of their employees.[29] The bill has
historically received support from both religious conservatives and some
of the most socially liberal members of Congress. The WRFA is backed by
the Coalition for Religious Freedom in the Workplace, a 50-member
strong partnership of organizations affiliated with a wide spectrum of
religions. It is opposed, at least in its current form, by the Chamber of
Commerce, the American Civil Liberties Union (ACLU), and a variety of
women's advocacy groups, including the National Women's Law Center.

The WRFA makes three significant changes to Title VII's religious
accommodation requirement. First, the WRFA requires employers to
accommodate three specific categories of employees' religious practices:
practices related to wearing religious clothing, practices related to taking
time off to observe religious holidays, and other religious practices that
may have "a temporary or tangential effect on the ability to perform job
functions." This third category is intended to accommodate cases like that
of a Muslim who requests to take brief time during the day to pray. According to the WRFA, these three types of practices do not conflict with the
"essential functions" or "core requirements" of the employment position.

Second, the WRFA defines "undue hardship" as "an accommodation
requiring *significant* difficulty or expense." The WRFA models its understanding of undue hardship on the standard articulated in the Americans with Disabilities Act (ADA) of 1990 (42 U.S.C. §§ 12101–12213),
which is the only other federal statute to impose a duty of accommodation on employers. Employers are required to accommodate disabled
employees—for example, by modifying facilities—unless doing so would
cause the employer undue hardship. However, the standard applied to
determine undue hardship under the ADA is much more rigorous than
the standard applied under Title VII of the CRA per *Hardison*.[30] The
ADA lists a number of factors to be considered in determining whether
an accommodation for a disabled employee would impose an undue
hardship on the employer. These factors include the nature and cost of
the accommodation, the overall financial resources of the employer, and
the type of operations of the employer. Although the factors for determining undue hardship set forth in the WRFA are not identical to those
of the ADA, they do require the cost of accommodation to be quantified
and considered in relation to the size of the employer.

Finally, the WRFA requires that, for an accommodation to be considered reasonable, it must fully remove the conflict between employment requirements and the religious observance or practice of the employee. This provision makes it clear that a reasonable accommodation, by definition, cannot require any compromise of the employee's religious beliefs.

Proponents of the bill claim that the WRFA will ensure that American workers of all creeds are accorded respect by employers and are able to remain true to their faith in the workplace. For example, Morgan (2005) writes, "If enacted, the WRFA could play a significant role in bringing the legal and business communities' perception of religion and its practice at work in line with the expectations of an increasingly religious workforce and a society that exhibits growing religious pluralism" (p. 75). Opponents of the bill worry that the WRFA will sanction proselytizing and harassing behavior by religious employees. The ACLU (2005) claims that the WRFA threatens critical personal and civil rights of coworkers, customers, and patients. For example, if the bill becomes law, pharmacists with religious objections to contraception might refuse to fill birth-control prescriptions, or police officers might refuse to protect abortion clinics. Other critics argue that there are good reasons to distinguish religious observance from disabilities. Thompson (2005), for example, writes: "Religious employees forced to decide whether to honor a religious belief or stay at a job face a difficult choice, to be sure. But people with disabilities have no choice at all." Because religious observance is a matter of choice and disability is not, Thompson argues it is appropriate that the law should require less by way of accommodating employees' religious practices.

PART IV

If the prevailing policy of separating religion from the workplace fails to acknowledge that the "whole person" comes to work, what are the alternatives? Are there any theoretical models for fostering spirituality in the workplace? And, if there are, what sorts of reasons are there for organizations to adopt these models given that the law does not require it? Is it good for business? Is it morally incumbent upon organizations to promote the spiritual development of their workers?

As noted in this chapter's opening, much of the literature tends to take for granted a strict distinction between spirituality and religion (for example, see Conger, 1994). Again, spirituality is understood to address many of the same concerns as religion—concerns about the nature and purpose of life, transcendence, and moral values as these all manifest themselves in daily life. But, in contrast to conventional religion, spirituality is not formally organized or denominational; it is broadly inclusive in accepting all ways of experiencing the sacred. Most authors take for granted the notion that spirituality unites while religion divides, and, hence, a good deal of the literature embraces spirituality while rejecting religion.[31] Proponents of workplace spirituality typically appeal to a "person-centered" approach to management. This approach recognizes that the worker is a complex individual who brings all of her beliefs, commitments, and motivations with her to work, and that her multifaceted identity impacts her potential and actual job performance. This approach is distinguished from classic management theories as typified by Taylor's "scientific management," which view workers as one-dimensional and motivated mainly by rational self-interest. Despite this shift in management paradigms, Sheep (2006, p. 368) has noted that there is still a distinct instrumental rationality that runs through the workplace spirituality literature: The ultimate rationale for promoting workplace spirituality is its alleged link to better organizational performance. This final section critically evaluates the model of workplace spirituality as it is exemplified in the work of Mitroff and Denton (1999). This model, it is argued, is inadequate for a number of reasons. This section and chapter concludes by pointing to a more promising model for accommodating *both* the spiritual and religious convictions of workers.

Mitroff and Denton (1999), as with Wuthnow (1994) and Nash and McClennan (2001), have conducted pioneering empirical studies of religion and spirituality in the workplace. They have documented spiritual employees' tendency to compartmentalize their lives, and they mount a compelling case against "the usual way in which organizations respond to spiritual matters and concerns of the soul by declaring them inappropriate or out of bounds" (p. 5). The "Chinese wall" that organizations erect between the so-called private concerns of their employees and the public demands of their businesses, they argue, creates both an external and an internal division: "It is external in that it walls off the organization from the deepest sources of creativity and productivity of its members. It is internal in that it produces a fundamental split in the souls of its members" (p. 6). Mitroff and Denton advise organizations to tear down this wall and "seek ways to tie together and integrate the potential inherent in the soul with the realities of the workplace"; for doing so will unleash "the immense energy or potential that lies at the core of each of us yet remains largely unacknowledged and untapped in our places of work" (p. 5).

But while Mitroff and Denton (1999) believe that spirituality should be welcomed into the workplace, they also believe that religion should be turned away. They report that the majority of the participants in their study indicated that "any and all expression of religion in the workplace is highly inappropriate" (p. 73). Commenting on this finding, Mitroff and Denton write:

> We are inclined strongly to agree with them, even though we realize it may be difficult to ban all religious talk because it can be construed as

protected speech. Nonetheless, in spite of the legal difficulties, the vast majority of our respondents felt that it was highly desirable to set clear limits on religious expression and talk in the workplace. Many felt even more strongly that zero-based tolerance policies should be set. In other words, no religious talk at all should be tolerated. However unfortunate this attitude may be, it means that employees who consider religion extremely important in their lives will not be able to realize their full potential in most environments. The most desirable if not the only alternative may be for them to seek employment in expressly religious organizations. (p. 73f.)

Setting aside the complex issue of protected speech, this analysis is problematic for two reasons. First, it appears to commit the "is/ought fallacy" to the extent that it assumes that because things are a certain way, they ought to be that way—precisely, it assumes that because people disapprove of religious expression in the workplace, religious expression ought to be banned. But perhaps Mitroff and Denton, by indicating that their respondents' general attitude toward religion in the workplace is "unfortunate," do not intend any such inference to be drawn. Even if this is so, it is not clear how their view that religious expression in the workplace is inappropriate is to be reconciled with their more general view that organizations should acknowledge the whole person. To admit spirituality into the workplace while turning away religion looks to be inconsistent, particularly when they themselves acknowledge that "Christianity, Hinduism, Judaism, and Islam are all historically important ways in which spirituality has been experienced and celebrated" (p. 23). In light of the discussion in part one, it should be clear that religion is a fundamental dimension of the religious workers' identity, and, moreover, that positive outcomes are typically associated with the successful integration of faith and work.

Perhaps Mitroff and Denton could respond that the benefits of permitting religious expression in the workplace are outweighed by the potential for acrimony and conflict that would result. But there are problems with this response. First, it uncritically assumes that religious expression in the workplace generally would be divisive and that the overall impact on the organization in terms of efficiency would be negative. The court cases described previously, and the media in general, tend to focus our attention on those cases of religious expression that involve deep conflict. Perhaps these cases are the exception, though, and religious expression in the workplace typically does not lead to disagreement. But even if it were established that religious expression frequently leads to conflict, it may be the case that the moral value associated with religious expression trumps the loss of economic value.

This last consideration leads to questions about the underlying rationale that Mitroff and Denton (1999) posit for promoting workplace spirituality. Like many proponents of the "spiritual organization," they defend their view primarily in terms of instrumental reasons—that is, they argue that organizations should acknowledge the whole person, including her spiritual dimensions, because doing this translates into superior organizational performance. Thus, at the heart of Mitroff and Denton's argument are their findings that

> those organizations that identify more strongly with spirituality or have a greater sense of spirituality have employees who (1) are less fearful of their organizations, (2) are far less likely to compromise their basic beliefs and values in the workplace, (3) perceive their organization as signifi- cantly more profitable, and (4) report that they can bring significantly more of their complete selves to work, specifically their creativity and intelligence. (p. xiv)

The cover-flap of their book tells managers, executives, and organiza- tion designers that they will learn how to "harness the power of spirit- ual energy ... in order to make [their organizations] more creative, competitive, and profitable."[32] Now, it might well be the case that organizations that accommodate the spiritual dimensions of their employees' lives do experience these benefits (note that Mitroff and Denton's (1999) findings do not prove that organizations *are in fact* more profitable, but only that employees of these organizations *perceive* them to be); but a number of theorists find this approach to justifying workplace spirituality troubling. From the point of view of spiritual and religious employees, the focus should be on exploring how work can be an extension of spirituality and faith, rather than on how spiri- tuality and faith can be profitable tools for business. Sheep (2006) dubs the attempt to justify workplace spirituality in terms of the odd admix- ture of concerns about spirituality and profitability the "instrumentality dilemma." Spiritual and religious employees are likely to develop the sense that their spirituality and faith are being exploited for the sake of the bottom line rather than being accorded the moral respect that they rightly deserve.

Some theorists have already formed this impression. Joanne Ciulla (2000), for example, offers a scathing appraisal of the workplace spiri- tuality movement.

> While this interest in religion and spirituality at work is admirable, it is also problematic.... From management's perspective, the spiritual approach picks up where the psychological approach left off. In the 1950s management theorists cultivated workers' "need" for belonging- ness. In the 1990s they are cashing in on their need for spirituality and meaning. The nonreligious spiritual approach [i.e., Mitroff and Denton's approach] is most interesting. It offers a combination of religion "lite" and therapy "lite." This approach attempts to satisfy what some want from religion without the work of faith and what some want from ther- apy without the work of changing. But the biggest problem is that

behind this desire for spirituality often lurk serious ethical problems about how employers and employees treat each other. In the end, spirituality at work does what pop psychology and management fads have always done: It attempts to make people feel good and adapt, not address the serious problems of power, conflict, and autonomy that make people feel bad in the first place. (p. 222f)

According to Ciulla's broader analysis, employers often use progressive concepts—like workplace spirituality—to develop new, more subtle, ways to dominate employees. The workplace spirituality movement is the just latest attempt to harness the motivation, goodwill, and energy of employees for the purpose of improving organizational performance. Workplace spirituality, in other words, is the newest opiate that employers have to offer employees. In Ciulla's view, the growing interest in religion and spirituality in the workplace is symptomatic of a deeper problem involving the nature of modern work.

The real problem is that their work zaps them of the energy, the time, and perhaps even the will to take part in meaningful activities and communities outside of work. If employers want to fill this need for something more, the answer is not a prayer meeting or a seminar on finding your soul. They need to rethink the structure of the workplace and give employees more time and flexibility to lead good lives outside of work without fear of losing promotions, bonuses, or jobs. (p. 223f)

There is a good deal of truth in this analysis, but to the extent that it suggests that spiritual and religious concerns are matters to be pursued *outside* of work, it perpetuates the customary view that religion is a private matter and the workplace is a secular domain.

What is needed in light of the discussion to this point is a framework that acknowledges the significant *non-instrumental* value of spiritual *and* religious expression *within* the workplace. A promising model is offered by Hicks (2003), who argues that organizations have a moral obligation to adopt a policy of "respectful pluralism."

The guiding principle of respectful pluralism is termed the *presumption of inclusion*. It can be stated as follows: To the greatest extent, workplace organizations should allow employees to express their religious, spiritual, cultural, political, and other commitments at work, subject to the limitations of noncoercion, nondegradation, and nonestablishment, and in consideration of the reasonable instrumental demands of the for-profit enterprise (p. 173).[33]

This framework is intended to be responsive to the circumstances of the contemporary American workplace: It acknowledges that religious diversity among employees is steadily growing, that religious and spiritual beliefs are a fundamental and inseparable part of many employees' lives, that the workplace is increasingly becoming a public site, that the place of religion in public life is highly contested, and that companies are for-profit enterprises. The ultimate aim of this model is to foster mutual respect amidst diversity in the workplace.

Hicks (2003) intentionally eschews an instrumental justification of his principle and defends it exclusively on moral grounds. The presumption of inclusion is premised on the moral values of human dignity and respect, which, Hicks argues, entail a basic right of religious exercise. Like other basic rights, such as the right to physical security, which entails the right to safe working conditions, the right to religious freedom is part of the structure in which employment occurs. The moral obligation to respect workers' dignity is *prior to* considerations of economic efficiency; so, the worker does not forfeit her basic rights, including the right to religious expression, simply by entering the workplace. "The essential point is that the moral status of employees, possessing dignity and deserving respect, builds a presumption for a high degree of 'personal' expression," Hicks explains (p. 173).[34] There is a stark difference between the presumption of inclusion involved in respectful pluralism and the presumption of exclusion that is tacit in the current understanding of the workplace as a secular domain. The default assumption of respectful pluralism is that it is legitimate for a worker to bring her religious convictions to work, and the moral burden is on the organization to justify policies that would limit personal expression.

Respectful pluralism does not warrant any and all expression simply because it is religious. Just as the religious employee is entitled to dignity and respect, so are others in the organization. Hence, the same moral values that justify the presumption of inclusion also imply several norms limiting personal expression. First, religious employees may not illegitimately impose their religious values on others. Second, religious employees may not employ speech or action that shows clear disrespect for particular individuals or groups of coworkers or third parties. Third, the organization as an institution may not endorse or promote any particular religious tradition, because employees from differing religious (or secular) backgrounds may understandably feel compelled to assent to the privileged viewpoint. Clearly, determining whether these norms have been violated—determining whether some instance of personal expression is coercive or degrading, or whether some institutional policy gives preferential treatment to a particular religious outlook—will require the exercise of moral judgment.

Respectful pluralism acknowledges that, within the bounds of legality and morality, companies have a legitimate right to seek profits. This entails the employers' right to limit personal expression for legitimate reasons related to efficiency, as long as they do so on an equal basis for all employees. But the presumption of inclusion entails that costs in efficiency would have to be significant before limits on personal expression would be warranted. "Respectful pluralism's approach,"

Hicks writes, "requires accommodation—on moral grounds—that goes beyond the standard *de minimis* interpretation of the legal framework required in Title VII of the Civil Rights Act" (p. 176). Hicks does not discuss the WRFA, but on the basis of his discussion it seems that his understanding of what would constitute an undue burden is generally in line with the proposed legislation.

Religion is an essential and healthy aspect of the identity of many women in the American workforce. But the traditional policy of separating religion and work—grounded in the distinction between "private" and "public" spheres—makes it very difficult for religious women in the workforce to live an integrated life. Many women respond by compartmentalizing, which often leads to significant psychological and moral strain. There are alternative models of public and organizational policy, however, that would accord religious women greater freedom to live and express their faith in the context of work.

NOTES

1. Spilka et al. (2003, p. 11) also point out that, in the current social and behavioral sciences, there is no commonly accepted way of distinguishing the meaning of "spirituality" from that of "religion"—indeed, some theorists maintain that it is not possible to distinguish the two—and, hence, the use of these terms is highly ambiguous in the literature. So, one must check what an investigator actually measures, regardless of the investigator's usage of these terms, to determine what is being researched.

2. Hicks also points out that this literature tends to focus on the views and experiences of business executives, and, to the extent that men are disproportionately represented in this group, this literature tends to focus on the views and experiences of men.

3. Nobel Prize winning economist Robert Fogel (2000) argues that the rise of the Religious Right is symptomatic of the "Fourth Great Awakening" in American history.

4. An excellent introduction to this literature is Douglas Hicks's *Religion and the Workplace* (2003).

5. According to the U.S. Department of Labor's Bureau of Labor Statistics (2006), in 1970, 43% of women age 16 and older were in the labor force. By the late 1990s, the labor force participation rate of women had risen to 60%. From 1975 to 2000, the labor force participation rate of mothers with children under age 18 rose from 47% to 73%. Moreover, during the past several decades, women have been increasingly employed in higher paying occupations. In 2000, half of all the workers in management, professional, and related occupations were women. The Department of Labor's Women's Bureau (2006) notes that in 2006 a record 67 million women were employed in the U.S., and women comprised 46% of the total U.S. labor force.

6. Wuthnow's analysis was based upon a very detailed survey of more than 2,000 members of the U.S. labor force. This research was supplemented with in-depth interviews of 175 people.

7. Woodhead (2001, p. 73) summarizes the three most frequently offered hypotheses: (1) Women are more religious than men because of their structural locations in society (religion, like housework, has become one of the gendered institutions created by the division of labor); (2) women are differently socialized; (3) women's greater religiosity is a compensatory response to their material and social deprivation. (See also Spilka et al., 2003, p. 154f).

8. Consider, for example, Hassan (2003): "Many traditional societies—including the Muslim—divide the world into private space (that is, the home, which is the domain of women) and public space (that is, the rest of the world, which is the domain of men). Muslims, in general, tend to believe that it is best to keep men and women segregated, in their separate, designated spaces, because the intrusion of women into men's space is seen as leading to the disruption, if not the destruction, of the fundamental order of things. If some exigency makes it necessary for women to enter into men's space, they must make themselves "faceless," or, at least, as inconspicuous as possible. This is achieved through veiling, which is thus an extension of the idea of the segregation of the sexes" (p. 226).

9. Just as Gilligan criticized Kohlberg's theory for its failure to deal with the unique aspects of women's *moral* development, some (e.g., Schweitzer, 1997) have criticized the leading theories of *religious* development for their failure to address the unique aspects of women's religious experience. For a discussion of this issue, see Spilka et al., 2003, p. 81.

10. This position—sometimes dubbed the "different voice" position—is not without its critics. For an overview of the controversies related to this line of work, see Donelson (1999, p. 319ff).

11. When asked "what do you find most satisfying about your work," the most common answer offered by participants in the USCCB focus groups was helping and serving others. Though this answer was especially common for educators and those in the health professions, it dominated *all* occupational categories.

12. Josselson's subjects were college educated women of the boomer generation. It is likely that the experience of women with different educational and socioeconomic backgrounds, and, perhaps, younger women, would be very different.

13. See Juliet B. Schor's *The Overworked American: The Unexpected Decline of Leisure* (1992). A more recent analysis by the Organisation for Economic Cooperation and Development indicates that during 1970–2002 the number of hours worked per capita declined in 14 of 19 nations surveyed. France recorded the sharpest drop among declining nations with 23.5%. Germany dropped 17.1%; Japan dropped 16.6%; and the United Kingdom dropped 7.2%. For the five nations whose per capita hours rose, the U.S. led the way with a 20.0% increase in hours (OECD, 2004, p. 6).

14. A number of commentators attribute declining attendance at religious services to the increased participation of women in the labor force. In his introduction to *Gender and Religion* (1994), sociologist William Swatos writes, "I would be willing to offer the hypothesis that virtually the entire "decline" of "the churches" in America can be "explained" by the entrance of women into the workforce, certainly more so than by anything like a "crisis of belief" (p. xi).

15. The definitive work in the field of religious coping is Kenneth Pargament's *The Psychology of Religion and Coping* (1997).

16. Those attending religious services every week were 32 points more likely to pray or meditate to relieve feelings of stress from their job; 11 points more likely to discuss stress with others (9 points more likely to discuss stress with their spouses, 6 points more likely to talk to a member of the clergy, and 3 points more likely to talk with friends); 5 points less likely to come home and watch television; and 4 points less likely to drink alcohol (p. 321).

17. According to Gallup (2006b), nearly one in three Americans say that business executives have "low" or "very low" ethical standards.

18. An emerging body of empirical evidence supports, in varying degrees, a positive relationship between religiousness and well-being *in general* (see Spilka et al., 2003, Chapter 15; and Miller & Thoresen, 2003), and as researchers have made advances in conceptualizing and measuring religion, some potential reasons for this positive association are starting to emerge (see Hill & Pargament, 2003).

19. The author is unaware of any investigation into whether religious and spiritual factors may play some role in the "gender/job satisfaction paradox"—that is, the finding that women report levels of job satisfaction that are comparable to and often exceed those of men, although, in objective terms, women do not fare as well as men in the workplace.

20. The Civil Rights Act (CRA) applies to all private employers of 15 or more persons whose business affects interstate commerce. (Virtually all states have similar fair employment laws that reach smaller employers than does the CRA. Many of these state laws are more stringent than federal law or address areas not covered by federal law.) The CRA also applies to public employers and labor unions. Religious entities are exempted from the provisions of the CRA prohibiting hiring based on religion.

21. Note that Title VII also prohibits discrimination against atheists. So, an employer may not refuse to hire, or fire, an individual simply because she has no religious belief or affiliation.

22. This case is described by Cummins, H.J. (2005, August 24). Sea of faith washing over the workplace. *Star Tribune*. Minneapolis-St. Paul, MN.

23. See *Wilson v. US West Communications*, 58 F. 3d 1337 (8th Cir. 1995), citing *Bhatia v. Chevron, U.S.A.* 734 F.2d 1382 (1984). Note that atheists can appeal to the reasonable accommodation provision of Title VII if their rejection of religion is the source of a workplace conflict. See, for example, *EEOC v. Townley Engineering and Mfg. Co.*, 859 F.2d 610 (9th Cir. 1988).

24. See *Wilson v. US West Communications*, 58 F. 3d 1337 (8th Cir. 1995).

25. See *Noesen v. Med. Staffing Network*, No. 06-2831 (7th Cir. 2007).

26. See *McDaniel v. Essex Int'l.*, 696 F. 2d 34, 35 (6th Cir. 1982).

27. As in *Hardison*, employers often invoke the provisions of collective bargaining agreements, which are enforced by federal labor laws, in refusing to accommodate employee accommodation requests.

28. For example, in *Protos v. Volkswagen of America* (797 F. 2d 129 (3d. Cir. 1986)) the court refused to find undue hardship when an employee of a large automobile manufacturer requested time off for his Sabbath, and in *EEOC v. Ilona of Hungary* (198 F. 3d 1569 (7th Cir. 1997)) the court held that a beauty salon faced no undue hardship in accommodating two Jewish employees' request

for unpaid leave to participate in Yom Kippur, even though the day the employees requested off happened to be the busiest day of the week for the salon.

29. In the spring of 2007, the WRFA was reintroduced in the House as H.R. 1431 by Rep. Carolyn McCarthy (D, NY). The bill is cosponsored by 13 Representatives. The bill currently rests in committee, where it has died every year that it has been introduced.

30. One of the main reasons why the ADA has such a strong definition of undue hardship is because its drafters saw how the Court had eviscerated the religious accommodation requirement through its narrow interpretations of Section 701(j) of Title VII.

31. Consider, for example, Fairholm (1998): "While important, the religious nature of spirituality is not considered here. This aspect of spirituality is better accommodated in doctrinaire religions and their social instrumentalities. Indeed, many, including this author, would object to matters of personal religion being introduced in the workplace" (p. 113).

32. To be fair, although an economic mode of justification dominates their book, Mitroff and Denton do hint at other sorts of arguments in favor of developing workplace spirituality. Although they do not explicitly say so, it seems clear that they believe it is morally wrong for organizations to force spiritual employees to compartmentalize their lives. (But, again, why is it not similarly morally wrong for organizations to force *religious* employees to compartmentalize their lives?) They also suggest that fostering workplace spirituality will promote ethical organizational cultures, which benefits society more generally.

33. Respectful pluralism provides a framework for all forms of personal expression in the workplace. This is advantageous for it does not require managers to discriminate between religious, spiritual, cultural, and political expressions. Consider, for example, does a "pro-life" button constitute religious or political speech?

34. It seems any moral system that regards living an integrated, noncompartmentalized life as a fundamental moral value would support the presumption of inclusion. If people should live integrated, noncompartmentalized lives, then there is a presumption that they should be allowed to express their religious convictions in the workplace. So, while Hicks defends the presumption of inclusion in terms of moral concepts such as "dignity," "respect," and "rights," one could make a case for the presumption of inclusion in terms of other moral frameworks, including Aristotelian ethics and some forms of feminist ethics.

REFERENCES

American Civil Liberties Union (2005). *ACLU letter to the House of Representatives on the harmful effects of the Workplace Religious Freedom Act.* Available at: http://www.aclu.org/religion/gen/16256leg20050315.html.

Bacchus, D.N.A., & Holley, L. C. (2004). Spirituality as a coping resource: The experiences of professional black women. *Journal of Ethnic & Cultural Diversity in Social Work, 13,* 65–84.

Beit-Hallahmi, B., & Argyle, M. (1996). *The social psychology of religion.* London: Routledge.

Bridges, R. A., & Spilka, B. (1992). Religion and the mental health of women. In J. Schumaker (Ed.), *Religion and mental health* (pp. 43–53). New York: Oxford.

Chodorow, N. (1978). *The reproduction of mothering: Psychoanalysis and the sociology of gender*. Berkeley: University of California Press.

Ciulla, J. B. (2000). *The working life: The promise and betrayal of modern work*. New York: Times Books.

Conger, J. (1994). *Spirit at work*. San Francisco: Jossey-Bass.

Cornwall, M. (1989). Faith development in men and women over the life span. In Bahr & Peterson (Eds.), *Aging and the family*. Lexington, MA: Lexington Books.

Donelson, F. E. (1999). *Women's experiences: A psychological perspective*. Mountain View, CA: Mayfield.

Eck, D. (2001). *A new religious America: How a "christian country" has become the most religiously diverse nation*. San Francisco: Harper.

Fairholm, G. W. (1998). *Perspective on leadership: From the science of management to its spiritual heart*. Westport, CT: Quorum.

Fenn, R. K. (2001). Religion and the secular; the sacred and the profane: The scope of the argument. In R. K. Fenn (Ed.), *The Blackwell companion to sociology of religion* (pp. 3–22). Malden, MA: Blackwell.

Fogel, R. W. (2000). *The fourth great awakening & the future of egalitarianism*. Chicago: University of Chicago Press.

Ford, R. T. (2005). Take God to work day: Why the law shouldn't bend over backwards for religious employees. Slate.com. Available at: http://slate.com/id/2120789.

Francis, L. (1997). The psychology of gender differences in religion: A review of empirical research. *Religion, 27*, 68–96.

Galinsky, E., Bond, J. T., Kim, S. S., Backon, L., Brownfield, E., & Sakai, K. (2005). *Overwork in America: When the way we work becomes too much, executive summary*. New York: Families and Work Institute.

Gallup Poll (2006a). *Religion*. Available at: http://www.galluppoll.com/content/?ci=1690&pg=1.

Gallup Poll (2006b). *Honesty and ethics in the professions*. Available at: http://www.galluppoll.com/content/?ci=1654&pg=1.

Gallup Poll (2007). *Americans more likely to believe in God than the devil, heaven more than hell*. Available at: http://www.galluppoll.com/content/?ci=27877&pg=1.

Gilligan, C. (1982). *In a different voice*. Cambridge, MA: Harvard.

Gunther, M. (2001). God & business. *Fortune, 144*(1), 58–80.

Gutek, B. (1993). Asymmetric change in men's and women's roles. In B. Long & S. Kahn (Eds.), *Women, work, and coping: A multidisciplinary approach to workplace stress* (pp. 11–31). Montreal: McGill-Queen's University Press.

Hassan, R. (2003). Islam. In A. Sharma & K. Young (Eds.), *Her voice, her faith: Women speak on world religions*. Boulder, CO: Westview.

Hicks, D. (2003). *Religion and the workplace: pluralism, spirituality, leadership*. New York: Cambridge University Press.

Hill, P., & Pargament, K. (2003). Advances in the conceptualization and measurement of religion and spirituality. *American Psychologist, 58*, 64–74.

Josselson, R. (1996). *Revising herself: The story of women's identity from college to midlife*. New York: Oxford.

Miller, J. B. (1976). *Toward a new psychology of women*. Boston: Beacon Press.

Miller, W., & Thoresen, C. (2003). Spirituality, religion, and health: An emerging research field. *American Psychologist, 58*, 24–35.

Mitroff, I., & Denton, E. (1999). *A spiritual audit of corporate America: A hard look at spirituality, religion, and values in the workplace*. San Francisco: Jossey-Bass.

Morgan, J. F. (2005). In defense of the Workplace Religious Freedom Act: Protecting the unprotected without sanctifying the workplace. *Labor Law Journal, 56*, 68–81.

Nash, L., & McLennan, S. (2001). *Church on Sunday, work on Monday: The challenge of fusing Christian values with business life*. San Francisco: Jossey-Bass.

Nasr, S. H. (1993). Islam. In A. Sharma (Ed.), *Our religions* (pp. 425–532). San Francisco: Harper.

National Institute for Occupational Safety and Health. *Stress . . . at work*. DHHS (NIOSH) Publication No. 99–101.

Organisation for Economic Cooperation and Development (2004). *Clocking in and clocking out: Recent trends in working hours*. Available at: http://www.oecd.org/dataoecd/42/49/33821328.pdf.

Ozorak, E. W. (1996). The power, but not the glory: How women empower themselves through religion. *Journal for the Scientific Study of Religion, 35*, 17–29.

Pargament, K. (1997). *The psychology of religion and coping*. New York: Guilford Press.

Pollard, C. W. (1996). *The soul of the firm*. Grand Rapids, MI: Harper Business.

Prothero, S. (2006). *A nation of religions*. Chapel Hill, NC: The University of North Carolina Press.

Putnam, R. D. (2000). *Bowling alone: The collapse and revival of American community*. New York: Simon & Schuster.

Rayburn, C. A., & Richmond, L. J. (2002). Women, whither goest thou? To chart new courses in religiousness and spirituality and to define ourselves! In L. H. Collins et al. (Eds.), *Charting a new course for feminist psychology* (pp. 167–189). Westport, CT: Praeger.

Reinke, M. J. (1995). Out of order: A critical perspective on women in religion. In J. Freeman (Ed.), *Women: A feminist perspective* (pp. 430–447). Mountain View, CA: Mayfield.

Roof, W. C. (1993). *A generation of seekers: The spiritual journeys of the boom generation*. San Francisco: Harper.

Schor, J. B. (1992). *The overworked American: The unexpected decline of leisure*. New York: Basic Books.

Schweitzer, F. (1997). Why we might still need a theory for the religious development of women. *International Journal for the Psychology of Religion, 7*, 87–91.

Sheep, M. L. (2006). Nurturing the whole person: The ethics of workplace spirituality in a society of organizations. *Journal of Business Ethics, 66*, 357–375.

Silverman, M. K., & Pargament, K. (1990). *God help me: Longitudinal and prospective studies on effects of religious coping efforts*. Paper presented at the annual meeting of the American Psychological Association, San Francisco.

Smith, D. (2004). Workplace religious freedom: What is an employer's duty to accommodate? A review of recent cases. *The ALSB Journal of Employment and Labor Law, 10*, 49–65.

Spilka, B., Hood, Jr., R.W., Hunsberger, B., Gorsuch, R. (2003). *The psychology of religion: An empirical approach*. New York: Guilford Press.

Sullivan, S. C. (2006). The work-faith connection for low-income mothers: A research note. *Sociology of Religion, 67*, 99–108.

Swatos, Jr., W. H. (Ed.). (1994). *Gender and religion.* New Brunswick, NJ: Transaction.

U.S. Conference of Catholic Bishops, Committee on Women in Society and in the Church. *Women's spirituality in the workplace: A compilation of diocesan focus group reports.* Available at: http://www.usccb.org/laity/women.

U.S. Department of Labor, Bureau of Labor Statistics (2006). *Women in the labor force: A databook* (2006 edition). Available at: http://www.bls.gov/cps/wlf-databook2006.htm.

U.S. Department of Labor, Women's Bureau (2006). *Quick stats 2006.* Available at: http://www.dol.gov/wb/stats/main.htm.

U.S. Equal Employment Opportunity Commission, Office of Research, Information, and Planning (2007). *Enforcement statistics and litigation.* Available at http://www.eeoc.gov/stats/enforcement.html.

Walter, T., & Davie, G. (1998). The religiosity of women in the modern west. *British Journal of Sociology, 49*, 640–669.

Williams-Nickelson, C. (2006). Balanced living through self-care. In J. Worell & C. D. Goodheart (Eds.), *Handbook of girls' and women's psychological health* (pp. 183–191). New York: Oxford.

Willits, F. K., & Crider, D. M. (1988). Religion and well-being: Men and women in the middle years. *Review of Religious Research, 29*, 281–294.

Wilson, J., & Sherkat, D. E. (1994). Returning to the fold. *Journal for the Scientific Study of Religion, 33*, 148–161.

Wolfteich, C. E. (2002). *Navigating new terrain: Work and women's spiritual lives.* New York: Paulist Press.

Woodhead, L. (2001). Feminism and the sociology of religion. In R. K. Fenn (Ed.), *The Blackwell companion to sociology of religion* (pp. 67–84). Malden, MA: Blackwell.

Wuthnow, R. (1994). *God and Mammon in America.* New York: Free Press.

Chapter 9

Workforce Issues: In My Own Voice

LuAnn Hart

I am currently an administrator for the Arthropod-Borne Disease Program (ABDP), which is located within the Bureau of Communicable Disease Control, Division of Epidemiology, New York State Department of Health (NYSDOH). It is clear to see by this description that I work within a bureaucratic organization, which most government agencies are. I have worked for this program for 6 years and am preparing for an imminent change in programs.

As an administrator I am responsible for day-to-day operations including human resource management, procurement, and oversight of contracts of a complex program that is charged with surveillance of arthropod-borne diseases throughout New York state. Arthropod-borne diseases are those that are transmitted by insects, primarily mosquitoes and ticks.

I started with the NYSDOH in early 1994, when I accepted an entry-level secretarial position (Keyboard Specialist grade 6). At the time, my husband was out of work due to a recession and we needed benefits. I had been working for a mortgage company where I held the position of new construction (residential) underwriter. The job was very challenging; however, the pay was equal to the entry-level secretarial position in state government. At the time, I held two associate degrees: legal secretarial science and business administration. I hadn't spent a single day as a secretary until I came to work for NYSDOH. I worked the equivalent of 50% effort or half-time (2 days one week, 3 days the next week). We also had two young daughters, ages 3 and 7 months.

It did not take long before I was completely bored and asked for more work. It never mattered to me if I was working beyond my pay scale—I needed to be busy, challenged, and constantly learning. Over time, I accepted a five-grade promotion to an entry-level administrative position. I took this job full-time because my husband was again out of work (he worked in the commercial construction industry, which was badly hurt during the early 1990s) and it was a requirement to get the promotion. I worked full-time for about 18 months, when I had my son. During that time, there was a reorganization and I was "saved" when I was assigned to another program, where I went on to receive two more promotions over the next 3 years. During that time, I went back to Siena College (yes, work, three young children, a home, a husband, a dog, and everything I had ever wanted) to earn a BS in Marketing/Management. This was difficult because I dealt daily with the pulls from demands of daily life. However, I knew that I needed this degree to advance further within the health department. It didn't take me long to realize how credentialed the health field was, and where I wanted to be. I graduated magna cum laude (my third degree with honors) from Siena College in May 2002.

Shortly before my graduation, I applied for and was awarded another promotion to a Health Program Administrator grade 18 (October 2001). This was a significant move and allowed me to utilize my BS degree months before graduation. I had negotiated working four days a week, which was vital to keeping up with school (I had taken three classes that fall to finish up my graduation requirements) and three small children. My son was not yet in school and my goal was to be able to stay home with him as much as possible. Within 18 months exactly, I applied for and was awarded another promotion to a Health Program Administrator 1 grade 23. This was amazing in that this is a professional title, and I had worked my way up from a G-6 to a G-23 in 9 years. This was a rare accomplishment in government, though I had worked very, very hard to develop my career to the level I am today. Thinking back on it all, I did not choose to go into this field. I only took advantage of opportunities available to me when I began work in the state health department. It didn't take long for me to see that there was an opportunity to do valuable work and that I wanted to play an important role in the field of public health. This was the driving force behind my decisions regarding my graduate education.

In 2005, I took a chance and met with the admissions staff at Union Graduate College (UGC). I had previously planned on working on a master's degree and started investigating programs. I wanted an MBA because it was in line with my undergraduate degree, but I did not want to study the stock market. UGC had an MBC with a health management concentration. Based on my GPA at Siena College, I was awarded a 50% scholarship, which made this graduate degree affordable when combined with my employer's tuition reimbursement program. Here I was, back in school again! Although there was reason to celebrate: No one in my family or my husband's had ever obtained a graduate degree, and it was Union!

MENTORS

During my time at NYSDOH, I participated in the Mentor/Protégé program twice. The first time I participated as a G-16, where I worked with a woman who was a G-18. She helped me rewrite my resume, discuss my career goals, and ultimately referred me to my next promotion to a G-18. She was a wonderful supporter and understood the complexities of my life and the need to balance my career aspirations. A year later, I had met with Dennis Murphy, then association director for the division of family health. Dennis and I went to a conference and met in the exhibition hall. We had dinner and spoke about my career at NYSDOH. He offered to mentor me formally in the Mentor/Protégé program. We were paired and worked together for a year formally. During that time, we met each month. Dennis put me in touch with key executive staff throughout NYSDOH, including the Deputy Commissioner Dennis Whalen (currently Secretary of Health for New York State). These meetings were very enriching; Dennis and I met shortly before each meeting to develop relevant interview questions and to go over the results from my previous interview. I met with about nine executives in total—all upper level executives. The interview questions I chose included their early career experiences (which were of great interest to me when I met with women whom I wanted to emulate), education, growth and promotional experiences, and advice for my career. Some meetings started rather uncomfortably, especially when the interviewee thought I was there to ask for a promotion or transfer. When I was able to explain my goals for the meeting, my questions were met with enthusiasm, warmth, and generosity of both time and advice. These meetings allowed me to network and to obtain information for my personal use in developing and implementing my career aspirations. To this day, Dennis Murphy remains a mentor for me and a confidant. In reflecting back to the development of this mentor relationship, I could easily say that I would not have guessed that my mentor would be a man. I will explain further in the gatekeeping section.

GATEKEEPERS

In the broadest sense, my first response when I am asked about gatekeepers would be that they were all women. All of them were key women in my life; however, I must say that my gatekeepers were only obstacles for me to overcome, and never seemed impassable to me.

My mom was a single mother of two. She divorced at a time when it was not politically correct to be divorced and wore a wedding ring after the divorce so as not to embarrass my grandmother. The thinking at the time was that your children were illegitimate, not that they were the product of a divorced couple. Mom worked as many as three jobs most of my adolescent life. She accepted government assistance until my younger brother and I were in school. When I was about 16, my boyfriend at the time (now my husband) was applying to colleges. This was exciting for me because I had every intention of doing the same the following year. My mother informed me that if I had intentions (note "if") of going to college that I had to start working on my planning because she couldn't help me, financially or otherwise: Gatekeeper #1. I got a job shortly thereafter as a clerk in a nursing home and began my college plans. At that time, I wanted to be a lawyer, but more than that I wanted to be a mom. I decided that I did not want to work in the health field! I felt that I couldn't do both well after seeing my mother working long hours at low-paying jobs and after gaining much of my own independence early. I decided I would do the next best thing, which was legal secretarial science. I was excellent in high school in my business classes and enjoyed and excelled in shorthand. I did receive my AAS degree (graduated magna cum laude) in legal secretarial science. I know that my mother was trying to help me in the only way she knew how.

The other gatekeepers I experienced were women who hired me at the G-13 and G-18 levels. I found over time that they had preconceived notions about the limit of my professional skills. These notions were revealed during the course of my employment when I appealed for increased challenge or responsibility. I am determined and many have called me driven. I overcame each gatekeeper with gentle persistence and a work ethic that has provided me with career growth and rewards. When I have discussed these women (three at different times of my career over the past 10 years) with male supervisors, their read was always that I was a threat to these women. I cannot agree that all three of these gatekeepers were threatened, but I can agree that at least two may have felt that I was competition. Ultimately, my response was to move on to other jobs, leaving on the best of terms with these women. I never felt driven away; I actually felt that I was in control of my own destiny and that I would choose my opportunities and movement when I felt that growth was limited.

INTEGRATION OF WORK AND FAMILY

Because my mom worked so hard, and still does, and was not the cookie-baking homeroom mom, I worked very hard to be able to balance my home and work life. When my children were little, my husband worked very hard so that I could work part-time and be home with my children. I knew that I could not babysit other people's children to make money, so I maintained a "foot in the working world" by working part-time. This meant that my advancement was stifled somewhat during those years, but my priority was and is my family. At the same time, they have supported me when I have taken on career and educational challenges. My children do not lose out on any (I mean any!) school, sport, or extracurricular opportunity. This takes a small army to accomplish, but there is no other option for me. My oldest daughter, Meghan (age 16), has been in dance, competitive cheerleading (requiring East Coast travel), and currently is in high school and competitive softball (requiring East Coast travel). My middle child, also a daughter, Jaclyn (age 14), has been in dance and sports throughout elementary and middle school (basketball, volleyball, and softball) as well as band, and has taken private drum lessons for five years. My youngest is Bobby (age 10), who has been involved in all kinds of sports.

I often worried that I wasn't doing the right thing by going back to college, and was even told so by one mother when she told me that she was a "better mother because she put her children before her career." In speaking with my daughters and other mothers, I thought and still feel that I was actually setting a better example for my girls by pursuing my career goals and working very hard to balance my responsibilities. I have to credit my husband with my success as well. He's a traditional guy, but he has been supportive at every step in my education and career. I know that going back to school put additional stress on our family—at least doubled the demands over working full time. Yet they have been nothing but supportive. They all attended my Siena graduation ceremony and cheered me on loudly. I know that it will be no time at all before I am doing that for my children! My experiences have also enriched my children. My current job allows me to bring my children to work occasionally and to have experiences in a professional setting and to learn about the research that is conducted. These experiences are ones that they would not otherwise have.

ADVICE

The very first piece of advice I would give anyone for work or otherwise is that there is no such thing as luck. There is only preparation for opportunity. I'll have to credit Oprah with this bit of advice, which is something I have always kept with me. Hard work, perseverance, and preparation are key elements to success, particularly control over your own destiny and ultimate success. Working hard at an education, learning new job skills, or remaining open to new experiences can provide preparation and skills necessary to take advantage of unforeseen opportunities.

Second, women should think like men. This sounds strange, but I will explain. I mean that women tend to develop emotional attachments to jobs and to people, which prevents them from making strategic professional moves. Men don't tend to make those emotional connections and are better at making changes that benefit them professionally in the long run.

Last, work hard to develop personal and professional networks and do not burn bridges. You never know who will be your next boss, so do not make enemies. And work hard to meet people and demonstrate your potential. Interviewing for jobs even when you are not necessarily in the market is a great way to make a good first impression and develop professional ties with people outside of your immediate work environment. Never forget that you may only have one first impression.

Chapter 10

Society's Gains: Economics of Women in the Workplace

Zhilan Feng
Maneechit Pattanapanchai

INTRODUCTION

Employed women have become a driving force in our modern economy. Women's contribution both to unpaid home services and to the labor market has contributed to recent economic growth and is believed to be the foundation for its future growth.

"A Guide to Womenomics" (2006) presented several statistics concerning employed women. For example, in developed economies, women produce just under 40% of the official gross domestic product (GDP). If the value of the domestic services at home is estimated and added to their contribution, however, "then women probably produce slightly more than half of total output" (p. 73). The GDP is a way for measuring the size of the country's economy. It is defined as the market value of all final goods and services produced within a country in a given period of time. *The Economist* (2006) also noted that women's importance is not limited to goods and homecare but also as "consumers, entrepreneurs, managers and investors." Women make about 80% of the buying decisions in areas such as housing, furniture, food, and health care. Furthermore, Catalyst (2007) reported that American companies with more women in senior management jobs earned a higher return on equity than those with fewer women in top managerial positions.

In this chapter, we discuss women's contribution to the economy. We begin with a general description of women's participation in the workforce and its contribution to productivity and GDP growth. We then investigate the income gender gap and its harmful consequences. Finally, we discuss women's contribution to long-term economic growth.

WOMEN'S LABOR PARTICIPATION RATE

Labor force participation rate is defined by the Bureau of Labor Statistics as "the proportion of a particular population group that is in the labor force—that is, either working (employed) or actively looking for work (unemployed)." This number is important because the GDP growth can be achieved by either increasing the productivity (output rate) or by labor utilization (labor participation rate).

According to data from the Bureau of Labor Statistics (Table 10.1), women's labor participation rate (for women aged 16 and older) in United States has steadily increased from 34% in 1950 to 59% in 2006. This participation rate reflects an increase of more than 50 million employees. On the other hand, the labor participation rate for men has dropped from 86% to 74% during the same time period. We also report the employment to population ratio in Table 10.1 as a comparison. Both the labor participation rate and employment rate share the same trends. This phenomenon is not unique to the United States. For example, Taiwan reported that women's labor force participation has grown from 33% in 1965 to 45% in 1995.[1] Men's labor force participation has declined from 83% to 72%.[2] Table 10.2 reports the labor force participation rate, and Table 10.3 reports the employment rate by sex of

Table 10.1
U.S. labor force 16 years and 1950–2006

Year	Employment to population ratio, %		Civilian labor force (thousands)		Labor participation rate, %	
	Male	Female	Male	Female	Male	Female
1950	81.98	31.98	43,820	18,390	86.4	33.9
1960	78.85	35.50	46,387	23,239	83.4	37.7
1970	76.18	40.80	51,228	31,543	79.7	43.4
1980	72.03	47.68	61,453	45,487	77.4	51.5
1990	72.15	54.40	69,049	56,860	76.4	57.5
2000	71.90	57.48	76,280	66,303	74.8	59.9
2001	70.88	57.03	76,886	66,848	74.5	59.8
2002	69.70	56.28	77,500	67,363	74.1	59.6
2003	68.90	56.13	78,238	68,272	73.5	59.5
2004	69.18	55.98	78,980	68,421	73.4	59.2
2005	69.58	56.25	80,033	69,288	73.3	59.3
2006	70.08	56.63	81,255	70,173	73.5	59.4

Source: U.S. Bureau of Labor Statistics.

Table 10.2
Labor force participation rates by sex 15 – 64 years (percentages)

Countries	Men						Women					
	1973	1983	1990	2000	2005	2006	1973	1983	1990	2000	2005	2006
Australia	91.1	85.9	85.9	82.0	82.7	82.9	47.7	52.1	62.1	65.5	68.4	69.0
Austria	83.0	82.2	80.1	80.1	79.3	80.4	48.5	49.7	55.4	62.5	65.6	67.0
Belgium	83.2	76.8	72.7	73.8	73.1	72.7	41.3	48.7	52.4	56.6	59.5	58.9
Canada	86.1	88.5	84.9	83.1	82.5	82.2	47.2	62.2	68.1	70.5	73.1	73.5
Denmark	89.6	87.6	89.6	84.0	83.6	83.4	61.9	74.2	78.4	75.9	75.1	76.7
Finland	80.0	82.0	80.6	76.5	75.7	76.2	63.9	72.7	72.9	72.0	72.9	73.2
France[a]	85.2	78.4	74.6	74.4	74.5	74.2	50.1	54.3	56.6	61.7	63.8	63.9
Germany[a]	89.6	82.6	80.8	81.1	80.6	81.4	50.3	52.5	57.0	63.2	66.9	68.5
Greece	83.2	80.0	82.1	77.1	79.2	79.1	32.1	40.4	39.9	49.7	54.6	55.0
Ireland	92.3	87.1	82.2	79.1	79.9	81.0	34.1	37.8	38.9	55.7	60.3	61.3
Italy	85.1	80.7	78.9	73.8	74.4	74.6	33.7	40.3	44.5	46.2	50.4	50.8
Japan	90.1	89.1	87.8	85.2	84.4	84.8	54.0	57.2	60.4	59.6	60.8	61.3
Luxembourg	93.1	85.1	95.1	76.4	76.0	NA	35.9	41.7	50.5	51.7	57.0	NA
Netherlands	85.6	77.3	79.9	83.9	81.4	81.9	29.2	40.3	53.0	65.7	68.6	69.4
New Zealand	89.2	84.7	82.2	83.2	84.4	85.1	39.2	45.7	62.1	67.5	70.8	71.4
Norway[b]	86.5	87.2	84.5	84.8	82.3	81.4	50.6	65.5	71.2	76.5	75.4	74.8
Portugal	NA	86.9	86.1	78.8	79.0	79.5	NA	56.7	61.3	63.6	67.9	68.4
Spain[c]	92.9	80.5	76.8	79.1	82.2	82.5	33.4	33.3	40.9	51.8	59.1	61.1
Sweden[b]	88.1	85.9	85.3	81.2	82.5	82.6	62.6	76.6	81.1	76.4	77.7	77.7
Switzerland	100.0	93.5	96.2	89.4	87.4	87.8	54.1	55.2	59.2	73.9	74.3	74.7
United Kingdom[b]	93.0	87.5	86.5	84.3	83.0	83.2	53.2	57.2	67.4	68.9	69.6	70.3
United States	86.2	84.7	85.8	83.9	81.8	81.9	51.1	61.9	68.2	70.8	69.2	69.3
OECD Europe[c]	88.7	82.3	80.6	78.0	77.9	78.0	44.7	49.8	53.5	60.2	58.1	58.6
Total OECD[c]	88.2	84.4	83.7	81.1	80.3	80.4	48.3	55.2	60.0	61.3	60.4	60.8

[a]Data for 2006 are Secretariat estimates obtained by applying changes between 2005 and 2006 estimates from the European Labour Force Survey to national estimates for 2005.

[b]Refers to persons age 16 to 64.

[c]For data under 2000, 2005, and 2006, OECD Europe also includes Czech Republic, Hungary, Iceland, and Slovak Republic.

Source: OECD Employment Outlook Statistical Annex, 1996, 2001, and 2007.

Table 10.3
Employment/population ratio by sex 15 – 64 years (percentages)

Countries	Men						Women					
	1973	1983	1990	2000	2005	2006	1973	1983	1990	2000	2005	2006
Australia	89.9	77.5	80.3	76.6	78.5	78.8	46.4	47.0	58.0	61.6	64.7	65.5
Austria	82.4	79.4	77.7	76.2	75.4	76.9	47.7	47.1	53.5	59.7	62.0	63.5
Belgium	81.6	69.2	68.4	69.8	67.7	67.0	39.9	39.8	45.7	51.9	54.1	53.6
Canada	81.9	77.8	82.3	76.3	76.7	76.8	44.1	55.0	65.1	65.8	68.3	69.0
Denmark	89.0	78.3	82.7	80.7	80.1	80.6	61.2	65.0	71.4	72.1	70.8	73.2
Finland	78.1	77.4	77.4	69.4	69.4	70.5	62.3	69.0	70.8	64.5	66.5	67.3
France[a]	83.8	73.4	70.3	68.1	67.8	67.5	47.9	48.3	50.9	54.3	56.9	57.1
Germany[a]	88.8	76.6	76.1	74.8	71.4	72.9	49.7	47.8	53.2	57.7	59.6	61.5
Greece	81.8	75.3	71.7	71.3	74.5	74.6	31.2	35.6	38.5	41.3	46.2	47.5
Ireland	86.5	73.8	69.5	75.6	76.2	77.3	32.8	33.6	35.0	53.3	58.0	58.8
Italy	81.6	75.7	73.7	67.6	69.7	70.5	29.9	34.2	37.9	39.3	45.3	46.3
Japan	88.8	86.7	86.1	81.0	80.4	81.0	53.4	55.7	59.1	56.7	58.1	58.8
Luxembourg	93.1	84.0	76.8	75.0	73.3	NA	35.9	40.9	43.9	50.0	53.7	NA
Netherlands	83.5	69.1	75.5	82.1	77.4	78.7	28.6	34.7	47.4	63.4	64.8	66.0
New Zealand	89.1	80.3	76.7	78.0	81.5	82.1	39.1	42.8	58.3	63.5	68.0	68.4
Norway[b]	85.6	84.4	79.8	81.5	78.3	78.6	49.3	63.0	67.8	74.0	72.0	72.3
Portugal	99.2	82.8	86.1	76.2	73.4	73.9	30.5	49.8	58.8	60.4	61.7	62.0
Spain[b]	90.5	67.9	68.4	71.4	76.4	77.3	32.5	26.5	31.4	41.1	51.9	54.0
Sweden[b]	86.2	83.0	83.0	76.1	75.9	76.8	60.8	73.9	78.8	72.3	71.8	72.1
Switzerland	100.0	92.7	95.7	87.3	83.9	84.7	54.1	54.7	59.3	71.6	70.4	71.1
United Kingdom[b]	90.3	75.9	80.3	79.1	78.8	78.4	52.7	52.6	63.4	65.5	66.7	66.8
United States	82.8	76.5	81.2	80.6	77.6	78.1	48.0	56.2	64.9	67.9	65.6	66.1
OECD Europe[c]	86.7	75.2	75.4	72.0	71.2	71.8	43.2	44.4	48.1	53.9	52.3	53.2
Total OECD[c]	85.8	77.6	79.1	76.3	75.0	75.6	46.4	50.3	55.6	57.1	56.1	56.8

[a]Data for 2006 are Secretariat estimates obtained by applying changes between 2005 and 2006 estimates from the European Labour Force Survey to national estimates for 2005.
[b]Refers to persons age 16 to 64.
[c]For data under 2000, 2005, and 2006, OECD Europe also includes Czech Republic, Hungary, Iceland, and Slovak Republic.
Source: OECD Employment Outlook Statistical Annex, 1996, 2001, and 2007.

countries around the world. We observe that these trends (increasing participation by women in the labor force and declining participation by men between the ages of 15 and 64) occur across all continents.

Child-care support programs such as on-site child care, child-care subsidy, and child-care credit have helped facilitate women's participation in the workforce. This fact has suggested that the increased participation of women's labor may contribute to the decline in the non-paid domestic home service. Braunstein (2003) investigated this issue using 30 years of labor force data from Taiwan from 1965 to 1995. Braunstein noted that Taiwan's high economic growth during this period is credited to the increase in women's labor participation rate, most especially for women with college and graduate school education. Women's participation in the market sector contributes to the increased public investment in human capital and hence leads to high productivity in the household sector as well.

In Table 10.4, we report the percentage of part-time[3] and full-time employees from 1950 to 2006 for individuals aged 16 years and older. The table indicates that 7.8% of men had a part-time job in 1968. This number has been increased to 10% since 1980 and has stayed relatively stable in the 1990s and during the first six years of the 21st century. For women, the percentage of part-time employment is in the range of 25% to 27% over the last 40 years. Certainly, women are more likely to take a part-time job relative to men because of maternity leaves and their responsibility as primary caregivers to children and elderly parents. This trend is likely to continue as employers offer flex time,

Table 10.4
U.S. labor force 16 years and over 1950–2006, %

	Male		Female	
Year	Full-time	Part-time	Full-time	Part-time
1968	92.2	7.8	75.1	24.9
1970	91.5	8.5	73.9	26.1
1980	90.4	9.6	73.2	26.8
1990	89.8	10.2	74.7	25.3
2000	89.9	10.1	74.8	24.6
2001	89.7	10.3	75.4	24.8
2002	89.4	10.6	75.2	25.3
2003	89.2	10.8	74.7	25.6
2004	89.2	10.8	74.4	25.7
2005	89.3	10.7	74.3	25.2
2006	89.4	10.6	74.8	24.7

Source: Bureau of Labor Statistics.

job sharing, telecommuting, and other flexible job designs (Paludi & Neidermeyer, 2007). In 2006, there were more than 100,000 customer-service representatives who worked from home. As Naylor (2006) observed, "in the face of political pressures and customer backlash, many companies are bringing call center operations back from over-seas." Hence, the number of part-time jobs is predicted to exceed 300,000 by 2010. The flexibility of the home-based jobs will certainly encourage more women's participation in the labor market.

WOMEN'S CONTRIBUTION TO SOCIETY

Human Capital

Tables 10.5 and 10.6 report the education levels for full-time, year-round employees aged 25 years old and older during the period of 1991 to 2005. The number of both men and women employees who received some college education and above (including associate degrees, bachelor's degrees, master's degrees, professional degrees, and doctoral degrees) have been increasing over the years. On average, women employees invest more in education than men. For example, the percentage of men employees who received less than a 9th grade education is always higher than the percentage of women employees who received the same amount of education. The story of the educa-tion levels for those employees who receive some college education or higher is more compelling. In 1991, about 54% of all full-time female workers had some college education, compared with 55% of men. In 2005, however, there were more women employees (about 65%) who received some college or higher education compared to 59% of men employees. These statistics suggest that women employees are more willing to invest in human capital development.

Supporting our previous finding, Figure 10.1 depicts the number of bachelor's degrees awarded in Science and Engineering (S&E) and non-Science and Engineering (non-S&E) fields by sex during the years 1966 to 2004. The dark dotted line is the number of degrees awarded to women in S&E, while the light dotted line is for men in S&E. Simi-larly, the dark solid line is the number of degrees awarded to women in non-S&E; the light solid line is for men in non-S&E. Over this pe-riod, there are more women who were awarded bachelor's degrees in non-S&E fields each year. The number of women with bachelor's degrees has grown at a faster pace compared to that of their male counterparts. In the S&E field, the number of women with bachelor's degrees started lower in 1966, but since then it has increased and caught up with the number of men with bachelor's degrees received in 2003. Even though there are fever master's and doctoral degrees awarded to women in the field of S&E during this period, the numbers

Table 10.5
Employment by educational attainment full-time, year-round workers 25 years old and over, 1991–2005 (thousands)

| | | | | | | Women | | | |
| | Elementary/secondary | | | College | | | | | |
Year	Less than 9th grade	9th to 12th Grade (no diploma)	High school graduate (includes equivalency)	Some college, no degree	Associate degree	Bachelor degree	Master degree	Professional degree	Doctorate degree
1991	733	1,819	10,936	5,621	2,523	5,251	2,022	311	206
1992	733	1,653	11,026	5,903	2,651	5,599	2,192	334	225
1993	764	1,576	10,505	6,276	3,061	5,733	2,166	323	260
1994	694	1,675	10,777	6,254	3,210	5,897	2,173	398	283
1995	774	1,760	11,059	6,328	6,334	6,432	2,268	421	283
1996	750	1,751	11,358	6,574	3,468	6,686	2,213	413	322
1997	791	1,761	11,470	6,628	3,536	7,172	2,447	488	318
1998	814	1,876	11,605	7,067	3,527	7,276	2,639	468	329
1999	905	1,921	11,984	7,524	3,844	7,712	2,857	479	353
2000	934	1,964	11,801	7,534	4,231	7,869	2,865	499	364
2001	927	1,869	11,686	7,281	4,190	8,253	3,089	531	392
2002	857	1,840	11,673	7,353	4,281	8,226	3,281	572	402
2003	876	1,738	11,586	7,340	4,397	8,327	3,376	567	462
2004	916	1,797	11,395	7,341	4,492	8,683	3,467	532	453
2005	900	1,736	11,412	7,451	4,751	9,072	3,589	657	437

continued

Table 10.5 Continued

	Men								
	Elementary/secondary			College					
Year	Less than 9th grade	9th to 12th Grade (no diploma)	High school graduate (includes equivalency)	Some college, no degree	Associate degree	Bachelor degree	Master degree	Professional degree	Doctorate degree
1991	1,807	3,083	15,022	8,034	2,899	8,455	3,073	1,147	674
1992	1,815	3,009	14,722	8,066	3,203	8,719	3,178	1,295	745
1993	1,790	3,083	14,599	8,490	3,555	9,178	3,131	1,231	808
1994	1,895	3,057	15,097	8,783	3,735	9,636	3,225	1,258	868
1995	1,944	3,335	43,3351	8,908	3,926	9,597	3,395	1,208	853
1996	2,041	3,440	15,838	9,172	3,931	9,898	3,272	1,277	893
1997	1,914	3,548	16,220	9,169	4,086	10,349	3,228	1,321	966
1998	1,870	3,613	16,442	9,375	4,347	11,058	3,414	1,264	998
1999	2,095	3,407	16,797	9,786	3,398	11,253	3,783	1,291	1,033
2000	2,159	3,476	16,735	9,837	4,813	11,654	3,788	1,268	1,086
2001	2,207	3,503	16,314	9,492	4,714	11,29	3,961	1,298	1,041
2002	2,154	3,677	16,002	9,603	4,399	11,829	4,065	1,308	1,065
2003	2,209	3,366	16,283	9,337	4,696	11,846	4,124	1,348	1,037
2004	2,427	3,464	17,052	9,255	4,906	11,705	4,244	1,308	1,090
2005	2,425	3,651	17,258	9,532	5,020	12,032	4,275	1,369	1,144

Source: U.S. Census Bureau, Housing and Houshold Economic Statistics Division.

156

Table 10.6

Employment by educational attainment full-time, year-round workers 25 years old and over, 1991–2005 (%)

	Women								
	Elementary/secondary				College				
Year	Less than 9th grade	9th to 12th Grade (no diploma)	High school graduate (includes equivalency)	Some college, no degree	Associate degree	Bachelor degree	Master degree	Professional degree	Doctorate degree
1991	2.5	6.2	37.2	18.6	8.6	17.8	6.9	1.1	0.7
1992	2.4	5.5	36.4	19.5	8.7	18.5	7.2	1.1	0.7
1993	2.5	5.1	34.3	20.5	10.0	18.7	7.1	1.1	0.8
1994	2.2	5.3	34.4	19.9	10.2	18.8	6.9	1.3	0.9
1995	2.2	4.9	31.0	17.7	17.8	18.0	6.4	1.2	0.8
1996	2.2	5.2	33.9	19.6	10.3	19.9	6.6	1.2	1.0
1997	2.3	5.1	33.1	19.1	10.2	20.7	7.1	1.4	0.9
1998	2.3	5.3	32.6	19.9	9.9	20.4	7.4	1.3	0.9
1999	2.4	5.1	31.9	20.0	10.2	20.5	7.6	1.3	0.9
2000	2.5	5.2	31.0	19.8	11.1	20.7	7.5	1.3	1.0
2001	2.4	4.9	30.6	30.6	11.0	21.6	8.1	1.4	1.0
2002	2.2	4.8	30.3	19.1	11.1	21.4	8.5	1.5	1.0
2003	2.3	4.5	30.0	19.0	11.4	21.5	8.7	1.5	1.0
2004	2.3	4.6	29.2	18.8	11.5	22.2	8.9	1.4	1.2
2005	2.2	4.3	28.5	18.6	11.9	22.7	9.0	1.6	1.1

continued

Table 10.6 *Continued*

Men

Year	Elementary/secondary				College				
	Less than 9th grade	9th to 12th Grade (no diploma)	High school graduate (includes equivalency)	Some college, no degree	Associate degree	Bachelor degree	Master degree	Professional degree	Doctorate degree
1991	4.1	7.0	34.0	18.2	6.6	19.1	7.0	2.6	1.5
1992	4.1	6.7	32.9	18.0	7.2	19.5	7.1	2.9	1.7
1993	3.9	6.7	31.8	18.5	7.8	20.0	6.8	2.7	1.8
1994	4.0	6.4	31.7	18.5	7.9	20.3	6.8	2.6	1.8
1995	4.0	6.9	31.6	18.4	8.1	19.8	7.0	2.5	1.8
1996	4.1	6.9	31.8	18.4	7.9	19.9	6.6	2.6	1.8
1997	3.8	7.0	31.9	18.0	8.0	20.4	6.4	2.6	1.9
1998	3.6	6.9	31.4	17.9	8.3	21.1	6.5	2.4	1.9
1999	4.0	6.4	31.8	18.5	6.4	21.3	7.2	2.4	2.0
2000	3.9	6.3	30.5	17.9	8.8	21.3	6.9	2.3	2.0
2001	4.1	6.5	30.2	17.6	8.7	21.3	7.3	2.4	1.9
2002	4.0	6.8	29.6	17.7	8.1	21.9	7.5	2.4	2.0
2003	4.1	6.2	30.0	17.2	8.7	21.8	7.6	2.5	1.9
2004	4.4	6.2	30.8	16.7	8.8	21.1	7.7	2.4	2.0
2005	4.3	6.4	30.4	16.8	8.9	21.2	7.5	2.4	2.0

Source: U.S. Census Bureau, Housing and Houshold Economic Statistics Division.

Figure 10.1

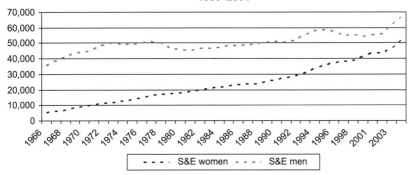

Master's degree awarded in Science and Engineering and
Non-Science and Engineering Field by Sex
1966–2004

Source: National Science Foundation.

of women who received master's degrees and PhDs have grown at faster rates compared to those of their male counterparts (see Figures 10.2 and 10.3).

The high level of education of women employees has contributed to their improved position in the labor market. In Table 10.7, we report the change of occupation by women employees (aged 16 years and older) from 1984 to 2004. More women are in positions that require a high degree of education. These positions include executives, administrators and managers, professional specialists, engineering and related technologists and technicians, health technologists, and science technicians. For example, the percentage of female employees in the executive, administrator, and manager positions has increased from 8.4% in 1984 to 13.2% in 2004. Likewise, the percentage of women employees

Figure 10.2

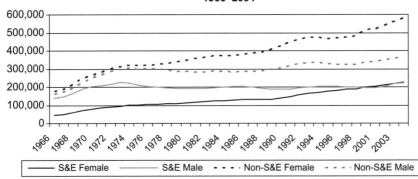

Bechelor's degree awarded in Science and Engineering and
Non-Science and Engineering Field by Sex
1966–2004

Source: National Science Foundation.

Figure 10.3

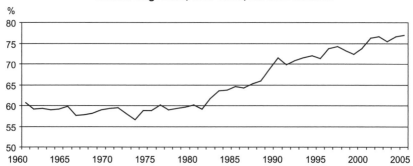

Gender wage ratio, 1960–2005, full-time workers

Note: Data based on median earnings of full-time, year-round workers 15 years old and over as of March of the following year. Before 1989 earnings are for civilian workers only.

Source: U.S. Census Bureau, Housing and Household Economic Statistics Division.

in the professional specialty positions has increased from 14.4% to 21.6% during the same period.

Another measure of human capital is healthiness. Research has found that women's participation in the workforce has positive impacts on their own as well as their children's health. McMunn, Bartley, Hardy, and Kuh (2006), for example, investigated the relationship between long-term social role and healthiness of women in the United Kingdom. They reported women who have multiple roles—wife, mother, and actively involved in the labor market for longer period of time—are in relatively good health at age 54. Moreover, they find that women who are less active in the labor market are more likely to be obese at age 53. Only 23% of working mothers were overweight when they reached their fifties, while 38% of stay-at-home moms were.

Reducing Poverty

The investment in human capital by women employees has earned them deserved returns and improved their economic position. Table 10.8 reports the median family income by family types from 1950 to 2005 according to the U.S. Census Bureau, Housing and Household Economic Statistics Division. The numbers are reported in current dollars. Without adjusting for inflation, we can calculate the annual growth rate for each family type during this 55-year period. On average, the annual growth rate is 5.28% for all families. The married-couple families with the wife in paid labor force enjoys the highest annual growth rate at 5.57%, followed by the single-female families with an annual growth rate of 4.94%. The married-couple families with only

Table 10.7A
Employed females 16 years and older by occupation in selected years, 1984–2004 annual averages

	All occupations	Executives, administrators, and managers	Professional specialty	Engineering and related technologists and technicians	Health technologist and technician	Science technician	Other occupation
1984	46,094	3,889	6,619	157	927	71	34,431
1986	48,893	4,653	7,059	166	945	58	36,012
1988	51,879	5,590	7,643	175	1,013	67	37,391
1990	53,906	5,931	8,287	196	1,086	77	38,329
1992	54,235	6,110	8,771	162	1,241	87	37,864
1994	56,771	7,014	9,411	179	1,298	98	38,771
1996	58,674	7,767	10,160	183	1,293	92	39,179
1998	60,946	8,469	10,776	202	1,414	123	39,962
2000	63,100	8,960	11,570	205	1,388	112	40,865
2002	63,737	9,446	12,154	204	1,531	138	40,264
2004	64,728	8,517	13,979	141	1,639	120	40,332

Source: National Science Foundation.

Table 10.7B
Employed females 16 years and older by occupation in selected years, 1984–2004, % of total employed

	Executives, administrators, and managers	Professional specialty	Engineering and related technologists and technician	Health technologist and technician	Science technicians	Other occupation
1984	8.4	14.4	0.3	2.0	0.2	74.7
1986	9.5	14.4	0.3	1.9	0.1	73.7
1988	10.8	14.7	0.3	2.0	0.1	72.1
1990	11.0	15.4	0.4	2.0	0.1	71.1
1992	11.3	16.2	0.3	2.3	0.2	69.8
1994	12.4	16.6	0.3	2.3	0.2	68.3
1996	13.2	17.3	0.3	2.2	0.2	66.8
1998	13.9	17.7	0.3	2.3	0.2	65.6
2000	14.2	18.3	0.3	2.2	0.2	64.8
2002	14.8	19.1	0.3	2.4	0.2	63.2
2004	13.2	21.6	0.2	2.5	0.2	62.3

Source: National Science Foundation.

the husband working have an annual growth rate in median income of 4.83%, and single male households have an annual growth rate of 4.80%. Obviously, there are multiple factors that contribute to growth in women's wages (such as efforts to reduce the gender gap). The investment in human capital by women employees is certainly one of them.

In 2001, the poverty rate for families with children in the United States was 13%. Using census data and a simulation technique, a study by the Brookings Institute (2003) reported that if all heads for non-elderly and non-disabled families have full-time jobs, the poverty rate would be reduced by 5% to 7.5%. According to the U.S. Census Bureau, families with two or more working members are less likely to live in poverty than those with only one working member. In a study sponsored by the United Kingdom Department of Trade and Industry, Walby and Olsen (2002) reported that women's participation in the labor force helped reduce child poverty. Especially for single-female household families that are reported in Table 10.8, an increase in median income means fewer children are living in poverty in the short run. In the long run, a mother who does not live in poverty herself is likely to raise productive workers for the next generation.

Improving Child Welfare

Another notable benefit of female participation in the workforce is their contribution to their children's well-being. In the United States,

Table 10.8
Median family income by family type, all races 1950–2005 (current dollars)

Year	All families	Married couple families		No spouse families	
		Wife in paid labor force	Wife not in paid labor force	Male housholder	Female housholder
1950	3,319	4,003	3,315	3,115	1,922
1960	5,620	6,900	5,520	4,860	2,968
1970	9,867	12,276	9,304	9,012	5,093
1980	21,023	26,879	18,972	17,519	10,408
1990	35,353	46,777	30,265	29,046	16,932
2000	50,732	69,235	39,982	37,727	25,716
2001	51,407	70,834	40,782	36,590	25,745
2002	51,680	72,806	40,102	37,739	26,423
2003	52,680	75,170	41,122	38,032	26,550
2004	54,061	76,854	42,215	40,361	26,969
2005	56,194	78,755	44,457	41,111	27,244

Source: U.S. Census Bureau, Housing and Houshold Economic Statistics Division.

more than 70% of women with children under 18 years of age were in the labor force in 2005. Mothers with children ages 6 to 17 years were more likely to participate in the labor force than mothers with pre-school children (age 6 or under). In 1975, 55% of mothers with children ages 6 to 17 years were in the labor force, and this number rose to 76.5% in 2005. During the same period, mothers of preschool children who were in the labor force rose from 39% to 62.8% (Child Health USA, 2006).

Furthermore, Hong and White-Means (1993) reported that maternal employment is a significant factor affecting children's physical health. Similar results were reported by Heyman (2001). A 2003 study by the Henry J. Kaiser Family Foundation indicated that almost 60% of women with children received their insurance through either their or their spouses' employers. Of these women, approximately half received coverage through their own employers, and half received coverage as dependents. In 2005, job-based insurance was the major form of health insurance for women ages 18 to 64, accounting for approximately 34%.

Heck and Parker (2002) examined the impact of family structure on the characteristics of health insurance coverage for children in the United States. They reported that, in two-parent families, 9% of children with both working parents are uninsured, while 15.1% of children do not have insurance coverage when the father is the only one working in the family. A report by the Institute for Women's Policy Research (Lee, 2004) indicated that mothers are more likely to stay on their job longer if the job provides child care or health insurance.

INCOME GENDER GAP

As we documented above, women have been and continue to be the driving force of economic growth. To ensure a prosperous future, policy makers should remove barriers and detriments that discourage women's participation in the market. One such barrier is the existence of the income gender gap. In the updated "Womenomics Revisited" (2007), the authors reported a study by the United Nations Economic and Social Commission for Asia and the Pacific which concluded that "sex discrimination cost[s] the region $42 billion to $47 billion a year by restricting women's job opportunities" (p. 88). They also cited findings in a recent report by Kevin Daly (an economist at Goldman Sachs), which suggested that under the assumption that GDP grew in proportion with employment and if the women's employment rates were raised to the same level as men's, then "America's GDP would be 9 percent higher, the Euro zone's would be 13 percent more, and Japan's would be boosted by 16 percent" (p. 88). Hence, minimizing the gender gap is crucial to sustainable growth in the future economy. In this section, we will

Figure 10.4

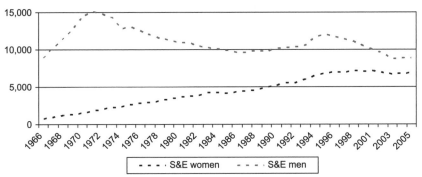

Doctoral's degree awarded in Science and Engineering and
Non-Science and Engineering Field by Sex
1966–2004

Source: National Science Foundation.

document the income gender gap in the United States and around the world, and we will discuss the importance of gender equality.

Figure 10.4 shows the changes in the income/gender wage ratio for full-time employees from 1960 to 2005. The gender/wage ratio is calculated based on median earnings of full-time, year-round employees 15 years of age and older. Obviously, we have made substantial improvement in reducing the income gender gap over this period. However, the situation is less impressive if we consider the annual income by education levels. In Tables 10.9A and 10.9B we report the median annual income of men and women by the amount of education they attained from 1991 to 2005. In 10.9A, the numbers are in thousands of dollars, while in 10.9B, the numbers are percentage of women's median income to men's median income. On average, we observe reducing gaps between women's median income and men's median income in all levels of education. The income gap between men and women who have professional degrees has reduced most during this period. In 1991, women with professional degrees earned less than 61% compared with men in the same professions. The situation has been improved and by the end of 2005 they earned more than 80% of the men's income in the same category. However, the numbers are less comforting for other education levels. For example, the income gaps between men and women are widened during this period for those who have master's degrees and associate's degrees. For all other levels of education, the reductions in income gaps are almost stalled. The situation is even more pronounced when we look at the women's income globally. The fact-sheet reported by the United Nation's web site stated that "women earn on average slightly more than 50 percent of what

Table 10.9A
Median annual income by educationa attainment full-time, year-round workers 25 years old and over, 1991–2005 (current thousands $)

Sex and year	Elementary/secondary			Some college, no degree	College				
	Less than 9th grade	9th to 12th Grade (no diploma)	High school graduate (includes equivalency)		Associate degree	Bachelor degree	Master degree	Professional degree	Doctorate degree
Men									
1991	16,880	20,994	26,218	31,034	32,221	39,894	47,002	70,284	54,626
1992	16,853	21,057	26,699	31,341	32,340	40,344	47,227	73,602	56,346
1993	16,380	21,402	26,820	31,278	32,616	41,416	49,826	77,185	61,347
1994	17,151	21,748	27,237	31,344	35,121	42,049	51,354	72,090	60,270
1995	17,492	21,887	28,542	32,363	33,468	42,602	51,814	75,283	61,700
1996	17,246	22,206	30,090	33,293	36,072	43,780	56,076	78,144	66,159
1997	18,551	24,241	30,655	35,087	36,677	46,255	57,553	78,290	70,706
1998	18,553	23,438	30,868	35,949	38,483	49,982	60,168	90,653	69,188
1999	19,532	23,946	32,028	37,166	40,422	50,994	61,816	76,722	76,722
2000	20,250	24,646	32,432	38,175	40,983	5,280	65,280	93,276	75,366
2001	21,139	25,857	33,037	40,159	41,658	53,108	66,934	100,000	81,077
2002	20,919	25,903	33,206	40,851	42,856	56,077	67,281	100,000	83,305
2003	21,217	26,468	35,412	41,348	42,871	56,502	70,640	100,000	87,131
2004	21,646	26,280	35,726	41,906	44,395	57,199	71,434	100,000	82,397
2005	22,330	27,189	36,302	42,418	47,180	60,020	75,025	100,000	85,864

continued

Table 10.9A Continued

Sex and year	Elementary/secondary			Some college, no degree	College					
	Less than 9th grade	9th to 12th Grade (no diploma)	High school graduate (includes equivalency)		Associate degree	Bachelor degree	Master degree	Professional degree	Doctorate degree
Women										
1991	11,637	13,538	18,042	21,328	23,862	27,654	32,122	42,604	40,172
1992	12,153	13,705	18,615	21,951	24,817	29,206	35,001	44,313	43,778
1993	11,876	14,700	19,168	21,997	25,067	30,344	36,924	48,406	46,420
1994	12,029	14,474	19,529	22,171	25,214	30,740	37,546	48,284	46,479
1995	12,776	15,103	19,649	22,512	26,281	30,798	38,593	48,111	41,920
1996	13,572	16,132	20,501	23,832	26,773	31,910	40,415	56,431	51,989
1997	13,447	15,907	21,291	25,035	27,206	33,432	41,856	54,528	50,758
1998	14,132	15,847	21,963	26,024	28,377	35,408	46052	55,460	52,167
1999	14,420	16,328	21,956	26,419	30,108	56,685	45,360	56,685	56,322
2000	15,622	17,186	23,571	27,304	30,701	38,456	46,987	60,481	57,351
2001	16,170	17,937	24,217	28,839	31,194	39,818	48,276	60,093	60,425
2002	16,510	19,307	25,182	29,400	31,625	40,853	48,890	57,018	65,715
2003	16,907	18,938	26,074	30,142	32,253	41,327	50,163	66,491	67,214
2004	17,015	19,167	26,045	30,822	33,489	41,703	51,319	75,100	68,387
2005	16,142	20,125	26,289	31,399	33,939	42,172	51,412	80,458	66,852

Source: U.S. Census Bureau, Housing and Houshold Economic Statistics Division.

167

Table 10.9B
Gender/wage ratio by educational attainment full-time, year-round workers 25 years old and over, 1991–2005, %

| | Elementary/secondary | | | | | College | | | |
Year	Less than 9th grade	9th to 12th Grade (no diploma)	High school graduate (includes equivalency)	Some college, no degree	Associate degree	Bachelor degree	Master degree	Professional degree	Doctorate degree
1991	68.9	64.5	68.8	68.7	74.1	69.3	70.5	60.6	73.5
1992	72.1	65.1	69.7	70.0	76.7	72.4	74.1	60.2	77.7
1993	72.5	68.7	71.5	70.3	76.9	73.3	74.1	62.7	75.7
1994	70.1	66.6	71.7	70.7	71.8	73.1	73.1	67.0	77.1
1995	73.0	69.0	68.8	69.6	78.5	72.3	74.5	63.9	67.9
1996	78.7	72.6	68.1	71.6	74.2	72.9	72.1	72.2	78.6
1997	72.5	65.6	69.5	71.4	74.2	72.3	72.7	69.6	71.8
1998	76.2	67.6	71.2	72.4	73.7	70.8	69.8	61.2	75.4
1999	73.8	68.2	68.6	71.1	74.5	71.2	73.4	59.0	73.4
2000	77.1	69.7	72.7	71.5	74.9	73.2	72.0	64.8	76.1
2001	76.5	69.4	73.3	71.8	74.9	75.0	72.1	60.1	74.5
2002	78.9	74.5	75.8	72.0	73.8	72.9	72.7	57.0	78.9
2003	79.7	71.6	73.6	72.9	75.2	73.1	71.0	66.5	77.1
2004	78.6	72.9	72.9	73.6	75.4	72.9	71.8	75.1	83.0
2005	72.3	74.0	72.4	74.0	71.9	70.3	68.5	80.5	77.9

Source: U.S. Census Bureau, Housing and Houshold Economic Statistics Division.

men earn" worldwide. Also, the majority of the 1.5 billion people living on $1 a day or less are women. Hence, we certainly have a long way to go in reducing the gender gaps in terms of income.

There are other factors restricting women's economic opportunities. Women assume major responsibility in taking care of their families. Caregiving demands their time and increases their workload, and thus reduces their availability to participate in the workforce (Paludi et al., 2007). To encourage more participation of women in the labor force, affordable child care has to be made available, and favorable tax rates and policies have to be put in place. If incomes are high and some household care can be purchased at a reasonable price (maybe with subsidies), more women will likely join the labor force.

Women are less likely to return to work full-time after they give birth (Barrow, 1999; Paul, 2006). In the United Sates, women are offered a 12-week maternity leave without any pay. This policy obviously contributes to the gender gap in income that we observed above. Women are forced to choose between having children and continuity of their career. The fact that 49% of high-achieving women in the United States are childless compared to 19% of their male colleagues suggests that lack of provisions for child rearing hinders women's career achievement and restricts their economic opportunities (Hewlett, 2002).

It is important for policy makers to see that there is a clear correlation between gender equality (measured by economic participation, education, health, and political empowerment) and GDP per head. Also, inequality between the sexes harms long-term growth. As a reminder for the policy makers, *The Economist* stated "men run the world's economics; but it may be up to the women to rescue them" (p. 88). To achieve and maintain economic growth, it is critical to continuously fight to minimize the income gender gap.

CONCLUSION

As we demonstrated, women's participation in the workforce is not only instrumental to GDP growth and long-term economic success, it also has profound secondary social benefits. It helps to reduce poverty, increases the investment in human capital, and improves children's welfare. We also show that homecare responsibility and the existence of the income gender gap have been detrimental to women's active involvement in the market. The failure of the United States in removing obstacles to employment for women is noted. The United States is among the handful of countries that do not guarantee payment to mothers during their maternity leaves. The female economic activity rate, which is defined as the percentage of the economically active population (both employed and unemployed) out of the total population for those aged 15 and older was 58.8% for the United States in 2000, ranking 58 out of 157 countries. We hope that these numbers serve as an alarm to the policy makers and prompt their actions to encourage women's participation in the market. If the United States wants to keep its leadership role in the world economy, we have to be more active and aggressive in facilitating women's involvement.

NOTES

1. The author does not mention ages for the labor participation rates. For a comparison we report the employment and labor participation rate for the age group 15–64 years across the world in Tables 10.2 and 10.3.

2. In the United States, the labor participation rate was 59% for women and 75% for men aged 16 and older in 1995.

3. Those who work less than 35 hours per week (U.S. Department of Labor and U.S. Bureau of Labor Statistics).

REFERENCES

Barrow, L. (1999). An analysis of women's return-to-work decisions following first birth. *Economic Inquiry, 37*, 432–451.

Braunstein, E. (2003). Shifting women's work from the home to market: Assessing policies for economic growth in Taiwan, University of Massachusetts, Political Economy Research Institute. http://www.peri.umass.edu/filead min/pdf/research_brief/RB2003-2.pdf.

The Brookings Institute (2003). Welfare reform & beyond #28, The Brookings Institute Policy Brief, September. http://www3.brookings.edu/es/wrb/publications/pb/pb28.pdf.

Catalyst. (2007). Catalyst.org/pressroom/press_bottom_line_2shtml.

Child Health USA (2006). Rockville, MD: U.S. Department of Health and Human Services Administration, Maternal and Child Health Bureau.

The Economist (2006, April 15). A guide to womenomics. http://www.ecomomist. com, 73–74.

The Economist (2007, April 21). Womenomics revisited. http://www.economist. com, 88.

Heck, K., & Parker, J. (2002). Family structure, socioeconomic status, and access to health care for children. *Health Services Research, 37*, 171–184.

The Henry Kaiser Family Foundation (2003, April). Women's issue brief, an update on women's health policy, women, work, and family health: A balancing act. http://www.kff.org/womenshealth/loader.cfm?url=/common spot/security/getfile.cfm&PageID=14293.

Hewlett, S. A. (2002). Executive women and the myth of having it all. *Harvard Business Review, 80*, 66–73.

Heyman, J. (Ed.). (2000). *The widening gap: Why American working families are in jeopardy and what can be done about it*. New York: Basic Books.

Hong, G., & White-Means, S. I. (1993). Do working mothers have healthy children? Abstract, Handbook of the Sociology of gender. As appears on http://www.springerlink.com/content/v8j0387821r2t121.

Lee, S. (2004). Women's work supports, job retention, and job mobility: Child care and employer-provided health insurance help women stay on jobs. Institute for Women's Policy Research, November. http://www.iwpr.org/pdf/C359.pdf.

McMunn, A., Bartley, M., Hardy, R., & Kuh, D. (2006). Life course social roles and women's health in mid-life: Causation or selection. *Journal of Epidemiology and Community Health, 60,* 484–489.

Naylor, M. (2006). There's no workforce like home. Business Week. http://www.businessweek.com/technology/content/may2006/tc20060502_763202.htm.

Paludi, M., & Neidermeyer, P. (Eds.). (2007). *Work, life and family imbalance: How to level the playing field.* Westport, CT: Praeger.

Paludi, M., Vaccariello, R., Graham, T., Smith, M., Allen-Dicker, K., Kasprzak, & White, C. (2007). Work/life integration: Impact on women's careers, employment, and family. In M. A. Paludi & P. E. Neidermeyer (Eds.), *Work, life and family imbalance: How to level the playing field.* Westport, CT: Praeger.

Paul, G. (2006). The impact of children on women's paid work. *Fiscal Studies, 27,* 473–512.

Walby, S., & Olsen, W. (2002, November). Report to Women and Equality Unit, Department of Trade and Industry, UK.

Index

Page numbers followed by *f* indicate figures; *t* indicates tables.

About the Editor and Contributors

Michele A. Paludi, PhD, is the author/editor of 27 college textbooks, and more than 140 scholarly articles and conference presentations on sexual harassment, psychology of women, gender, and sexual harassment and victimization. Her book, *Ivory Power: Sexual Harassment on Campus* (1990, SUNY Press), received the 1992 Myers Center Award for Outstanding Book on Human Rights in the United States. Dr. Paludi served as chair of the U.S. Department of Education's Subpanel on the Prevention of Violence, Sexual Harassment, and Alcohol and Other Drug Problems in Higher Education. She was one of six scholars in the United States to be selected for this subpanel. She also was a consultant to and a member of former New York State Governor Mario Cuomo's Task Force on Sexual Harassment. She is the series editor for Praeger's Women's Psychology Series.

Dr. Paludi serves as an expert witness for court proceedings and administrative hearings on sexual harassment. She has had extensive experience in conducting training programs and investigations of sexual harassment and other equal employment opportunity issues for businesses and educational institutions. In addition, Dr. Paludi has held faculty positions at Franklin & Marshall College, Kent State University, Hunter College, Union College, and Union Graduate College, where she directs the human resource management certificate program. She teaches courses in the School of Management: Foundations of Human Resource Management, Managing Human Resources, and International Human Resource Management.

Linda Dillon is currently the director of human resources for the New York State Higher Education Services Corporation. She has over 30 years of service in the New York state government. Ms. Dillon earned a BS from Russell Sage College and has completed several master's level courses from both Russell Sage College and Union College. Ms. Dillon resides outside Albany, New York, with her husband William. Their son Christopher is a recent graduate of Harvard Business School, and their daughter Stephanie is a recent graduate of the Roger Williams University School of Architecture.

Donna Lee Faulkner is currently completing the requirements for the Master of Science degree in clinical psychology at the University of Texas at Tyler, and she plans to become a licensed professional counselor in the state of Texas. Shelly L. Marmion, PhD, and Ms. Faulkner co-authored the chapter entitled "Effects of Class and Culture on Intimate Partner Violence," which was included in *Intimate Violence Against Women: When Spouses, Partners and Lovers Attack*. In addition, Ms. Faulkner has assisted Dr. Marmion in experimental research at the University of Texas at Tyler and has collaborated with Dr. Paula Lundberg-Love on several research projects.

Zhilan Feng received her master's and doctoral degrees from the University of Connecticut. She has been an assistant professor for Union Graduate College since September 2003, and has published papers in several real estate and finance journals. Her current research topics are corporate governance, asset pricing in capital markets, capital structure policy, and real estate investment and securitization.

Susan Fineran is an associate professor at the University of Southern Maine School of Social Work. Her professional career includes clinical experience in the areas of aging, substance abuse, child and family treatment, sex discrimination, and women's issues. Her research interests include sexual harassment and bullying that affects adolescents in schools and in the workplace and the implications for child and adolescent mental health.

James Gruber is a professor of sociology at the University of Michigan–Dearborn. He has published extensively on workplace sexual harassment and has presented workshops and expert witness testimony on the topic since the early 1980s. He co-edited a book in 2005 with Dr. Phoebe Morgan (*In The Company of Men: Male Dominance and Sexual Harassment*) that offers new directions in theory and research on the topic. Currently, he is conducting research with Dr. Susan Fineran on bullying and sexual harassment in middle and high school. Also, they are studying the impact of sexual harassment on girls who hold jobs while attending high school.

LuAnn Hart is an administrator for the Arthropod-Borne Disease Program for the Bureau of Communicable Disease Control, Division of Epidemiology, New York State Department of Health. She is also earning her MBA in health administration at Union Graduate College.

Susan Lehrman has been president and dean of the faculty of Union Graduate College since it was spun off from Union College in 2003. Prior to that time she served as dean of Union College's graduate programs and as a faculty member in its MBA program. Dr. Lehrman is a nationally known health services researcher focusing on the evaluation of services for the HIV infected and affected population, providing research and evaluation services at the national, regional, and local levels. Prior to her academic career, she had a successful 15-year career in health care management. Dr. Lehrman holds a BS in education from Oregon State University and MPH and PhD degrees from the University of California at Berkeley. She currently is the dean of the business school at Providence College.

Paula Lundberg-Love is a professor of psychology at the University of Texas at Tyler and the Ben R. Fisch Endowed Professor in Humanitarian Affairs for 2001–2004. Her undergraduate degree was in chemistry and her doctorate was in physiological psychology with an emphasis in psychopharmacology. After a 3-year postdoctoral fellowship in nutrition and behavior in the Department of Preventive Medicine at Washington University School of Medicine in St. Louis, she assumed her academic position at University of Texas at Tyler, where she teaches classes in psychopharmacology, behavioral neuroscience, physiological psychology, sexual victimization, and family violence. Subsequent to her academic appointment, Dr. Lundberg-Love pursued postgraduate training and is a licensed professional counselor. She is a member of Tyler Counseling and Assessment Center, where she provides therapeutic services for victims of sexual assault, child sexual abuse, and domestic violence. She has conducted a long-term research study on women who were victims of childhood incestuous abuse, constructed a therapeutic program for their recovery, and documented its effectiveness upon their recovery. She is the author of nearly 100 publications and presentations and is co-editor of *Violence and Sexual Abuse at Home: Current Issues in Spousal Battering and Child Maltreatment*. As a result of her training in psychopharmacology and child maltreatment, her expertise has been sought as a consultant on various death penalty appellate cases in the state of Texas.

Michael B. Mathias (PhD, University of Rochester) is a clinical assistant professor of management at Union Graduate College and lecturer in the philosophy department at Union College. His teaching and research interests include business ethics and ethical, political, and legal theory. He also works as an ethics consultant and conducts workshops on teaching ethics.

Maneechit Pattanapanchai was born and raised in Bangkok, Thailand. She received a doctoral degree in environmental economics from the

University of Connecticut. Her research interests include economic forecasting, public policies, and corporate restructuring. She is currently working as an economist for the Ways and Means Committee of the New York State Assembly in Albany, New York.

Tina Stern grew up in Cleveland, Ohio, and has lived in Atlanta, Georgia, since 1987. She earned her undergraduate degree from Boston University, her master's degree from Cleveland State University, and her PhD from the University of Georgia. She is a professor of psychology at Georgia Perimeter College, where for many years she has taught courses on the psychology of women. In addition, as a licensed psychologist, Tina maintains a clinical practice specializing in women's issues. Since her days at Boston University, Tina has been interested in and has written about issues related to women and, in particular, the psychology of women.

Susan Strauss, RN, EdD, is a national and international speaker, trainer, and consultant. Her specialty areas include harassment and workplace bullying, organizational development, and management/leadership development. Her clients are from business, education, health care, law, and government organizations from both the public and private sector. Dr. Strauss has authored book chapters and articles in professional journals, written curriculum and training manuals, as well as authored the book *Sexual Harassment and Teens: A Program for Positive Change*. Ms. Strauss has been featured on *The Donahue Show, CBS Evening News,* and other television and radio programs and has often been interviewed for newspaper and journal articles such as for the *Times of London, Lawyers Weekly,* and *Harvard Education Newsletter.* Ms. Strauss has presented at international conferences in Botswana, Egypt, Thailand, Israel, and the United States. She has consulted with professionals from other countries such as England, Australia, Canada, and St. Maarten. She has her doctorate in organizational leadership, is a registered nurse with a bachelor's degree in psychology and counseling, a master's degree in public health, and a professional certificate in training and development.

Christa White is majoring in psychology at Union College and is expected to graduate in June, 2008. She has conducted research in work/life integration, especially the impact of maternal employment on children and elder care responsibilities for women.